5 STEPS TO A 5™

500
AP European History
Questions
to know by test day

Also in the 500 Questions to Know by Test Day series

5 Steps to a 5: 500 AP Biology Questions to Know by Test Day

5 Steps to a 5: 500 AP Calculus Questions to Know by Test Day

5 Steps to a 5: 500 AP Chemistry Questions to Know by Test Day

5 Steps to a 5: 500 AP English Language Questions to Know by Test Day

5 Steps to a 5: 500 AP English Literature Questions to Know by Test Day

5 Steps to a 5: 500 AP Environmental Science Questions to Know by Test Day

5 Steps to a 5: 500 AP Human Geography Questions to Know by Test Day

5 Steps to a 5: 500 AP Microeconomics/Macroeconomics Questions to Know by Test Day

5 Steps to a 5: 500 AP Physics Questions to Know by Test Day

5 Steps to a 5: 500 AP Psychology Questions to Know by Test Day

5 Steps to a 5: 500 AP Statistics Questions to Know by Test Day

5 Steps to a 5: 500 AP U.S. Government & Politics Questions to Know by Test Day

5 Steps to a 5: 500 AP U.S. History Questions to Know by Test Day

5 Steps to a 5: 500 AP World History Questions to Know by Test Day

5 STEPS TO A >5™

500

AP European History Questions
to know by test day

Sergei Alschen

New York Chicago San Francisco Lisbon London Madrid Mexico City
Milan New Delhi San Juan Seoul Singapore Sydney Toronto

CONTENTS

Introduction   vii

Chapter 1 **Recovery and Expansion**   1
Questions 1–28

Chapter 2 **The Renaissance, 1350–1550**   7
Questions 29–65

Chapter 3 **The Reformation, 1500–1600**   17
Questions 66–90

Chapter 4 **The Rise of Sovereignty, 1600–1715**   25
Questions 91–112

Chapter 5 **The Scientific Revolution During the
17th Century**   31
Questions 113–123

Chapter 6 **The Enlightenment: A Cultural Movement During
the 18th Century**   35
Questions 124–154

Chapter 7 **Social Transformation and State-Building in the
18th Century**   43
Questions 155–212

Chapter 8 **The French Revolution and the Rise of Napoleon,
1789–1799**   57
Questions 213–249

Chapter 9 **The Fall of Napoleon and the Post-Napoleonic Era,
1800–1848**   67
Questions 250–283

Chapter 10 **The Second Industrial Revolution, 1820–1900**   77
Questions 284–311

Chapter 11 **The Rise of New Ideologies in the 19th Century**   85
Questions 312–336

Chapter 12 **Nationalism and State-Building, 1848–1900**   91
Questions 337–365

Chapter 13 **Mass Politics and Imperialism in Africa and Asia, 1860–1914   97**
Questions 366–392

Chapter 14 **Politics of the Extremes and World War I, 1870–1918   105**
Questions 393–443

Chapter 15 **The Interwar Years and World War II, 1918–1945   117**
Questions 444–467

Chapter 16 **The Cold War and Beyond, 1945–Present   123**
Questions 468–500

Answers   131

Bibliography   213

INTRODUCTION

Congratulations! You've taken a big step toward AP success by purchasing *5 Steps to a 5: 500 AP European History Questions to Know by Test Day*. We are here to help you take the next step and score high on your AP Exam so you can earn college credits and get into the college or university of your choice!

This book gives you 500 AP-style multiple-choice questions that cover all the most essential course material. Each question has a detailed answer explanation. These questions will give you valuable independent practice to supplement your regular textbook and the groundwork you are already doing in your AP classroom.

This and the other books in this series were written by expert AP teachers who know your exam inside out and can identify the crucial exam information as well as questions that are most likely to appear on the exam.

You might be the kind of student who takes several AP courses and needs to study extra questions a few weeks before the exam for a final review. Or you might be the kind of student who puts off preparing until the last weeks before the exam. No matter what your preparation style, you will surely benefit from reviewing these 500 questions, which closely parallel the content, format, and degree of difficulty of the questions on the actual AP exam. These questions and their answer explanations are the ideal last-minute study tool for those final few weeks before the test.

Remember the old saying "Practice makes perfect." If you practice with all the questions and answers in this book, we are certain you will build the skills and confidence needed to do great on the exam. Good luck!

—Editors of McGraw-Hill Education

CHAPTER 1

Recovery and Expansion

1. Which of the following was NOT a result of the Hundred Years' War?

    (A) France became more united.
    (B) England became more united.
    (C) Cannons and firearms became more commonly used in war.
    (D) The British Parliament expanded its powers as the monarch needed money for war.
    (E) Large numbers of nobles on both sides died.

2. Which of the following was a decisive weapon of the Hundred Years' War?

    (A) crossbow
    (B) rifle
    (C) trebuchet
    (D) longbow
    (E) mace

3. The Black Death appeared in a Europe that

    (A) had already been weakened by local famines
    (B) was in the midst of the Renaissance
    (C) had been experiencing a time of peace and stability
    (D) had just emerged from the Dark Ages
    (E) was in the middle of the Scientific Revolution

4. Which of the following did Europeans NOT believe was (were) responsible for the Black Death?

    (A) Jews
    (B) sin
    (C) fleas
    (D) bad air
    (E) a comet

5. The Black Death is generally credited with

(A) raising wages
(B) lowering wages
(C) reducing social mobility
(D) ending the Hundred Years' War
(E) beginning the Scientific Revolution

6. What was the reason for the conflict that brought about the Avignon papacy?

(A) the controversy over indulgences
(B) French concern over church corruption
(C) a desire to bring the church away from the influence of the Medici
(D) the desire of the king of France to be able to try clergy in court
(E) the desire of the king of France to tax the clergy

7. The period of the "Babylonian Captivity" was characterized by

(A) shock at the church's extravagance
(B) a new sense of piety
(C) a strengthening of the church's influence
(D) the creation of new orders of monks
(E) the increase of the influence of the Holy Roman Emperor

8. The Conciliar Movement got its start from

(A) the outrage against simony
(B) reaction against the Hussite movement
(C) the immoral behavior of the clergy
(D) increased use of annate payments
(E) the desire to be rid of two simultaneous papacies

9. Which of the following was a result of the Conciliar Movement?

(A) reform of controversial church practices
(B) reunification of the Catholic East and Orthodox West
(C) movement to venerate Catholic saints
(D) increased power for papal authority
(E) the adoption of recommendations of the Council of Trent

10. Which of the following is true about the Wars of the Roses?

(A) They were a clear ideological struggle between the combatants.

(B) They were the first time conscription of ordinary men was used widely.

(C) They began with the end of the Thirty Years' War.

(D) They ended with the accession of Henry VIII to the throne.

(E) They began with the end of the Hundred Years' War.

11. Which is a result of the Wars of the Roses?

(A) They ended with the victory of the House of York.

(B) Many nobles died, hastening the end of feudalism.

(C) The Black Death was spread by the marauding armies.

(D) Many saw the importance of maintaining private armies for nobles.

(E) They led to the eventual English Civil War.

12. Which led to greater independence of the French Catholic Church from the pope?

(A) the Edict of Nantes

(B) the Peace of Augsburg

(C) the Pragmatic Sanction of Bourges

(D) the Council of Trent

(E) the Hundred Years' War

13. Louis XI of France and Henry VII of England had all of the following in common except

(A) religion

(B) suppression of the nobility

(C) subjects afraid of recent anarchy and civil war

(D) the power to tax

(E) a form of parliament

14. The unification of Spain is notable because it happened despite

(A) the power of the Catholic Church

(B) great linguistic differences

(C) the formidable military forces of the Moors

(D) constant invasion by the French

(E) the defeat of the Spanish Armada

15. Which emerging nation-state had the strongest parliament?

    (A) Spain

    (B) France

    (C) Russia

    (D) Netherlands

    (E) England

16. Crusades were said to have gone on in all of the following except

    (A) England

    (B) Spain

    (C) southern France

    (D) the Holy Land

    (E) eastern Europe

17. Which was the last area of Spain to be conquered from the Moors?

    (A) Castile

    (B) Aragon

    (C) Catalonia

    (D) Granada

    (E) Navarre

18. After 1492 the Spanish Inquisition focused on persecuting

    (A) Moriscos and Marranos

    (B) Huguenots and Puritans

    (C) Jews and Muslims

    (D) pagans

    (E) Hussites

19. Which of the following helped unite Spain after 1492?

    (A) language

    (B) the Inquisition

    (C) hatred of the Moors

    (D) defense against foreign invasion

    (E) Hapsburg rule

20. Which of the following proved to be the exception to the trend of centralization?

(A) England
(B) the Holy Roman Empire
(C) France
(D) Spain
(E) Sweden

21. Which of the following is NOT a reason for the decentralization of the Holy Roman Empire?

(A) the heterogeneous nature of the German states
(B) the fact that the emperor was elected
(C) a strong tradition of autonomy of German princes
(D) linguistic diversity within the empire
(E) the Holy Roman Emperor's preoccupation with struggles with the pope and others

22. Italy remained disunited for many reasons, EXCEPT

(A) the pope could not unite Italy because of the Avignon papacy
(B) religious conflict in the 16th century
(C) conflicting economic interests of the various city-states
(D) constant attacks and occupations by foreign powers
(E) the local power of merchant classes in each city-state

23. Italy managed to avoid the worst of the Middle Ages because

(A) it had been temporarily conquered by the Muslims
(B) Rome remained a center of learning throughout the Middle Ages
(C) its geographic position enabled merchants to prosper
(D) it was geographically isolated from barbarian invasion
(E) people honored it as a center of the Catholic Church

24. Which of the following was NOT ruled by Charles V in the 16th century?

(A) Spain
(B) Austria
(C) Holy Roman Empire
(D) France
(E) Netherlands

25. The Spanish financed the voyage of Columbus because

    (A) they wanted to get to India before the Portuguese

    (B) they wanted to get to America before the Portuguese

    (C) Spanish clergy wanted to prove the world was flat

    (D) America was believed to be rich in gold and silver

    (E) the English had announced their plan to explore the Atlantic

26. Spanish colonies in the Americas were notable for their

    (A) religious freedom

    (B) self-government

    (C) extractive economies

    (D) adoption of native culture

    (E) cooperation with native governments

27. The Spanish *encomienda* was modeled on the

    (A) Catholic Church

    (B) medieval university

    (C) Cortes

    (D) Inquisition

    (E) feudal manor

28. Which of the following made up the smallest section of the population in Spanish America?

    (A) creoles

    (B) *peninsulares*

    (C) mulattos

    (D) mestizos

    (E) natives

CHAPTER 2

The Renaissance, 1350–1550

29. Which of the following is NOT characteristic of the Italian Renaissance?

(A) emphasis on the individual

(B) glorification of human achievement

(C) steadfast support for the church's leading role in society

(D) new attempts to reconcile the pagan philosophy of the Greco-Roman world with Christian thought

(E) a movement that featured the proliferation of art

30. Persecution and forced conversions of religious minorities in Spain after 1478 happened under the aegis of the

(A) Muslim rulers

(B) Inquisition

(C) conquistadors

(D) *encomienda*

(E) Moriscos and Marranos

31. Florence was to the Italian Renaissance what

(A) Constantinople was to the development of the Islamic cultural revival of the 13th century

(B) Moscow was to the northern Renaissance

(C) Athens was to classical Greek culture

(D) Madrid was to western European Jewish intellectual life after 1492

(E) Stockholm was to the Protestant Reformation

32. All of the following reasons best describe why Poland experienced the Renaissance and Russia didn't EXCEPT

(A) Poland was a Roman Catholic country while Russia was Eastern Orthodox and under the cultural influence of the Byzantine Empire

(B) Poland was at the heart of the Holy Roman Empire while Russia wasn't

(C) Russia was cut off from cultural and intellectual trends coming from western Europe by the Mongol occupation (1240–1480)

(D) Poland was geographically closer to Rome and the Italian city-states where the Renaissance began

(E) the Polish used Latin letters in their alphabet while Russians used Cyrillic

33. Italian humanism gave rise to

(A) Greek becoming the official literary language of the Renaissance writers

(B) the welfare state

(C) a rebirth in church literature and hymns

(D) the movement toward writing in the vernacular in Europe

(E) the movement known as liberation theology

34. According to Baldassare Castiglione, the goal of the education system in the 16th century was to

(A) provide a practical education in construction and commerce

(B) offer the same learning opportunities to boys and girls

(C) phase out the study of the classics in favor of more practical "career" and technical disciplines

(D) provide a young man with a well-rounded education including knowledge of the arts, mathematics, and oration skills

(E) make the system compulsory to all until the age of 18

35. Charles V was one of a long line of Austrian rulers of the Holy Roman Empire (1452–1806) from which family?

(A) Hapsburg

(B) Tudor

(C) Valois

(D) Hohenzollern

(E) Piast

36. All of the following were from Florence EXCEPT

(A) Machiavelli
(B) Boccaccio
(C) Erasmus
(D) Petrarch
(E) Brunelleschi

37. The Renaissance began in Italy for all of the following reasons EXCEPT

(A) Italian unification was achieved, and the state actively financed art and cultural development
(B) Italy held a key strategic position in the growing East-West trade
(C) Italian intellectuals became increasingly aware of their Roman traditions during this time
(D) wealthy Italian middle-class merchants and bankers increasingly used their wealth to commission Renaissance art and literature
(E) Byzantine intellectuals escaped Constantinople and Ottoman conquest and brought knowledge of ancient Greek achievements with them to Italy

38. Peasants comprised approximately _____ of the population of Renaissance Europe.

(A) 10–15 percent
(B) 25 percent
(C) 45–50 percent
(D) 85–90 percent
(E) 95–98 percent

39. Which of the following best describes the overall influence the Renaissance had on the people of Europe during the 15th and 16th centuries?

(A) It was a mass movement that encompassed significant segments of all social classes.
(B) It was the preserve of the wealthy upper classes that constituted a small percentage of the population.
(C) Gender discrimination became less noticeable because many women became prominent in politics, universities, and merchant guilds.
(D) The influence of the Renaissance was a factor in leading to universal education in the 16th century.
(E) It was a movement that lashed out against the growing materialism and individualism pervading society.

40. Which of the following contributed the most to Italy's demise in general, and Rome's fall in particular, in 1527?

    (A) The decadent culture unleashed by the Renaissance tore at the moral fiber of Italian society.
    (B) The Italian city-states and republics' inability to unify in the face of foreign invasion left the country open to conquest.
    (C) Italy's imperial ambitions outstripped the country's ability to finance colonial wars.
    (D) Papal intrigue with the French, Germans, and Spanish consisted of a "fifth column" in Italy.
    (E) Civil war broke out between the Medici and Sforza families.

41. All of the following were reasons why Germany and Flanders were the center of the northern Renaissance EXCEPT

    (A) increased commercial contacts between Bruges and Antwerp strengthened cultural contacts between Italy and Flanders
    (B) German banking families were among the wealthiest in Europe
    (C) the conquest of Constantinople by the Ottoman Turks resulted in a mass exodus of Byzantine scholars to the Holy Roman Empire and Flanders
    (D) the German-speaking world was the center of European intellectual life during this period
    (E) the invention of the printing press by Johannes Gutenberg in 1450 greatly facilitated the spread of humanist writing

42. All of the following were methods that monarchs in Russia, France, and Spain employed to consolidate their rule EXCEPT

    (A) promoting ethnic and religious nationalism
    (B) establishing the right to make laws and raise armies on their own initiative
    (C) breaking the independent power of the nobility
    (D) securing control over levying taxes
    (E) establishing a close but dominant relationship with the Christian Church in their lands

43. The major obstacle preventing the growth of monarchies in southeastern Europe was

    (A) the conquest and occupation of that part of Europe by the Ottoman Turks

    (B) the patriarchs of the various Eastern Orthodox Churches worked to limit the power of monarchs

    (C) the low education level of the ruling dynasties

    (D) the mountainous terrain of the Balkans, which prohibited large-scale consolidation of territory

    (E) their enthusiastic support of Ottoman rule

44. More often than not, which group or person wielded the most political power in Poland?

    (A) the monarch

    (B) the landed nobility

    (C) the clergy

    (D) the peasantry

    (E) the proletariat

45. The typical family in 16th-century western Europe

    (A) was an extended household of parents, children, and grandparents

    (B) was a broken family caused by a high divorce rate

    (C) toiled in the urban factories for miserable wages

    (D) was a nuclear family comprised of husband, wife, and their children

    (E) was familiar with the works of da Vinci and Michelangelo

46. The Medici family was best known for

    (A) its opposition to papal infallibility and leading the Protestant Reformation

    (B) opening the long commercial relations between the Genoese and the Persians along the Silk Road

    (C) leading the *Reconquista* of Spain against the Muslims

    (D) sacking Rome in 1527

    (E) being the most famous Florentine patrons of arts and architecture

47. Sandro Botticelli's two most famous works, *The Birth of Venus* and
La Primavera,

(A) convey the spiritual appeal of the afterlife
(B) evoke sympathy for the plight of the serfs
(C) portray nature and humans realistically
(D) are dominated by pagan themes
(E) illustrate the dominance of males over females

48. Which of the following best characterizes the Byzantine Empire during
the 15th century?

(A) successful commercial competition with Venice
(B) declining size and strength as a result of Arab and Turkic incursions
(C) republican government
(D) financial center of Europe
(E) reassertion of control over Asia Minor

49. Which of the following was NOT incorporated into the kingdom of Spain
by Ferdinand and Isabella?

(A) Portugal
(B) Castile
(C) Aragon
(D) Granada
(E) Catalonia

50. The three orders of people in medieval Europe consisted of

(A) aristocracy, bourgeoisie, and proletariat
(B) clergy, bourgeoisie, and peasants
(C) royalty, nobles, and clergy
(D) professionals, bourgeoisie, and peasants
(E) clergy, nobles, and peasants

51. Beginning in 1438, which family traditionally gained election as Holy
Roman Emperors?

(A) Valois
(B) Hapsburg
(C) Carolingian
(D) Hohenzollern
(E) Stuart

52. As a result of the Treaty of Tordesillas (1494),

    (A) Spain claimed all of the Americas except Brazil while Portugal claimed all rights of trade in Africa, Asia, and the East Indies
    (B) the last of the Moors were forced to leave Spain in 1492
    (C) Portugal took control over parts of coastal India
    (D) the British were given exclusive rights to the slave trade between Africa and the Spanish colonies in the Western Hemisphere
    (E) Portugal gained most favored nation trade status with Japan

53. The reason Bartolome de Las Casas wrote his book chronicling the conduct of the Spanish in Latin America was

    (A) to agitate for the overthrow of the Spanish monarchy
    (B) to expose the flawed principles that Roman Catholicism was founded on
    (C) in revenge for not being named viceroy of Cuba
    (D) to inform the authorities in Spain about the abuses committed in Latin America
    (E) to be named viceroy of all of Spain's Latin American possessions

54. Prior to the Age of Discovery in the 15th century, Europe's major attempt at expansion and colonization beyond the confines of the continent was

    (A) the Viking landing in Greenland
    (B) the Crusaders brief occupation of the Middle East
    (C) Britain's occupation of India
    (D) Russia's expansion into Central Asia
    (E) Belgian colonization of the Congo

55. All of the following were factors that prompted the Portuguese to explore overseas trade routes and establish colonies EXCEPT

    (A) the desire to spread Christianity to non-Christians
    (B) the search for African gold
    (C) advances in navigational technology either developed by the Portuguese or assimilated from advances of the Muslims and Chinese
    (D) the hope of finding a shorter route to Japan
    (E) Portugal was inhospitable to agriculture

56. Which of the following stimulated the need to find a route to the Indies?

(A) Goods passing through Ottoman and Venetian territories became too expensive as a result of heavy taxation.

(B) Once the Ottoman Turks brought down the Byzantine Empire, they cut off all East-West trade between Europe and Asia.

(C) There were difficulties in traversing the vast deserts of the Silk Road.

(D) Constant wars between the Ottomans and the Mongols made the Middle East and Central Asia too dangerous to travel for European merchants.

(E) European countries needed a source of cheap labor to work in the new factories sprouting up in the urban areas.

57. All of the following resulted from the discovery of new trade routes during the 16th century EXCEPT

(A) the Silk Road declined as a major trade route uniting Asia and Europe

(B) the monarchies of Spain and Portugal became wealthier

(C) the cost of goods were reduced for Europeans

(D) demand in Europe was stimulated for overseas goods

(E) Germany rose as a European power

58. The importation of African slaves to the Americas dramatically increased as a result of the growing need for labor to harvest

(A) mutton

(B) wheat

(C) sugarcane

(D) maize

(E) coal

59. Which of the following countries had the largest population in Europe in 1600?

(A) Spain

(B) Poland

(C) England

(D) France

(E) Russia

60. In the mid-16th century, Charles V's empire included all of the following territories EXCEPT

(A) Venice
(B) Austria
(C) South America
(D) Naples
(E) Spain

61. Portugal and Spain were able to attain overseas colonies because of

(A) cooperation with Portuguese and Spanish immigrants in foreign lands
(B) their superior firearms and sea power
(C) fair financial compensation to local rulers
(D) treaties with local leaders
(E) their ability to defeat England and France in mainland wars and acquiring their colonies

62. All of the following were middle-class professions in the 16th century EXCEPT

(A) army officers
(B) lawyers
(C) artisans
(D) bankers
(E) shopkeepers

63. The parallel transfer of people, cultures, animals, food, and disease between Europe, Africa, and the Western Hemisphere as a result of the Spanish colonization of the New World is known as the

(A) continental divide
(B) Cartesian swap
(C) Faustian bargain
(D) Columbian Exchange
(E) Middle Passage

64. Which of the following best describes the political and economic environments of much of 15th-century Italy?

(A) a few large states dominated by a wealthy landed nobility
(B) a strong, unified Italian monarchy that patronized the arts
(C) many independent city-states with prosperous merchant oligarchies
(D) control of most of Italy by the pope, who encouraged mercantile development
(E) support of the territorial unity of Italy by the kings of France and the Holy Roman Emperors, who were competing for influence

65. Which of the following most clearly distinguishes the northern Renaissance from the Italian Renaissance?

   (A) interest in science and technology
   (B) greater concern with religious piety
   (C) cultivation of a Latin style
   (D) growth of national language in literature
   (E) admiration for scholastic thought

CHAPTER 3

The Reformation, 1500–1600

66. What was the Catholic Church's position on indulgences after the Council of Trent?

(A) Indulgences were recognized as erroneous and abolished.

(B) The issue of indulgences was not brought up at the council.

(C) The practice of offering indulgences was blamed on the Protestants and, therefore, severely condemned.

(D) The corruption of indulgences was criticized but the principle was upheld.

(E) The sale of indulgences was justified when a Catholic was martyred fighting against Muslims.

67. The center of European Calvinism in the 16th century became

(A) Geneva

(B) Lyon

(C) Amsterdam

(D) Glasgow

(E) Wittenberg

68. What was the immediate "spark" that caused Luther to condemn Catholic practices?

(A) Pope Nicholas II's banning of marriage for Catholic clergy

(B) Spanish conquistadors' use of cruel methods to convert the native population in the Americas to Christianity

(C) a Catholic-inspired pogrom of the Jewish population in Mainz, Germany

(D) the selling of indulgences as a means to save a soul that was in purgatory

(E) Luther's strong opposition to Pope Gregory VII's opposition to "Lay Investiture"

69. The immediate cause for the Reformation is found in the activity of Martin Luther during the years
(A) 1492–1498
(B) 1517–1521
(C) 1545–1563
(D) 1555–1575
(E) 1618–1648

70. All of these were precursors to Martin Luther in their criticisms of the Catholic Church EXCEPT
(A) Wycliffe
(B) Knox
(C) Savonarola
(D) Erasmus
(E) Hus

71. What was Henry VIII's goal when he broke with the Roman Catholic Church?
(A) reform Catholic practices
(B) install a new pope that would obey him
(C) become the head of a newly formed Anglican Church
(D) destroy Roman Catholicism and replace it with Lutheranism
(E) institute the practice of parliamentary elections to determine the head of the English Catholic Church

72. All of the following threatened the power of the Roman Catholic Church in the 16th century EXCEPT
(A) ideas emanating from the Italian Renaissance
(B) the growing strength in southeastern Europe of the Muslim Ottoman Turks
(C) the growth of the national state
(D) the Protestant Reformation
(E) the scientific discoveries of Copernicus and Galileo

73. Besides religious doctrinal disputes, the major issue behind the wars in Europe in the 16th and 17th centuries was

(A) how to divide colonies between the emerging imperialist European powers

(B) how to contain the growing military threat of Sweden

(C) what country would emerge as the leader in the fight against the Ottoman Turks

(D) how to contain the expansionist ambitions of France

(E) the struggle between the decentralizing tendencies of local princes and the centralizing efforts of national monarchs

74. What was Elizabeth I's contribution to the religion controversy in England during her rule?

(A) She brought the English Catholic Church back under the control of Rome.

(B) She broke off relations with Rome because the pope would not annul her marriage.

(C) She reestablished the Church of England's independence from Rome.

(D) She sided with the Puritans and eliminated all remnants of Catholicism from the Church of England.

(E) She was responsible for expelling the Jews from England.

75. Which of the following did Martin Luther and King Henry VIII of England have in common?

(A) Both were married eight times.

(B) Neither wanted to split from the Roman Catholic Church at the outset of their activities.

(C) Both wanted to raise an army to crush Catholic Spain's crusading missions in Europe.

(D) Neither thought that the clergy should marry.

(E) Both believed in the concept of papal supremacy.

76. Why did France support the Protestant rebels fighting against the Catholics in the Holy Roman Empire?

(A) It wanted to weaken and fragment the Holy Roman Empire.

(B) King Henry IV of France was a Huguenot and, therefore, a supporter of the German Protestants.

(C) The German Protestants had helped King Henry IV, a Huguenot, assume the throne in France.

(D) The French merchants desired to control the mouth of the Rhine River for trade.

(E) Revenge was sought for the pope excommunicating the entire French clergy.

77. "We . . . take it for granted that you will release us from serfdom as true Christians, unless it should be shown us from the Gospel that we are serfs."

This statement was written by

(A) Turkish peasants in Asia Minor

(B) English peasants under Henry VIII

(C) conquered Aztecs in Mexico

(D) Emelian Pugachev in 1775

(E) German peasants in the 1520s

78. According to John Calvin, certain people were "predestined" to go to heaven. What did he mean by this?

(A) Only Calvinists would go to heaven.

(B) Every Christian was guaranteed salvation.

(C) People who did good works would go to heaven.

(D) Calvinists and Lutherans were destined to go to heaven but not Catholics.

(E) God has already chosen if one would be saved prior to one's death.

79. As a result of the Peace of Augsburg, the Holy Roman Emperor agreed that German princes should

(A) become Protestant

(B) execute anyone who had fought in the Peasants' Revolt

(C) burn all copies of the Ninety-Five Theses

(D) be able to choose whether their lands would be Catholic or Lutheran

(E) declare their independence from the Holy Roman Empire

80. The saying "Erasmus laid the egg that Luther hatched" refers to

(A) the agricultural revolution
(B) the Renaissance
(C) civic humanism
(D) the Reformation
(E) the baroque style

81. "Christians should be taught that, if the Pope knew the exactions of the preachers of Indulgences, he would rather have the basilica of St. Peter's reduced to ashes than built with the skin, flesh and bones of his sheep."

This passage was contained in which of the following?

(A) Thomas More's *Utopia*
(B) Erasmus's *In Praise of Folly*
(C) Loyola's *Spiritual Exercises*
(D) Luther's Ninety-Five Theses
(E) Calvin's *Institutes of the Christian Religion*

82. The Peace of Augsburg (1555) left unresolved which issue?

(A) the place of Calvinism in the settlement
(B) border divisions in Scandinavia
(C) construction of St. Peter's Basilica in Rome
(D) the Italian frontier with Switzerland
(E) restoration of Catholicism in France

83. Calvinism became an influential force in which of the following countries?

(A) Spain
(B) Italy
(C) Scotland
(D) Russia
(E) Portugal

84. The most important change instituted by the English Reformation was the

(A) abolition of the mass
(B) rejection of the Old Testament
(C) removal of all bishops from their sees
(D) replacement of the pope by the king of England as head of the church
(E) banning of marriage for Anglican clerics

85. "That no Christian is bound to do those things which God had not decreed, therefore one may eat at all times all food, wherefrom one learns that the decree about . . . fasting is a Roman swindle."

This passage refers to

(A) errors of the Catholic Church written by a leader of the Reformation
(B) Charles V's dietary instructions at the Diet of Worms
(C) revision of canon law by the Council of Trent
(D) Ignatius Loyola's denunciation of Calvin
(E) one of the principle reasons for the split between the Catholic and Orthodox Churches

86. Among Luther's most important beliefs were all of the following EXCEPT

(A) justification by faith
(B) authority of scripture
(C) the seven sacraments
(D) priesthood of the believer
(E) translation of the Bible in the vernacular

87. Besides religious issues, the other major cause of the Protestant Reformation and the religious wars that followed was

(A) the political struggle between monarchs imposing their centralized rule over their subjects and nobles fighting to keep their feudal independence
(B) the growing sense of belonging to a nation that has a common language, ethnicity, culture, and history
(C) the growing mercantilist competition for overseas colonies between the Holy Roman Empire, Spain, France, and Holland
(D) the bitterness that some European countries felt toward France for allying itself with the Ottoman Empire
(E) the growing threat to Sicily and Vienna from the Ottoman Empire

88. The main result of the Edict of Nantes (1598) was that

(A) it led to the disintegration of the Holy Roman Empire
(B) it confirmed England as the new master of the seas
(C) Calvinists recognized Geneva as their capital
(D) it established the principles of religious toleration and equal civil rights for French Protestants and Catholics
(E) it led to the arrest of those responsible for the St. Bartholomew's Day massacre

89. What effect did the Thirty Years' War have on the German-speaking
population between 1618 and 1650?

(A) About a third of the population perished.
(B) It stayed about the same.
(C) Soldiers from Sweden resettled in the Holy Roman Empire,
    increasing its population slightly.
(D) Sickened by the Christian infighting, many converted to Judaism.
(E) The population doubled.

90. The Peace of Augsburg represented the end of Charles V's hopes to

(A) defeat the Turks in Hungary
(B) contain French aggression in the Rhineland
(C) restore Catholicism in all parts of the Holy Roman Empire
(D) regain his title as Holy Roman Emperor
(E) prevent Henry VIII of England from leaving the Catholic Church

CHAPTER 4

The Rise of Sovereignty, 1600–1715

91. In 1640 Charles I called Parliament into session because he

(A) needed money to pursue his war against France
(B) became a supporter of democratic principles
(C) wanted to change his religion
(D) wanted a declaration of war against Spain
(E) needed money to suppress a rebellion in Scotland

92. In the 18th century the principal economic activity of the Netherlands was

(A) banking and maritime commerce
(B) tulip cultivation
(C) timber production and export
(D) agricultural production
(E) oil refining

93. An immediate effect of the Glorious Revolution in England was

(A) the return of the Tudors as rulers of England
(B) universal manhood suffrage
(C) the persecution of members of the Anglican Church
(D) the decline of England as a colonial power
(E) the supremacy of Parliament over the monarchy

94. Which of the following was the most significant factor in the rise of national states in western Europe?

(A) the end of serfdom
(B) the acquisition of colonies in the New World
(C) the rise of the feudal nobility
(D) the need for protection from barbarian invasions
(E) the rise and support of the middle class

95. Louis XIV supported all of the following EXCEPT
   (A) the building of the Palace of Versailles
   (B) cooperation with the Estates General
   (C) art and culture
   (D) the policies of Cardinal Mazarin
   (E) the theory of divine right of kings

96. Colbert's contributions to the economy of France included all of the following EXCEPT
   (A) encouraging new industries and colonial ventures
   (B) creating a national bank
   (C) improving the transportation and communication systems within France
   (D) creating the French East India Company
   (E) creating a powerful merchant marine to transport French goods

97. Which of the following is the correct order of the Stuart dynasty?
   (A) Charles I, James I, James II, Charles II
   (B) James I, Charles I, James II, Charles II
   (C) Charles I, James I, Charles II, James II
   (D) James I, Charles I, Charles II, James II
   (E) James I, James II, Charles I, Charles II

98. William of Orange ascended to the throne from which country?
   (A) England
   (B) the Netherlands
   (C) France
   (D) Spain
   (E) Belgium

99. What was Cardinal Richelieu's chief goal?
   (A) to become king
   (B) to destroy the nobles' and Huguenots' power
   (C) to increase papal influence over the French king
   (D) to avoid alliances with Protestant countries
   (E) to conquer England

100. What was the result of Louis XIV's persecution of Huguenots?

(A) They rose against him in war.
(B) They left France, causing a blow to the French economy.
(C) The entire group was killed off.
(D) They formed a new French state.
(E) The St. Bartholomew Day massacre occurred.

101. Who was the leader of the Roundheads in the English Civil War?

(A) Charles I
(B) Parliament
(C) Henry VIII
(D) Oliver Cromwell
(E) John Pym

102. Many English Protestants feared that James II would

(A) wage war on France
(B) invite William and Mary to come to England
(C) restore the Roman Catholic Church
(D) restore the Church of England
(E) grant Ireland its independence

103. William and Mary were required to accept the _____ before taking the throne.

(A) Levellers
(B) Magna Carta
(C) English Bill of Rights
(D) Long Parliament
(E) pope's permission

104. Which of the following groups of people would have most likely lived at Versailles?

(A) wealthy middle class
(B) peasants
(C) nobility
(D) clergy
(E) sansculottes

105. Mercantilism was principally characterized by
- (A) government efforts to build a strong, self-sufficient economy
- (B) the efforts of the merchant class to influence policy by subsidizing the government
- (C) the efforts of bankers and exporters to establish free trade
- (D) the theory that gold and silver were not real wealth
- (E) the view that labor ought to be able to seek its own market

106. In the first half of the 17th century, King Gustavus Adolphus of Sweden played a key role in European affairs by
- (A) opposing the expansionist plans of Cardinal Richelieu of France
- (B) acting as intermediary between Catholic and Lutheran governments
- (C) leading a Protestant coalition against Catholic Europe
- (D) allying with Habsburg Spain to challenge British sea power
- (E) arguing that state interest should take precedence over religious loyalties

107. Nobles were most numerous during the 18th century in
- (A) England
- (B) Prussia
- (C) Poland
- (D) Russia
- (E) France

108. The most serious problem confronting Poland in the 18th century was
- (A) the end of serfdom
- (B) Swedish expansionism after the death of Charles XII
- (C) resurgence of the Ottoman Empire
- (D) weak central government
- (E) the threat of civil war between Catholic Poles and Orthodox Slavs

109. Which of the following combination of states blocked Russian expansion during the 16th and 17th centuries?
- (A) Sweden, Poland, Ottoman Empire
- (B) Holland, England, Holy Roman Empire
- (C) Poland, Holy Roman Empire, Finland
- (D) Ottoman Empire, Persia, Hungary
- (E) Sweden, England, France

110. Among the principal characteristics of 17th- and 18th-century absolutist states were all the following EXCEPT

(A) large standing armies
(B) development of constitutions
(C) weakening of the nobility
(D) absolutist rule based on divine right
(E) strong centralized bureaucracies

111. Between the 15th and 18th centuries, the Ukraine became a focal point in the struggle between

(A) Prussia and Poland
(B) Lithuania and Belarus
(C) Latvia and Russia
(D) Estonia and Sweden
(E) Russia and Poland

112. The period of political instability in Russia known as the Time of Troubles

(A) led to the occupation of the country by the Mongols
(B) resulted in the beginning of the Romanov dynasty
(C) led to the split in the Russian Orthodox Church
(D) weakened the monarchy and led to the formation of a Duma
(E) led to the strengthening of serfdom

CHAPTER 5

The Scientific Revolution During the 17th Century

113. The view that was accepted in Europe until the 16th century that the sun and planets revolved around the earth was known as the

(A) Socratic concept of the universe
(B) Platonic concept of the universe
(C) Diocletian concept of the universe
(D) Ptolemaic concept of the universe
(E) Hippocratic Oath

114. Nicholas Copernicus's major contribution to scientific knowledge was

(A) the discovery of the laws of gravitational pull
(B) that the universe was heliocentric
(C) the discovery of penicillin
(D) the development of calculus
(E) the development of the periodic table of elements

115. Galileo helped to confirm Copernicus's major contribution to scientific knowledge

(A) with the development of advanced mathematics
(B) through dissection and mapping out the human anatomy
(C) with the discovery of the telescope
(D) by reading the Bible
(E) by making advances in alchemy

116. What effect did the Scientific Revolution have on the authority of the Catholic Church?

- (A) It strengthened its intellectual authority since most scientists of the 16th century were Catholic.
- (B) It weakened its authority since more natural phenomena that had been traditionally left to the clerical leaders were now being explained through scientific inquiry.
- (C) The Catholic Church worked closely with the scientific community to develop methods that would alleviate suffering on earth.
- (D) The Scientific Revolution was able to confirm the existence of a divinity in the heavens, thus strengthening the authority of the church.
- (E) It led to the Protestant Reformation.

117. The greatest achievement of the Scientific Revolution included

- (A) chemistry
- (B) medicine
- (C) astronomy
- (D) physics
- (E) all of the above

118. The Royal Society was founded in 1662 by King Charles II to

- (A) encourage the arts and culture
- (B) ennoble middle-class merchants
- (C) honor military achievement
- (D) improve scientific knowledge
- (E) confer Nobel prizes

119. Among the most important advances of the Scientific Revolution were all of the following EXCEPT

- (A) the development of a vaccine for influenza
- (B) emphasis on empirical research
- (C) the invention of the telescope
- (D) the development of the scientific method
- (E) the development of a vaccine for smallpox

120. The most serious conflict facing scientists of the 17th century, such as Galileo, was

(A) understanding the role of the king in national politics
(B) resolving the dilemma between Christianity and Islam
(C) rejecting mathematics in place of alchemy
(D) reconciling scientific discoveries with Christian teachings
(E) the cutback in government funding for scientific research

121. "I may well presume, most Holy Father that certain people, as soon as they hear that in this book about the Revolution of Heavenly Spheres I ascribe movement to the earthly globe, will cry out that, holding such views, I should at once be hissed off the stage."

This passage was written by

(A) Bacon
(B) Copernicus
(C) Pope Urban VIII
(D) Descartes
(E) Servantes

122. The scientist responsible for developing calculus and the theory of gravity was

(A) Johann Kepler
(B) Gottfried Leibniz
(C) Dmitry Mendeleyev
(D) Isaac Newton
(E) Edward Jenner

123. What major impact did the Scientific Revolution have on the Enlightenment?

(A) Through application of the concept of natural law to political theory, society could be governed in a more rational way.
(B) With the confirmation of the existence of a supreme divinity, the concept of the divine right of kings was strengthened.
(C) Failure to discover all of the laws that governed nature meant skepticism in separation of powers.
(D) The Scientific Revolution had a marginal impact on the Enlightenment since the latter encompassed political theory, education, and culture while the former dealt with mathematics and science.
(E) none of the above

CHAPTER 6

The Enlightenment: A Cultural Movement During the 18th Century

124. John Locke is most famous for advancing the concept of
- (A) the divine right of kings
- (B) a heliocentric concept of the universe
- (C) universal suffrage and a modern welfare state
- (D) all people having natural rights based on life, liberty, and property
- (E) economic justice for all

125. What impact did the view of Thomas Hobbes have on the development of political theory in the 17th and 18th centuries?
- (A) Although his ideas on absolutism were popular in absolutist countries, his atheism limited his appeal.
- (B) His ideas greatly influenced the trajectory of the American Revolution.
- (C) He has often been called the "father of the democratic revolutions."
- (D) He would have significant influence on thinkers such as Karl Marx.
- (E) He was a precursor to libertarian thought.

126. Which of the following philosophes believed that society should adhere to a "general will"?
- (A) Locke
- (B) Rousseau
- (C) Montesquieu
- (D) Voltaire
- (E) Kant

127. What type of government did Voltaire favor?
- (A) a representative democratic system where all classes, men and women, were allowed to vote
- (B) an absolute monarchy ruling according to divine right that maintained order, stability, and prosperity in the country
- (C) an enlightened despotism that secured freedom of religion and expression, kept the church in a subordinate position, and advanced the cause of material and technical progress
- (D) a direct democracy where all citizens would take part in all the decision-making functions of government
- (E) a dictatorship of the sansculottes

128. Baron de Montesquieu is best known for
- (A) his opposition to Parliament's power
- (B) his support for enlightened despotism
- (C) his support of governments where power is separated between three branches
- (D) calling for the abolition of private property
- (E) none of the above

129. Montesquieu greatly admired
- (A) England
- (B) France
- (C) Prussia
- (D) Spain
- (E) Russia

130. In Rousseau's *The Social Contract*, the contract was between the
- (A) established church and the monarchy
- (B) government and the people
- (C) church and the people
- (D) people themselves
- (E) nobles and the bourgeoisie

131. The center of the Enlightenment was
- (A) France
- (B) England
- (C) Austria
- (D) Prussia
- (E) Russia

132. The major tax burden in France in the 18th century fell on the
  (A) landed nobility
  (B) Catholic Church
  (C) peasantry
  (D) monarch
  (E) none of the above

133. _____ has often been called the "father of rationalism."
  (A) Descartes
  (B) Hobbes
  (C) Voltaire
  (D) Kant
  (E) Newton

134. Which of the following called for equal rights for women in her book *Vindication of the Rights of Woman*?
  (A) Catherine the Great
  (B) Maria Theresa
  (C) Mary Wollstonecraft
  (D) Mary Astell
  (E) Mary Shelley

135. Voltaire was most outspoken and vehement in his denunciation of
  (A) Great Britain
  (B) the Roman Catholic Church
  (C) Catherine the Great
  (D) modern science
  (E) Frederick II of Prussia

136. Enlightened monarchs were LEAST likely to do which of the following?
  (A) surrender royal prerogatives
  (B) improve education
  (C) reduce the power of the church
  (D) reform legal codes
  (E) promote culture and science

137. All of the following were reforms enacted by enlightened monarchs during the 18th century EXCEPT

    (A) restricted the use of torture
    (B) ennobled Jews
    (C) abolished serfdom
    (D) abolished state churches
    (E) eased censorship

138. Which of the following did Maria Theresa of Austria NOT do?

    (A) pass laws against the abuse of peasants by their lords or overseers
    (B) implement a tariff union between Bohemia, Moravia, and Austria proper creating the largest free-trade zone in Europe
    (C) totally abolish serfdom
    (D) give birth to two future monarchs
    (E) become the only female monarch in Hapsburg dynastic history

139. All of the following were reforms of Joseph II EXCEPT

    (A) totally abolishing serfdom
    (B) granting universal suffrage
    (C) granting freedom of the press
    (D) granting religious freedom except for minor sects
    (E) decreeing absolute equality in taxation

140. One common concern of both Maria Theresa and Joseph II was

    (A) providing state social services to the needy
    (B) granting autonomy to the various ethnic groups in the Austrian Empire
    (C) industrializing the country
    (D) centralizing power
    (E) abolishing serfdom

141. Joseph's "Germanization" of the Austrian Empire led to

    (A) the Austrian War of Succession
    (B) growing nationalism among the non-German population
    (C) unification with Prussia
    (D) conflicts with Poland
    (E) conflict with Prussia

142. Why did Frederick the Great of Prussia only abolish serfdom on crown lands and not the lands held by the Junkers?

(A) The Junkers didn't possess serfs because they were a military caste.

(B) He wanted to keep the loyalty of the Junkers.

(C) Eighty-five percent of Prussia's serfs lived on crown lands.

(D) He thought it was immoral for the monarchy to keep peasants in serfdom.

(E) none of the above

143. All of the following are reasons why enlightened reform was limited in Prussia EXCEPT

(A) Frederick was a mediocre leader with limited intelligence and ambition

(B) political centralization had already been achieved by Frederick's predecessors

(C) the Lutheran Church was already subordinated to the state

(D) the relatively few burghers were heavily dependent on the crown

(E) the middle class was small and politically weak

144. What two major events limited the scope of Catherine's reforms in Russia?

(A) the Pugachev Rebellion and the French Revolution

(B) the wars against the Ottoman Empire and the partitions of Poland

(C) the Pugachev Rebellion and Catherine's active social life

(D) the American and French Revolutions

(E) none of the above

145. Catherine's foreign policy achievements were

(A) expanding Russia's control over Central Asia

(B) defeating France and England in the Crimean War

(C) gaining control of the Crimean peninsula and the Black Sea and expanding westward at the expense of Poland

(D) entering into an alliance with China that deterred the Ottoman Empire from starting a war with Russia

(E) defeating Sweden in the Great Northern War

146. European Jews benefited the most from which enlightened despot?

(A) Louis XVI

(B) Maria Theresa

(C) Frederick the Great

(D) Joseph II

(E) Philip II

147. As a result of the Pugachev Rebellion,
- (A) Catherine abolished serfdom in Russia
- (B) serfdom in Russia was strengthened to almost slave status and expanded into the Ukraine
- (C) St. Petersburg was sacked and Peter III was murdered
- (D) the Ottoman Turks invaded Russia and recaptured Odessa and Sevastopol
- (E) Emelian Pugachev became czar

148. Overall, the reforms of the enlightened despots
- (A) were not able to take hold because of limited support among the nobility
- (B) paved the way for democratic systems and the welfare state
- (C) led to a counterreaction and the return of absolutist rule all over Europe
- (D) led to the feudalization of Europe
- (E) none of the above

149. Among the goals of the revolutions of the 19th century were
- (A) to introduce limited suffrage
- (B) national unification in Italy and Germany
- (C) autonomy or self-determination of national minorities in the Austro-Hungarian, Ottoman, and Russian Empires
- (D) to limit monarchies
- (E) all of the above

150. Of the great powers in the 18th century, which of the following did NOT have a regular standing army?
- (A) Austria
- (B) Sweden
- (C) Britain
- (D) France
- (E) Ottoman Empire

151. The language of the Enlightenment and the aristocracy in 18th-century Europe was
- (A) French
- (B) German
- (C) English
- (D) Italian
- (E) Spanish

152. Officers in European armies in the 18th century usually came from

(A) the landed aristocracy
(B) the bourgeoisie
(C) mercenaries
(D) the peasantry
(E) monarch's sons

153. In the 18th century, the peasantry constituted about _____ percent of Europe's population.

(A) 20
(B) 35
(C) 50
(D) 85
(E) 95

154. Overall, the nobility in Europe constituted about _____ percent of the population in the 18th century.

(A) 5
(B) 20
(C) 35
(D) 50
(E) 80

CHAPTER 7

Social Transformation and State-Building in the 18th Century

155. All of the following were reasons why the Dutch were the commercial and financial leaders in Europe in the 17th century EXCEPT

(A) they standardized currency throughout Europe
(B) the Dutch government guaranteed the safety of the deposits
(C) their merchant marine was the largest in Europe
(D) the Dutch charged no interest on long-term loans
(E) depositors were allowed to draw checks against their accounts

156. The success of the Dutch Republic during the 17th century was due to all of the following EXCEPT

(A) banking and credit facilities in Amsterdam
(B) colonial possessions
(C) religious toleration
(D) political compromise between the Estates General and Orangist hereditary monarchy
(E) alliance with Spain

157. What impact did the British Navigation Acts (1651) have on Anglo-Dutch relations?

(A) Relations between the two worsened because the Dutch saw these acts as a direct threat to their commercial activities.
(B) Relations improved because the acts established a balance of power between the two in the newly discovered colonies in North America.
(C) They brought the Dutch into conflict with the French since France was England's biggest ally.
(D) Relations improved because the Dutch Republic was officially accepted into the United Kingdom.
(E) none of the above

158. Charles I of England faced a revolt against royal authority led by

 (A) Parliament
 (B) the Anglican Church
 (C) peasants
 (D) French agents
 (E) a renegade governor of Ireland

159. The immediate cause of conflict in England in the 17th century that led to the English Civil War was

 (A) the refusal on the part of the Stuart monarchs to raise taxes on the nobility, causing the peasantry to rise in rebellion
 (B) Tudor attempts to reclaim the throne with Spain's help
 (C) the potato famine in Ireland
 (D) the refusal by the Stuart monarchs to get Parliament's consent to raise taxes
 (E) the humiliating defeat to the Irish in the Great Potato War

160. Which of the following was the most significant outcome of Charles I's execution in 1649?

 (A) It was the first time in history that a Parliament had voted for the execution of a monarch.
 (B) The execution restored the Tudors on the throne.
 (C) The execution led to the abolition of monarchy in England.
 (D) Without a monarch, England was invaded and conquered by the Scots.
 (E) Charles's execution resulted in the independence of Ireland.

161. How did the execution of Charles I affect public opinion in Scotland?

 (A) The Scots used this event to take over England.
 (B) It turned public opinion strongly against the rule of Oliver Cromwell.
 (C) Scottish nobles were too busy putting down peasant riots to be affected.
 (D) It prompted Scotland and Ireland to join forces against England.
 (E) none of the above

162. After 1653 Cromwell transformed England into a

 (A) constitutional monarchy
 (B) theocracy
 (C) parliamentary republic
 (D) military dictatorship
 (E) fragmented feudal state

163. All of the following contributed to the growing opposition to Cromwell's rule in England EXCEPT

    (A) the increasing tax burden to pay for his wars alienated landowners and merchants
    (B) his strict Puritan social policies alienated moderate Anglicans
    (C) his growing reliance on France to prop up his government
    (D) his cruel treatment of Catholic dissenters in Ireland
    (E) his dissolution of the Rump Parliament

164. After the restoration of the Stuart dynasty, which of the following contributed the most to growing opposition to Charles II?

    (A) his growing alliance with the Dutch
    (B) his conversion to Calvinism midway through his rule
    (C) his inability to establish a rival commercial center in London
    (D) his growing admiration for Catholicism and Louis XIV
    (E) all of the above

165. Roundheads and Cavaliers fought each other during the mid-17th century in

    (A) England
    (B) France
    (C) Holland
    (D) Spain
    (E) Russia

166. Which of the following is the most significant result of the Glorious Revolution of 1688 and the English Bill of Rights?

    (A) Absolute rule based on the principle of divine right of kings was firmly established in England.
    (B) The United Kingdom was formed.
    (C) Equal rights and political representation were extended to subjects of the Crown in the English colonies.
    (D) Limited monarchy was firmly established in England.
    (E) England became the dominant European power until 1870.

167. Which of the following best illustrates Louis XIV's strong belief in national unity under the leadership of a strong monarch?
    (A) He revoked the Edict of Nantes.
    (B) All social classes must pay their fair share of taxes.
    (C) The Estates General must be convened regularly by the king, but the king has the final say in all matters.
    (D) French Catholics should be obedient to the monarch, who in turn answers only to the pope.
    (E) all of the above

168. "We forbid our subjects of the so-called Reformed religion to assemble any more for public worship."

    This statement was most likely issued as a result of the
    (A) Edict of Nantes
    (B) English Bill of Rights
    (C) Ninety-Five Theses
    (D) Edict of Fontainebleau
    (E) Peace of Augsburg

169. All of the following mercantilist policies were implemented by Jean-Baptiste Colbert between 1648 and 1653 EXCEPT
    (A) establish new industries
    (B) improve roads and build canals
    (C) increase internal tariffs
    (D) create the French East India Company
    (E) create a commercial code for businesses covering the entire country

170. Which of the following French kings is acknowledged as the embodiment of an absolute monarch?
    (A) Henry IV
    (B) Louis XIII
    (C) Louis XIV
    (D) Louis XV
    (E) Louis XVI

171. The main cause of the War of the Spanish Succession was

(A) Charles II of Spain had no legitimate heir to the throne
(B) the dispute over who would divide the spoils of the Spanish Empire as a result of Spain's defeat at the hands of England in 1588
(C) the European powers joining together to prevent a return to Muslim rule in Spain
(D) Portugal's struggle for independence from Spain
(E) Portugal's claim to the Spanish throne after the death of Charles II

172. The War of the Spanish Succession ended with

(A) the Hapsburgs reign in Spain
(B) the grandson of Louis XIV remaining king of Spain
(C) Italy's unification under French rule
(D) Britain's defeat and loss of Canada
(E) none of the above

173. The term "United Provinces" was used to describe

(A) East and West Prussia
(B) Belgium, the Netherlands, Luxemburg, parts of northern France, and western Germany
(C) Scotland, England, and Wales
(D) Castile, Aragon, and Navarre
(E) Belgium and the Netherlands only

174. "Divine right" monarchy was a term used to refer to

(A) a king's power derived from God
(B) the pope's authority over bishops
(C) the rights of subjects under a king
(D) the requirement that kings be ordained by the pope
(E) the theory that justified the rise and fall of kings

175. In the first half of the 17th century, the hub of the business world in Europe was located in

(A) Vienna
(B) Rome
(C) Amsterdam
(D) Paris
(E) London

176. Which of the following is an accurate characterization of England in the period 1688–1715?

(A) a Puritan theocracy
(B) an absolute monarchy
(C) a democracy practicing religious toleration
(D) a constitutional monarchy controlled by an aristocratic oligarchy
(E) a presidential democracy

177. After 1688, England forbade Catholics in _____ from sitting in Parliament, teaching, purchasing land, and exporting anything except agricultural goods to England.

(A) Scotland
(B) Ireland
(C) France
(D) Holland
(E) Wales

178. Which of the following became a British possession as a result of the treaty that ended the War of the Spanish Succession?

(A) Jamaica
(B) Gibraltar
(C) Manhattan
(D) Canada
(E) India

179. Which of the following stipulated that no Catholic could be king of England?

(A) Solemn League and Covenant
(B) Triennial Act
(C) Act of Settlement
(D) Petition of Right
(E) English Bill of Rights

180. All of the following were leaders of the British Parliament's revolt against Charles I EXCEPT

(A) Thomas Grey
(B) John Pym
(C) John Churchill
(D) John Hampden
(E) Oliver Cromwell

181. Which of the following was successful at establishing absolute monarchy in the 17th century?

(A) France
(B) Holland
(C) Italy
(D) Poland
(E) England

182. In which pair listed below did the institution of Parliament succeed in confirming the right to share power with the monarch?

(A) France and Spain
(B) Italy and the Holy Roman Empire
(C) England and Holland
(D) Sweden and Bavaria
(E) none of the above

183. The partitions of Poland 1772–1795

(A) created three independent Polish states
(B) eliminated Poland as an independent state
(C) divided Poland between Sweden, Finland, and Lithuania
(D) divided Poland between Russia, Hungary, and Austria
(E) led to the emergence of an independent Lithuanian state

184. Nobles were most numerous during the 18th century in

(A) England
(B) Prussia
(C) Russia
(D) France
(E) Poland

185. In 1713 Emperor Charles VI sought approval of the Pragmatic Sanction in order to guarantee

(A) indivisibility of the Hapsburg lands
(B) political privileges for Catholics
(C) borders between Holland and the Austrian Netherlands
(D) the dynastic union of the Hapsburgs and Romanovs
(E) succession of the Bourbons to the Spanish throne

186. Typically the largest expenditure item in the budget of an 18th-century state—excluding interest on the national debt—was
(A) military
(B) royal palaces
(C) education
(D) subsidies for the poor
(E) infrastructure projects

187. The most serious problem confronting Poland in the 18th century was
(A) the end of serfdom
(B) Swedish expansionism after the death of Charles XII
(C) the resurgence of the Ottoman Empire
(D) a weak central government
(E) the Protestant Reformation

188. Which of the following states successfully occupied Moscow in the 17th century?
(A) France
(B) Sweden
(C) Poland
(D) Ottoman Empire
(E) Holland

189. "The victory which the king of Poland hath obtained over the Infidels, is so great and so complete that past Ages can scarce parallel the fame; and perhaps future Ages will never see anything like it."

This passage comes from an account of the defeat of the
(A) Turks at Vienna
(B) Russians at Poltava
(C) Dutch at Utrecht
(D) French at Blenheim
(E) Poles at Tannenbaum

190. Among the principal characteristics of 17th- and 18th-century absolutist states were all the following EXCEPT
(A) politically powerful monarchs
(B) large standing armies
(C) written constitutions
(D) a weakening of the nobility
(E) strong centralized bureaucracies

191. With the exception of Russia, in 17th-century Europe a sure sign of high social standing included all of the following EXCEPT

(A) tax exemption
(B) large cash reserves
(C) extensive landed estates
(D) a title of nobility
(E) high positions in government and the military

192. Prussia was able to expand successfully during the 17th and 18th centuries because of all of the following EXCEPT

(A) a series of able rulers
(B) the willingness of the nobility to subordinate itself to the crown
(C) a large navy
(D) the creation of an army out of proportion to the size of the state
(E) no geographical barriers to expansion

193. The establishment and growth of St. Petersburg during the 18th century was part of Peter the Great's attempt to do which of the following?

(A) strengthen his alliance with the Baltic states
(B) remake Russian institutions to be as effective as those in western Europe
(C) reduce the high cost of government in the old capital of Moscow
(D) discourage Russian expansion farther eastward into Asia
(E) move Russia's capital out of Kiev away from Poland

194. During the 18th century, Russia expanded in Europe primarily by gaining territory from

(A) Austria
(B) the Ottoman Empire
(C) Poland
(D) Prussia
(E) Sweden

195. By the mid-18th century all of the following were ruling dynasties in Europe EXCEPT

(A) the Hohenzollerns
(B) the Romanovs
(C) the Medici
(D) the Hapsburgs
(E) the Hanovers

196. The nobility of _____ prevented both absolutism and parliamentary government, which eventually led to its downfall.

(A) Prussia
(B) Holland
(C) Russia
(D) Poland
(E) Austria

197. Hungary, Transylvania, Croatia, and Slovenia were incorporated into Austria as a result of the

(A) Treaty of Karlowitz
(B) Union of Lublin
(C) Treaty of Kuchuk Kainarji
(D) Treaty of Utrecht
(E) Treaty of Rastatt

198. The majority of people of the emerging Austrian Hapsburg Empire were

(A) Slavs
(B) Germanic
(C) Latin
(D) Magyars
(E) Turkic

199. The core of the early Prussian state was

(A) Kiev
(B) Danzig
(C) Bavaria
(D) Brandenburg
(E) Tyrol

200. Which of the following countries did NOT sacrifice territory to the Prussians in the long-term process of the first unification of Germany in 1870?

(A) France
(B) Austria
(C) Denmark
(D) Poland
(E) Holland

201. Sweden lost its position as a formidable European power as a result of

    (A) the Thirty Years' War
    (B) the Great Northern War
    (C) the War of the Spanish Succession
    (D) weak central government
    (E) the Seven Years' War

202. Frederick I (1701–1713) became king of Prussia during the

    (A) War of the Spanish Succession
    (B) Seven Years' War
    (C) French Revolution
    (D) English Civil War
    (E) Fronde Rebellion

203. Which of the following Petrine reforms exemplifies the consolidation of absolute rule in Russia in the 18th century?

    (A) the creation of the Table of Ranks whereby all material and social advantages of the nobility depended on serving the crown
    (B) the construction of St. Petersburg and the order to all landowners possessing more than 40 serf households to build a house in the new capital
    (C) the abolition of the position of patriarch of the Russian Orthodox Church and its replacement with the Holy Synod and Procurator
    (D) the strengthening of serfdom
    (E) all of the above

204. Between the 15th and 18th centuries, the Ukraine became a focal point in the struggle between

    (A) Russia and Poland
    (B) Lithuania and Belarus
    (C) Sweden and the Ottoman Empire
    (D) Latvia and Russia
    (E) Prussia and Poland

205. How did the Time of Troubles affect absolutism in Russia?

(A) This period had the effect of strengthening Polish absolutism when King Wladislaw declared himself czar.

(B) The chaos of the period convinced most Russians that absolutism was necessary to keep order and stability and to protect the country from foreign intervention.

(C) The Times of Troubles convinced Russians that their monarchs needed to have their power limited by a written constitution.

(D) Hereditary monarchy was abolished as a result of the Times of Troubles.

(E) none of the above

206. As a result of the Ottoman victory in the major battle _____, Serbia came under Turkish control.

(A) Battle of Vienna

(B) Battle of Poltava

(C) Battle of Kosovo

(D) Battle of Taganrog

(E) Battle of Tannenbaum

207. The Ottoman sultans organized non-Muslims according to religious communities called

(A) viziers

(B) millets

(C) Janissaries

(D) harems

(E) Divans

208. The "golden age" of Ottoman rule came under

(A) Hakan I

(B) Bayezid II

(C) Vlad the Impailer

(D) Suleiman the Magnificent

(E) Mustafa Kemal Ataturk

209. One of the main sources of conflict between the Ottoman Empire and Russia in the 18th and 19th centuries was

(A) the equal partition of Poland

(B) the poor treatment of ethnic Turks in Russia

(C) Russia's desire to control Constantinople and have guaranteed access to the Bosphorus and Dardanelle Straits

(D) the destruction of Orthodox churches in Istanbul

(E) the competition to secure oil in the Caspian Sea

210. Peter the Great's reforms in large measure were determined by

(A) his inner circle of foreign advisors

(B) the needs of the Russian war efforts against the Swedes and Turks

(C) the needs of the Russian Orthodox Church

(D) pressure from Poland

(E) the desire to alleviate the suffering of the peasants

211. All of the following are true about the Russian nobility under Peter the Great EXCEPT

(A) they were forced to undergo compulsory secular primary education

(B) they gained more rights and became more independent of monarchial authority

(C) their service to the state was mandatory to keep their noble status

(D) they were given full authority over their peasants

(E) none of the above

212. The battle in the Great Northern War that was the turning point that helped determine the outcome in favor of Russia was the

(A) Battle of Poltava

(B) Battle of Kosovo

(C) Battle of Kursk

(D) Battle of Stockholm

(E) Battle of Narva

CHAPTER 8

The French Revolution and the Rise of Napoleon, 1789–1799

213. The ideals of the French Revolution were best expressed in the phrase

(A) nobility, power, aristocracy
(B) equality, humanity, godliness
(C) liberty, equality, fraternity
(D) justice, honor, socialism
(E) pure race, pure blood, pure nation

214. The king's primary opponents in the initial struggle that led to the French Revolution were the

(A) nobles
(B) clergy
(C) British and Dutch
(D) middle-class members of the Third Estate
(E) Haitian slaves

215. The Estates General convoked in 1789 by Louis XVI was the first meeting of the legislature in France since

(A) 1215
(B) 1485
(C) 1614
(D) 1715
(E) 1788

216. The Tennis Court Oath, taken by the members of the new National Assembly at Versailles in 1789,

(A) avowed loyalty to absolutism
(B) defied royal absolutism by committing to a constitution
(C) was taken only by the clergy
(D) proposed the institution of state terror
(E) planned to reinstate the Treaty of Nantes

217. Voting in the Estates General was traditionally

(A) based on the principle of one person/one vote
(B) done by estate
(C) in the form of a national referendum
(D) the exclusive reserve of the nobility
(E) none of the above

218. The Declaration of the Rights of Man and Citizen proclaimed all of the following EXCEPT

(A) the emancipation of women
(B) an elective legislature
(C) protection of rights of property
(D) religious toleration
(E) equal protection under the law

219. The Bastille in Paris was stormed on July 14, 1789,

(A) in order to capture the royal family
(B) to defend against Austrian invasion
(C) to free the Marquis de Lafayette
(D) to arrest refractory priests opposing the revolution
(E) to seize arms to defend against royal reprisals

220. The Woman's March on Versailles on October 4, 1789, was a crucial turning point in the French Revolution because it

(A) brought the king and assembly back to Paris
(B) was embraced and supported by the king and queen
(C) was a peace offering to the monarchy after the storming of the Bastille
(D) forced the renunciation of feudal privileges
(E) called for replacing Louis XVI with Marie Antoinette

221. The term *émigrés* was used to describe

    (A) nobles who stayed in France to fight against the revolution

    (B) supporters of the revolution who came from other countries

    (C) members of mobs in the Paris streets

    (D) nobles who fled France

    (E) nobles who advised the king to sanction reforms

222. The French Revolution was set on a new course by the declaration of war in April 1792 against

    (A) Italy

    (B) Austria

    (C) Great Britain

    (D) Russia

    (E) Holland

223. Each of the following contributed to the inability of the anti-French alliance to defeat France EXCEPT

    (A) Prussia and Austria were more preoccupied with the partitions of Poland

    (B) Britain's military strength was mostly concentrated in the navy

    (C) the Dutch army was not a large enough force to make a difference in the fighting

    (D) the revolutionary zeal of the French forces

    (E) mass desertions from the anti-French coalition

224. Which of the following best summarizes the impact of Rousseau's ideas on the development of the French Revolution?

    (A) Rousseau's advocacy of full participatory democracy led to France establishing a form of direct democracy.

    (B) Rousseau's suggestion that property should be held by the "community" led to the Jacobins confiscating the property of nobles and distributing it to poor peasants.

    (C) The Jacobins took Rousseau's concept of the "general will" to mean all the people in France must support the ideals of the revolution.

    (D) Rousseau's rejection of separation of power is what influenced the Constitution of 1791.

    (E) none of the above

225. All of the following called for serious fiscal reform to ease the debt crisis in France prior to the revolution in 1789 EXCEPT

(A) Necker
(B) Maupeou
(C) Calonne
(D) de Brienne
(E) Lemaire

226. How many constitutions were written in France between 1789 and 1799?

(A) one
(B) two
(C) three
(D) four
(E) five

227. Which of the following were most adversely affected by the increases in the price of food?

(A) urban workers
(B) wealthy merchants
(C) the clergy
(D) the nobility
(E) none of the above

228. The largest portion of France's pre-1789 debt came from

(A) expenditures on the royal court
(B) costs of welfare programs
(C) military expenditures
(D) costs for developing infrastructure (roads, bridges, canals, ports)
(E) foreign aid payments to the American colonial rebels

229. The bourgeoisie belonged to which of the following groups?

(A) the First Estate
(B) the Second Estate
(C) the Third Estate
(D) the aristocracy
(E) émigrés

230. Which of the following became a symbol of the French Revolution?

(A) the Tennis Court Oath

(B) the Reveillon riots

(C) the guillotine

(D) French fries

(E) the National Assembly

231. What was the significance of the August 4, 1789, meeting of the National Assembly?

(A) The first constitution in France's history was established.

(B) The decision to execute Louis XVI was made.

(C) The Tuileries were stormed.

(D) The National Assembly declared war on Austria.

(E) Feudalism, with positions based on heredity and titles, was abolished.

232. The Civil Constitution of the Clergy

(A) placed the French Catholic Church under state control

(B) abolished the Catholic Church in France

(C) made Catholicism the official religion in France

(D) made the clergy part of the Third Estate

(E) none of the above

233. All of the following measures were taken against the Catholic Church in France by the National Assembly EXCEPT

(A) the clergy were forced to take a loyalty oath to the state

(B) the priests and bishops were to be elected by all French eligible to vote, including atheists, Protestants, and Jews

(C) the independence of the church was taken away and put under the jurisdiction of the Roman Catholic pope

(D) church lands were confiscated and sold to those who could afford it

(E) priests and bishops were to become salaried officials of the state

234. The Constitution of 1791

(A) abolished the monarchy

(B) established a constitutional monarchy

(C) gave the vote to all citizens

(D) reestablished the old provinces

(E) guaranteed income equality

235. During the Reign of Terror, Robespierre tried to
(A) execute all French nobles
(B) restore the Catholic Church
(C) crush all opposition to the revolution
(D) reinstate the monarchy
(E) sign a separate peace treaty with countries fighting against France

236. Besides the violence, how was the Jacobin phase of the revolution more radical than the previous National Assembly phase?
(A) The Jacobins called for universal male suffrage and an end to all forms of monarchy.
(B) The Jacobins called for the elimination of private property and the redistribution of wealth.
(C) The Jacobins called for women of talent to hold key government positions.
(D) The Jacobins called for the abolition of all borders for a united Europe.
(E) The Jacobins called for worldwide revolution and the abolition of colonialism.

237. Which of the following figures from the revolutionary era advocated using violence and terror to destroy enemies of France and promote the virtuous ideals of the French Revolution?
(A) Napoleon Bonaparte
(B) Marquis de Sade
(C) Maximilien Robespierre
(D) Maurice Richard
(E) Marquee de Lafayette

238. Which of the following best explains the attitude of many European monarchs toward the French Revolution?
(A) Since the revolution was strictly the internal affair of the French government, European monarchs paid little attention.
(B) Many rushed to aid Louis XVI.
(C) On the one hand they welcomed anything that would weaken France's position; on the other, they feared the revolution spreading to their countries.
(D) Many felt that it was time that radical reform came to France; therefore, they supported the revolution.
(E) none of the above

239. Which of the following classes, through its demands for universal male suffrage and its violent street tactics, kept the revolution moving in a more radical phase?

(A) the peasants
(B) the Parisian sansculottes
(C) rank-and-file soldiers in the army
(D) the émigrés
(E) the slaves

240. Which of the following classes was the "brains of the revolution" from 1789 to 1799?

(A) the bourgeoisie
(B) the nobility
(C) the sansculottes
(D) the royal family
(E) none of the above

241. Which French city was the center of radical politics during the French Revolution?

(A) Versailles
(B) Marseille
(C) Toulon
(D) Paris
(E) Vendee

242. The Committee of Public Safety was successful in all of these areas EXCEPT

(A) stabilizing wages and prices
(B) bringing political violence to an end
(C) conducting the war effort
(D) providing a consistent food supply to the army and city workers
(E) not requiring peasants to pay compensation for lands seized from the beginning of the revolution

243. Which French colony was inspired by and used the instability of the revolution to declare and eventually gain its independence?

(A) Haiti
(B) Vietnam
(C) Algeria
(D) Guadeloupe
(E) French Guiana

244. Which of the following is in the correct sequence?

(A) storming of the Bastille/Constitution of 1791/Reign of Terror/French declaration of war on Austria

(B) establishment of the Legislative Assembly/September Massacres/ execution of Louis XVI/establishment of the Committee of Public Safety

(C) Tennis Court Oath/French declaration of war on Britain and Holland/execution of Robespierre/storming of the Tuileries

(D) formation of the Jacobins/firing of Necker as finance comptroller/the ascension to power of the Directory/the overthrow of the Directory

(E) none of the above

245. What became apparent after the Directory asked Napoleon to suppress pro-Royalist sympathizers in 1797?

(A) Pro-Royalist sympathizers lost their final battle to try to turn the clock back in France to 1789.

(B) The Directory came to rely more and more on the army for its power.

(C) France was vulnerable to foreign enemies since the army was asked to establish order within France.

(D) all of the above

(E) none of the above

246. Which class made up 90 percent of the Third Estate?

(A) sansculottes

(B) peasants

(C) bourgeoisie

(D) bureaucrats

(E) clergy

247. Which of the following events contributed to the radicalization of the French Revolution?

(A) France's declaration of war on Austria

(B) the September Massacres

(C) the execution of Louis XVI

(D) the storming of the Tuileries

(E) all of the above

248. All of the following were reasons why Napoleon was extremely popular in France from 1799 to 1804 EXCEPT

(A) he made peace with the French Catholic Church

(B) he voted against the execution of Louis XVI in 1793

(C) he granted amnesty to émigrés if they returned to France and were loyal to the new government

(D) he was an outstanding and very successful military commander

(E) his personality

249. The majority of victims of the Reign of Terror were

(A) nobles and clergy

(B) the bourgeoisie

(C) foreign enemies

(D) the peasants and laboring classes

(E) none of the above

CHAPTER 9

The Fall of Napoleon and the Post-Napoleonic Era, 1800–1848

250. Napoleon Bonaparte first entered the world of French politics by

  (A) swearing loyalty to the Tennis Court Oath
  (B) calling for the execution of Louis XVI
  (C) orchestrating a coup d'etat that overthrew the Directory
  (D) crowning himself emperor of France
  (E) none of the above

251. The Quadruple Alliance established at the Congress of Vienna in 1814 included all of the following countries EXCEPT

  (A) Dutch Republic
  (B) Austria
  (C) Russia
  (D) Prussia
  (E) Britain

252. Czar Alexander I's most successful strategy in countering Napoleon's invasion of Russia was to

  (A) stand and fight at the Neman River
  (B) summon mountain warriors from the Caucasus to fight in the Russian army
  (C) surrender St. Petersburg
  (D) make a stand in front of Moscow
  (E) retreat and destroy food supplies

253. Napoleon's social origins were

   (A) Parisian sansculottes
   (B) Girondin bourgeois
   (C) Corsican noble
   (D) Burgundian peasant
   (E) none of the above

254. The Napoleonic Code, enacted by Bonaparte in 1804, did all of the following EXCEPT

   (A) create laws that favored business and private enterprise
   (B) reaffirm the patriarchal nature of the traditional family
   (C) grant special privileges to the aristocracy
   (D) form a basis for civil law copied in many countries
   (E) assure legal equality

255. To strangle the British economy, Napoleon imposed an economic blockade on his rival called

   (A) the Napoleonic Code
   (B) the Bastille Embargo
   (C) the Continental System
   (D) Pepe le Pieu
   (E) Anti-British Economic Policy

256. Napoleon's costliest defeat in terms of manpower and materials came

   (A) against the Russians
   (B) in Egypt
   (C) at the Battle of Trafalgar
   (D) at Waterloo
   (E) at the Battle of Austerlitz

257. Overall, the general goal of the allies at the Congress of Vienna was to

   (A) spread the revolutionary gains made in France to the rest of Europe
   (B) anoint Russia as the new leader of Europe
   (C) establish boundaries and conditions in Europe to contain France
   (D) weaken France by recognizing Haitian independence
   (E) create a permanent "Holy Alliance" between Austria, Prussia, Russia, and Great Britain

258. Which of the following was the key aim of the British Corn Laws in the early 1800s?

(A) export grain at cheaper prices to France
(B) weaken the power of the middle class in finance and banking
(C) improve the quality of British grain
(D) protect the interests of British grain producers from foreign imports
(E) set up a free-trade zone among farmers in western Europe

259. Following the death of Alexander I in 1825, Russia under Nicholas I became

(A) a police state due to Nicholas's fear of revolution
(B) the most liberal of the European powers
(C) a major imperialist power with colonies in Asia and Africa
(D) a limited monarchy under the control of the Duma
(E) an industrial power following the abolition of serfdom

260. After Napoleon was defeated by the Allies in 1815, they demanded

(A) greater legislative restraints placed on the emperor
(B) abdication in favor of his son Napoleon II
(C) a regency under his wife, Marie Louise
(D) abdication and exile to St. Helena
(E) establishment of a republic

261. The issue that precipitated a split between Napoleon and Czar Alexander I and that eventually led to war was

(A) Alexander's refusal to allow his daughter to marry Napoleon
(B) Russia's backing out of the Continental System
(C) a quarrel between France and Russia over how to partition Finland
(D) a promise by Prussia and Austria to Russia that they would give up their Polish possessions in exchange for Russia leaving the Continental System
(E) Alexander I's dissatisfaction with being simply the "emperor of the East" and not all of Europe as well

262. All of the following were results of the Congress of Vienna EXCEPT
- (A) the unification of Germany was finally realized
- (B) the restoration of hereditary monarchs that were in power in 1792 or at the time of their overthrow by Napoleon
- (C) the creation of the Netherlands out of Belgium, Luxembourg, and Holland to serve as a counterweight to France in the north
- (D) the formation of the Quadruple Alliance
- (E) the end of two centuries of colonial rivalry between France and Britain

263. Which of the following countries was the biggest supporter of Napoleon and why?
- (A) Spain was the biggest supporter because Spaniards welcomed Napoleon's moves to limit the Catholic Church's grip on all aspects of Spanish society.
- (B) Austria was the biggest supporter because Francis I offered Napoleon his daughter Maria Louise in marriage, cementing an alliance between the Bonapartes and Hapsburgs that lasted until 1914.
- (C) Poland was the biggest supporter because Napoleon offered the Poles hope of autonomy or independence by creating the Duchy of Warsaw.
- (D) Russia was the biggest supporter because Napoleon offered Alexander the title of Emperor of the East, and they both shared a dislike for the British.
- (E) Belgium was the biggest supporter because it shared similar cultural traits such as language and religion.

264. Besides turning back the clock to 1792, what foreign policy goal did Klemens von Metternich support at the Congress of Vienna?
- (A) continuation of the economic blockade against Britain
- (B) ascension of a Hapsburg to the French crown
- (C) a French-Austrian alliance against Prussia
- (D) Metternich's willingness to give Belgium to France in return for Austrian occupation of Prussia
- (E) containment of Russia and Prussia

265. All of the following were major artistic and literary contributors to the period of Romanticism EXCEPT

(A) Louis David
(B) Eugene Delacroix
(C) Lord Byron
(D) William Wordsworth
(E) Alexander Pushkin

266. What major event in Europe determined if one was a Liberal, Republican, or Conservative in 19th-century Europe?

(A) the English Civil War
(B) the American Revolution
(C) the French Revolution (1789)
(D) the Revolutions of 1830
(E) none of the above

267. One of the overriding principles of the Congresses of Aix-la-Chapelle, Troppau, and Verona promoted by Austrian Prime Minister Metternich was

(A) the necessity to implement constitutional reforms to save the monarchs of Europe
(B) the need to isolate France and force it to be regular with its indemnity payments
(C) how to fairly distribute the spoils of war taken from France at the Congress of Vienna
(D) the importance of gaining an agreement on a collective security arrangement from the Great Powers that would stamp out revolutionary uprisings in Europe
(E) none of the above

268. Britain's policy toward continental Europe from 1815 to 1850 was characterized by

(A) a refusal to be constrained by alliances
(B) leadership in creating the Holy Alliance
(C) military aid to revolutionary forces
(D) a complete neglect of the continent in favor of its colonies
(E) none of the above

269. By refusing to support the Greek uprising in 1821

    (A) Czar Alexander I forever lost the chance for Russia to play a major role in Balkan politics

    (B) Alexander I sacrificed Russian national interests to stand together with Metternich and oppose revolutionary upheavals in Europe

    (C) Russia avoided a possible two-front war with the Ottoman Empire and Austria

    (D) the Ottoman Empire agreed to recognize Russia as the sole protector of Christian property in Palestine

    (E) Russia turned its sights on consolidating its control over Poland

270. As a result of the _____, France was given permission to intervene militarily in Spain to suppress the revolutionaries and return the king and church to prominence.

    (A) Congress of Aix-la-Chapelle

    (B) Congress of Troppau

    (C) Congress of Verona

    (D) July Ordinances

    (E) July Days

271. Which of the following Serbian-dominated territories was placed under Austro-Hungarian occupation after the country's formal independence was recognized at the Treaty of Berlin in 1878?

    (A) Croatia

    (B) Bosnia

    (C) Kosovo

    (D) Slovenia

    (E) Montenegro

272. What was one of the main issues that sparked the Revolution of 1830 in France?

    (A) a vote by the French legislature to compensate émigrés who lost their property 30 years earlier in the first revolution

    (B) protestors who defied a ban on demonstrations

    (C) the crushing burden of government reparations stipulated by the Congress of Vienna

    (D) the election of Louis Napoleon Bonaparte as the president of France

    (E) Belgium's vote by a slim margin to appoint Louis Philippe's son as the new king

273. How was Marquis de Lafayette able to offer up Louis Philippe to the Liberals and Republicans as a "compromise candidate" in 1830?

(A) He said that if Louis wasn't chosen, the Great Powers might partition a leaderless France.

(B) Louis spent some years in America as the French ambassador to the United States before the French Revolution broke out.

(C) Louis Philippe served in the Republican army in 1792 but was also a Bourbon.

(D) Louis Philippe was a Capet.

(E) Louis Philippe was born after the revolution and, therefore, had no memory of it.

274. Which of the following can be credited for saving the Belgians' independence movement?

(A) the Netherlands

(B) Russia

(C) Prussia

(D) Poland

(E) Great Britain

275. As a result of the Polish uprising in 1830,

(A) Nicholas I abrogated Poland's constitution and fully incorporated it into the Russian Empire

(B) Poland became independent minus its ethnic lands in Prussia

(C) Poland's constitution was reinstated

(D) the Polish Catholic Church was closed down by Russian authorities

(E) Russia took all of Ukraine and Belarus under its control

276. Three days of violent class war in the streets of Paris, June 24–26, 1848, had an impact on the writings of

(A) Beau Babeuf

(B) Edmund Burke

(C) Karl Marx

(D) Friedrich Nietzsche

(E) Thomas Paine

277. The Reform Act of 1832 in Britain

(A) created a standing army for the first time

(B) expanded the number of voters

(C) abolished the House of Lords

(D) replaced William IV with Queen Victoria

(E) granted the right to vote to women of aristocratic background

278. Liberalism was likely to win the most support among which of the following groups?

(A) peasants
(B) factory workers
(C) nobles
(D) bourgeoisie
(E) enlightened despots

279. All of the following were considered Utopian Socialists EXCEPT

(A) Karl Marx
(B) Etienne Cabet
(C) Robert Owen
(D) Charles Fourier
(E) Count Saint Simon

280. Friedrich Engels considered his and Marx's version of Socialism "scientific" because

(A) it could be proven through the scientific method
(B) he felt that through the use of dialectical materialism, he could explain the inevitability of the coming of Socialism
(C) Charles Darwin had come to the same conclusions about the inevitability of Socialism
(D) none of the above
(E) all of the above

281. The repeal of the Corn Laws in Britain in 1846

(A) virtually destroyed British agricultural production and made the country reliant on Indian production
(B) encouraged British farmers to abandon corn
(C) was a concession to bourgeois industrialists
(D) was yet another step in erecting a protective tariff
(E) led to more imports of corn from the Balkans

282. What was the significance of the election following the French Revolution of 1848?

(A) It was the first in Europe to be based on universal male suffrage.
(B) It was the first time women were allowed to vote.
(C) It was the first time a Socialist was elected.
(D) Napoleon Bonaparte's son was elected as president.
(E) all of the above

283. England avoided revolution in the 1800s for all of the following reasons EXCEPT

(A) the government extended voting rights twice in 1832 and 1867
(B) the government enacted labor and industrial reforms to lessen the pain caused by the Industrial Revolution
(C) instead of being inspired by the revolutions, most people were turned off by the violence and chose reform
(D) there was universal suffrage and an extensive social welfare system in place to help the poor
(E) the long-standing tradition of parliamentary representation

CHAPTER 10

The Second Industrial Revolution, 1820–1900

284. Industrialization in the textile industry resulted in

(A) better paying jobs
(B) the establishment of factories
(C) improved working conditions
(D) slower production times
(E) more reliance on silk from China

285. In which of the following ways did Britain's colonial empire contribute to the country's industrialization?

(A) Industrial technology was shared with the colonies, thus improving the empire's overall industrial output.
(B) Colonial laborers worked for much cheaper wages than unionized British workers.
(C) The colonies provided a growing market for British manufactured goods.
(D) British companies established factories in the colonies that produced inexpensive goods for export.
(E) The colonies provided iron and coal, which Britain was lacking.

286. Which of the following was NOT a factor that contributed to Britain's Industrial Revolution?

(A) extensive colonial possessions
(B) agricultural innovations that led to more food production
(C) no internal tariffs inhibiting trade within Great Britain
(D) extensive and diverse supply of natural resources
(E) an effective central bank and well-developed credit markets

287. Which of the following does NOT describe Britain's enclosure movement?
- (A) It led to commercial farming.
- (B) Enclosure was legislated by Parliament.
- (C) It led to riots protesting the movement.
- (D) It was a means of collectivizing agricultural ownership.
- (E) It was a process led by large landowners.

288. Which of the following agricultural innovations is Charles Townshend most frequently associated with?
- (A) four-crop rotation
- (B) the three-field system
- (C) heavy use of manure for fertilizer
- (D) development of the tractor
- (E) invention of the steel plow

289. Which of the following characteristics did the putting-out and factory systems share?
- (A) scale of production
- (B) centralization of production
- (C) size of profits for successful entrepreneurs
- (D) production of textile-based finished goods
- (E) production for foreign export markets

290. The first factories in Britain's Industrial Revolution produced
- (A) textiles
- (B) tools
- (C) machines
- (D) cars
- (E) trains

291. Eighteenth-century inventions by James Hargreaves, Richard Arkwright, and Edmund Cartwright led to
- (A) a dramatic increase in the cotton textile industry
- (B) the extensive use of cottage industry in Great Britain
- (C) the need for oil as a new energy source
- (D) faster ships being manufactured
- (E) none of the above

292. As a consequence of mass-produced cotton textiles,

    (A) cotton goods became much cheaper and more affordable for people of all classes

    (B) shortages of this key raw material were experienced

    (C) India became an industrial power

    (D) working conditions in the factories improved

    (E) water remained the primary source of energy for factories

293. James Watt's improvement of the original steam engine in 1769 was significant because

    (A) factories could now use bulbs instead of candles for light

    (B) oil was no longer needed as an energy source

    (C) factories located near rivers now had an advantage over factories located away from water

    (D) new kinds of power equipment could be used to aid people in their work

    (E) Great Britain had abundant supplies of steam

294. All of the following were consequences of the development of the railroad EXCEPT

    (A) the cost of shipping freight overland was reduced

    (B) markets grew in size to nationwide

    (C) the number of urban workers grew

    (D) peasants were displaced

    (E) coal production decreased

295. All of the following are strong indicators of the success of the Industrial Revolution in Great Britain EXCEPT

    (A) Britain's share of the world's output of industrial goods increased from 2 percent in 1750 to 20 percent in 1860

    (B) the nation's GNP rose fourfold between 1780 and 1851

    (C) Britain's population rose from 9 million in 1780 to almost 21 million in 1851

    (D) Britain's iron production grew from 17,000 tons in 1740 to 3 million tons in 1844

    (E) between 1840 and 1850, Britain's railroads increased from 2,000 to 6,000 miles

296. In his book *National System of Political Economy* (1841), German journalist Friedrich List

(A) called for the overthrow of the bourgeoisie by the industrial proletariat
(B) supported high protective tariffs that would protect newly formed industries from advanced British ones
(C) argued that population would always grow faster than food supply
(D) believed that rapid population growth would depress wages to subsistence level
(E) advocated a completely free-market economy in Germany to compete with the British

297. Which 19th-century British handicraft workers protested against the Industrial Revolution by smashing machines that they felt put them out of work?

(A) utopians
(B) Fabians
(C) Marxists
(D) wreckers
(E) Luddites

298. Which of the following statements is true about the conditions of the working class in Great Britain around 1850?

(A) Workers' leisure time increased as a result of the advances in technology.
(B) Workers' pay increased without a significant rise in hours worked.
(C) Workers earned more because they worked more.
(D) Workers labored many more days a year without an increase in earnings.
(E) Workers saw no difference in the amount of days worked compared to agricultural workers.

299. Britain's Factory Act of 1833

(A) monitored pollution levels in factories
(B) addressed the issue of child labor by limiting their working hours
(C) encouraged entire families to seek employment in the same factory
(D) provided women with equal pay for equal work with men
(E) required employers to pay workman's compensation for injuries sustained in the factory

300. Friedrich Engels's *The Conditions of the Working Class in England in 1844*

- (A) brought attention to the appalling living conditions of the proletariat
- (B) lauded capitalism for raising the standard of living for regular workers
- (C) concluded that capitalist exploitation was necessary for improving the standard of living of the working class
- (D) called for the workers to return to agrarian life
- (E) ordered workers to destroy machines in protest against industrialization

301. The Mines Act of 1842

- (A) prohibited underground work for all women and for boys under 10 years old
- (B) gave women the right to work in coal mines
- (C) allowed children to work in mines after school and during summer breaks
- (D) called for coal mining quotas
- (E) closed coal mines down when oil became more prominently used

302. The Combination Acts of 1799

- (A) prohibited business monopolies
- (B) outlawed merchant guilds
- (C) prohibited men and women from working in mines together
- (D) outlawed unions and strikes
- (E) called for workers and owners to collectively bargain

303. Held in 1851, London's Crystal Palace Exhibition

- (A) showcased British technological and industrial achievements
- (B) featured the opening of the first factory that produced crystal
- (C) allowed the bourgeoisie to show off their opulence
- (D) was organized by skilled artisans as a way to stave off industrialization of their craft
- (E) was a venue where European countries exhibited their industrial superiority over the British

304. The creation of what customs union among the German states in 1834 facilitated industrialization and became the basis of the political unification of the German states?

- (A) the Bundestag
- (B) the Reichstag
- (C) the Maastricht Treaty
- (D) the Zollverein
- (E) the Bundeswehr

305. The population of Europe almost doubled between 1750 and 1850 mainly as a result of

(A) fewer deaths due to armed conflict

(B) shrinking death rates as a result of a declining number of famines and epidemics

(C) immigration from Africa and Latin America

(D) less use of contraceptives

(E) government programs that provided subsidies to families that had more than two children

306. Which of the following was the only European country to suffer a declining population in the 19th century?

(A) France

(B) Great Britain

(C) Ireland

(D) Russia

(E) Belgium

307. Which of the following countries was the most urbanized in 1850, with more than 50 percent of the population living in towns and cities?

(A) Holland

(B) Belgium

(C) Great Britain

(D) France

(E) Austria

308. All of the following were important industrial cities in England EXCEPT

(A) Birmingham

(B) Manchester

(C) London

(D) Rotterdam

(E) Liverpool

309. Edwin Chadwick's *Report on the Conditions of the Labouring Population of Great Britain* (1842)

(A) led to the creation of the National Board of Health, which established modern sanitary systems in Great Britain

(B) resulted in the British working class gaining the right to vote

(C) resulted in the creation of the National Health Service and universal health care

(D) created a minimum wage in Great Britain for the first time in history

(E) called on the British government to crack down on workers who created unsanitary living conditions

310. In 19th-century Britain, who among the following were NOT members of the middle class?

(A) factory owners

(B) lawyers

(C) factory workers

(D) bankers

(E) judges

311. The 19th-century Chartists

(A) were originally granted a charter to colonize India

(B) were Protestants looking to spread the faith to Britain's Caribbean colonies

(C) favored equal membership for women in all trade unions

(D) opposed Parliament's Factory Act of 1833

(E) demanded universal male suffrage and political representation in Parliament for the working class

CHAPTER 11

The Rise of New Ideologies in the 19th Century

312. All of the following are important principles of Romanticism EXCEPT

- (A) emphasis on moods and expressions
- (B) the relation of thought and feeling
- (C) emphasis on peculiar customs that the intellect could never classify
- (D) the importance of the subconscious
- (E) the use of dramatic imagery to provoke emotion

313. All of the following were major artistic and literary contributors to Romanticism EXCEPT

- (A) Jacques-Louis David
- (B) Eugene Delacroix
- (C) Lord Byron
- (D) William Wordsworth
- (E) Victor Hugo

314. During the 19th century, nationalism most often contributed to the _____ in Europe.

- (A) consolidation of multi-ethnic states
- (B) proliferation of multi-ethnic states
- (C) growth of the power of the Catholic Church
- (D) separatist tendencies that weakened the multi-ethnic states
- (E) clash of multi-ethnic states

315. One of the overriding principles of the congresses of Aix-la-Chapelle, Troppau, and Verona promoted by Austrian Prime Minister Metternich was

(A) the necessity to implement constitutional reforms to save the monarchs of Europe

(B) the need to isolate France and force it to be regular with its indemnity payments

(C) how to fairly distribute the spoils of war taken from France at the Congress of Vienna

(D) the importance of gaining an agreement on a collective security arrangement from the Great Powers that would stamp out revolutionary uprisings in Europe

(E) the necessity of working-class representation in the governments of Europe

316. Britain's policy toward continental Europe during the period of 1815–1850 was characterized by

(A) a refusal to be constrained by alliances

(B) leadership in creating the Holy Alliance

(C) military aid to revolutionary forces

(D) a complete neglect of the continent in favor of its colonies

(E) maneuvering to acquire land on the mainland of Europe

317. By refusing to support the Greek Uprising in 1821,

(A) Czar Alexander I forever lost the chance for Russia to play a major role in Balkan politics

(B) Alexander I sacrificed Russian national interests to stand together with Metternich and oppose revolutionary upheavals in Europe

(C) Russia avoided a possible two-front war with the Ottoman Empire and Austria

(D) the Ottoman Empire agreed to recognize Russia as the sole protector of Christian property in Palestine

(E) the Greek rebels lost respect for Russia

318. As a result of the _____, France was given permission to intervene militarily in Spain to suppress the revolutionaries and return the king and church to prominence.

(A) Congress of Aix-la-Chapelle

(B) Congress of Troppau

(C) Congress of Verona

(D) July Ordinances

(E) Congress of Vienna

319. Which of the following was a result of the Decembrist Revolt (1825)?

    (A) Greece gained its independence.

    (B) Charles X abdicated the throne and escaped to England.

    (C) Belgium gained its independence.

    (D) Nicholas I crushed all opposition to him and ruled like a despot.

    (E) Alexander II freed the serfs.

320. How was Greece able to get both conservatives in Russia and liberals in western Europe to support its drive for independence?

    (A) Greek leaders offered both the chance to join in an anti-Turkish campaign where they could share the spoils of a crumbled empire.

    (B) Western European liberals saw Greece as the foundation of western civilization while Russian conservatives identified with Greece as the country where Christian Orthodoxy was established.

    (C) The Greek leader of independence spent his early years in the Russian military but later studied at the Sorbonne in France.

    (D) Famine in Greece as a result of Turkish neglect galvanized sympathy for the Greek cause all over Europe.

    (E) Europeans knew about coal deposits in Greece that would be needed for the growing Industrial Revolution.

321. What issue sparked the Revolution of 1830 in France?

    (A) the French legislature's vote to compensate émigrés who lost their property 30 years earlier in the first revolution

    (B) protestors who defied a ban on demonstrations

    (C) the election of Louis Napoleon Bonaparte as president of France

    (D) Belgium's vote by a slim margin to appoint Louis Philippe's son as the new king

    (E) rumors that Charles X had raised taxes on the working class

322. How was Marquis de Lafayette able to offer up Louis Philippe to the Liberals and Republicans as a "compromise candidate" in 1830?

    (A) He said that if Louis wasn't chosen, the Great Powers might partition a leaderless France.

    (B) Louis spent some years in America as the French ambassador to the United States before the French Revolution broke out.

    (C) Louis Philippe served in the Republican army in 1792 but was also a Bourbon.

    (D) Louis Philippe had been a member of both circles.

    (E) Louis Philippe had proven his Republican sympathies by volunteering to fight in America like Lafayette.

323. Which of the following can be credited for saving the Belgian independence movement?

(A) the Netherlands
(B) Russia
(C) Prussia
(D) Poland
(E) Austria

324. As a result of the Polish uprising in 1830,

(A) Nicholas I abrogated Poland's constitution and fully incorporated it into the Russian Empire
(B) Poland became independent minus its ethnic lands in Prussia
(C) Poland's constitution was reinstated
(D) the Polish Catholic Church was closed down by Russian authorities
(E) Poland was allowed a subservient king to rule with the czar's authority

325. Which of the following was the most significant political aspect of the Revolution of 1848 in France?

(A) the number of people killed
(B) foreign intervention on the part of Austria and Russia to crush the rebellion
(C) British support for the revolutionaries
(D) the first time the Socialists play an important role in European political affairs
(E) the mobilization of the people of Paris for political change

326. A common aspect of the revolutions in France in 1830 and 1848 was

(A) the hostility to the institution of the monarch
(B) the destruction of Catholic Church property and the elimination of it from French political life
(C) attempts by bourgeois liberals to limit the revolution by keeping the working class and its leaders shut out of politics
(D) confiscation of noble property
(E) reintroduction of the French Republican calendar

327. Three days of violent class war in the streets of Paris June 24–26, 1848, had an impact on the writings of

(A) Gracchus Babeuf
(B) Edmund Burke
(C) Karl Marx
(D) Georg Hegel
(E) Otto von Bismarck

328. The revolution in Paris in 1848 called into question all of the following EXCEPT

    (A) the monarchy
    (B) bourgeois capitalism
    (C) the exclusive franchise
    (D) patriotism
    (E) dictatorship

329. The Reform Act of 1832 in Britain

    (A) created a standing army for the first time
    (B) expanded the number of voters
    (C) abolished the House of Lords
    (D) replaced William IV with Queen Victoria
    (E) gave voting rights to all adult males

330. Liberalism was likely to win the most support among which of the following groups?

    (A) peasants
    (B) factory workers
    (C) nobles
    (D) bourgeoisie
    (E) clergy

331. All of the following were considered Utopian Socialists EXCEPT

    (A) Karl Marx
    (B) Robert Owen
    (C) Charles Fourier
    (D) Count Saint Simon
    (E) Pierre-Joseph Proudhon

332. Karl Marx considered his version of Socialism "scientific" because

    (A) it could be proven through the scientific method
    (B) he felt that through the use of dialectical materialism, he could explain the inevitability of the coming of Socialism
    (C) Charles Darwin had come to the same conclusions about the inevitability of Socialism
    (D) none of the above
    (E) A, B, and C

333. The repeal of the Corn Laws in Britain in 1846

(A) virtually destroyed British agricultural production and made the country reliant on Indian production
(B) encouraged British farmers to abandon corn
(C) was a concession to bourgeois industrialists
(D) was yet another step in erecting a protective tariff
(E) resulted in an increase in the price of corn in Britain

334. Louis Blanc's "social workshops" were an example of

(A) laissez-faire economics
(B) the standard factory during the Industrial Revolution
(C) prison labor to rehabilitate criminals
(D) Utopian Socialism
(E) central planning

335. What was the significance of the election following the French Revolution of 1848?

(A) It was the first in Europe to be based on universal male suffrage.
(B) It was the first time women were allowed to vote.
(C) It was the first time a Socialist was elected.
(D) Napoleon Bonaparte's son was elected as president.
(E) Conservatives did not participate and tried to undermine the results.

336. England avoided revolution in the 1800s for all of the following reasons EXCEPT

(A) the government extended voting rights twice in 1832 and 1867
(B) the government enacted labor and industrial reforms to lessen the pain caused by the Industrial Revolution
(C) instead of being inspired by the revolutions, most British were offended by the violence and chose reform
(D) there was universal suffrage and an extensive social welfare system in place to help the poor
(E) gradual reform of voting districts and elimination of "rotten boroughs"

CHAPTER 12

Nationalism and State-Building, 1848–1900

337. Proponents of nationalism in the mid-19th century espoused

(A) adopting a common European language
(B) universal human rights
(C) creating Utopian Socialist communes throughout western Europe
(D) free trade to promote industrial development
(E) the idea that different peoples had distinct historical missions

338. The Concert of Europe was shattered as a result of

(A) the events of the Crimean War
(B) German unification
(C) the Danish War
(D) the Franco-Prussian War
(E) Italian unification

339. The nationalists of the first half of the 19th century were often

(A) conservatives waving the flag of hard-line politics
(B) radicals who called for working-class revolution
(C) liberals attempting to overthrow tyrannical regimes
(D) members of the Old Regime
(E) Romantics who valued the vernacular and folklore

340. The majority of nationalists in the 19th century would have also been considered

(A) Socialists
(B) conservatives
(C) liberals
(D) radicals
(E) religious zealots

341. *Volksgeist* refers to

    (A) the movement for German unification

    (B) a movement for Italian unification

    (C) a distinct national character

    (D) a German car

    (E) war reparations

342. The Troppau Protocol was invoked during a rebellion in which of the following places?

    (A) Austria

    (B) France

    (C) Italy

    (D) Germany

    (E) Russia

343. Which of the following countries came to the aid of the Greeks as they struggled for independence in the 1820s?

    (A) Spain

    (B) Italy

    (C) Russia

    (D) Austria

    (E) Ottoman Turkey

344. The "Eastern Question" refers to what to do with the declining _____ Empire.

    (A) Austrian

    (B) Russian

    (C) Ottoman

    (D) Chinese

    (E) Brazilian

345. After the Greeks achieved independence in 1832, what type of government was established?

    (A) a democratic republic with universal male suffrage

    (B) the first Socialist state

    (C) a monarchy

    (D) a democratic republic with limited suffrage

    (E) decentralized city-states reflecting classical Greece

346. In 1830 Poland attempted to achieve independence from

(A) Russia
(B) France
(C) Holy Roman Empire
(D) Austria
(E) Prussia

347. The Decembrist Revolt in Russia happened during the reign of

(A) Alexander I
(B) Nicholas I
(C) Nicholas II
(D) Peter I
(E) Catherine I

348. Belgium gained its independence from _____ in 1830.

(A) Spain
(B) the Netherlands
(C) France
(D) England
(E) Russia

349. Which of the following people was most responsible for building government-run workshops in France?

(A) Charles X
(B) Louis Napoleon
(C) Louis Blanc
(D) Louis Philippe
(E) Louis XVIII

350. Which of the following was the immediate cause of the "June Days" in France in 1848?

(A) Louis Philippe's conservativeness
(B) the coup executed by Louis Napoleon
(C) the closure of the Paris workshops
(D) an elected five-man executive that was quite moderate
(E) the failure to pay out pensions to French soldiers

351. Which foreign leader assisted Frederick Joseph in putting down the 1848 rebellions in Hungary?

(A) Napoleon III
(B) Kaiser Wilhelm
(C) Nicholas I
(D) Louis Philippe
(E) Elizabeth II

352. "In place of the old bourgeois society, with its classes and class antagonism, we shall have an association, in which the free development of each is the condition for free development of all."

These words express the ideas of

(A) Alexis de Tocqueville
(B) John Locke
(C) Jean-Jacques Rousseau
(D) Edmund Burke
(E) Karl Marx

353. Which of the following early 19th-century political figures was most closely identified with the concept of the "concert of Europe"?

(A) Castlereagh
(B) Napoleon I
(C) Talleyrand
(D) Alexander I
(E) Metternich

354. The Frankfurt Parliament of 1848 was an attempt to

(A) respond to Prussian aggression
(B) create the Zollverein, or customs union
(C) create a unified German state
(D) tie all independent German cities into a confederation
(E) mitigate growing tensions between Prussia and Austria

355. After the publication of Theodor Herzl's book *The Jewish State,*

(A) Jews began to immigrate to the United States
(B) the Ottoman Empire declared that there could be no Jewish immigration
(C) a Jewish state was immediately declared by Jews in Palestine
(D) a Zionist Congress proclaimed its aim to create that state in Palestine
(E) Jews in Arab countries began moving to Palestine

356. The worst persecution of the Jews in the late 19th century and early 20th century took place in

    (A) Italy
    (B) England
    (C) the Netherlands
    (D) Russia
    (E) Serbia

357. Otto von Bismarck was from the

    (A) bourgeoisie
    (B) Junkers
    (C) proletariat
    (D) clergy
    (E) Hohenzollern dynasty

358. Emperor Napoleon III of France lost his throne due to the

    (A) failure of his Mexican adventure
    (B) financial crash of 1857
    (C) unpopularity of his wife
    (D) defeat in the war with Prussia
    (E) Dreyfus Affair

359. All of the following opposed unification of Germany EXCEPT

    (A) the czar of Russia
    (B) the emperor of Austria
    (C) the emperor of France
    (D) the king of Hanover
    (E) the king of Denmark

360. The "dual monarchy" refers to which of the following pairs of countries?

    (A) England and Scotland
    (B) Prussia and Bavaria
    (C) Austria and Hungary
    (D) Holland and Belgium
    (E) Poland and Russia

361. Incentives for government-supported universal education in the 19th century included all of the following EXCEPT

- (A) more efficient military training
- (B) religious instruction
- (C) a liberal belief in social improvement
- (D) a more productive workforce
- (E) the Enlightenment ideal of an educated citizen being necessary for democracy

362. "In virtue of the new dispositions . . . the peasants attached to the soil will be invested within a term fixed by the law with all the rights of free cultivators."

This decree was issued by

- (A) Pope Leo XIII
- (B) Emperor Napoleon III
- (C) Czar Alexander II
- (D) Otto von Bismarck
- (E) Kaiser Wilhelm

363. Bismarck extended the vote to most adult male Germans because he

- (A) was a passionate democrat
- (B) wanted to copy the English
- (C) was convinced conservative peasants and artisans would outvote middle-class liberals
- (D) was forced by the emperor to do so
- (E) was forced to accept their demands in the face of demonstrations

364. The movement for women's rights that developed during the second half of the 19th century hoped to change all of the following EXCEPT

- (A) laws concerning ownership of property
- (B) divorce laws
- (C) the system of military service
- (D) laws of adultery
- (E) reproductive rights

365. An anarchist would be most likely to do which of the following?

- (A) assassinate a king
- (B) vote for a Communist candidate
- (C) join the police
- (D) support a dictator
- (E) support a war

CHAPTER 13

Mass Politics and Imperialism in Africa and Asia, 1860–1914

366. Which country gained control of much of southern Africa during the 1800s?

(A) France
(B) Italy
(C) Spain
(D) Britain
(E) Belgium

367. Kipling's justification of imperialism in *The White Man's Burden* is a good example of

(A) laissez-faire capitalism
(B) Social Darwinism
(C) a defense of native traditions
(D) scientific Socialism
(E) anarchism

368. The countries of northern Africa are

(A) culturally closer to the Middle East
(B) the only ones to escape imperialism on the continent
(C) culturally identical to the countries of sub-Saharan Africa
(D) among the most economically developed in the world
(E) the most agriculturally productive in Africa

369. Which of the following were the most important reasons why European imperialist governments were interested in Africa in the 17th and 18th centuries?

(A) natural resources and slaves

(B) to educate and provide health care to all Africans

(C) to spread industrial and technical advancements to Africans so that they may become independent and strong countries

(D) to spread democratic ideas and learn the benefits of African tribal culture

(E) to prevent the advancement of Islam in Africa

370. Why did Christian missionary groups follow explorers to Africa?

(A) to gather slaves

(B) to convert Africans to Christianity

(C) to study African culture

(D) to map out the courses of rivers

(E) to make icons out of ivory and other native materials

371. Why was the Berlin Conference held in 1884?

(A) to stop Leopold II from taking over Africa

(B) to include Africans on plans for dividing the continent

(C) to carve up Africa between the major European imperialist powers

(D) to stop trading practices on the Congo River

(E) to settle the rivalry between France and Germany

372. Which African country did Leopold II of Belgium turn into his own personal possession in the mid-1800s?

(A) Zimbabwe

(B) Mozambique

(C) Egypt

(D) Togo

(E) Congo

373. What was/is the strategic importance of the Suez Canal?

  (A) It greatly shortened the sea route between Europe and the west coast of North America.
  (B) Many oil refineries are located along the 100-mile length of the canal.
  (C) It brought enormous revenues to the Saudi Arabian government.
  (D) It greatly shortened the sea route from Europe to South Asia and East Asia.
  (E) It allowed ships to easily cross from the Atlantic Ocean to the Pacific Ocean.

374. In 1875 which country bought Egyptian shares of the Suez Canal?

  (A) Turkey
  (B) France
  (C) Britain
  (D) Saudi Arabia
  (E) Germany

375. After 1908 the major reason the world became interested in the Middle East was

  (A) the discovery of gold
  (B) to defeat the growing strength of Saddam Hussein's Iraq
  (C) the discovery of oil
  (D) to start a new crusade to win back Jerusalem from the infidels
  (E) because new wealth created a demand for oriental rugs and spices

376. After World War I, Palestine, Syria, Lebanon, Jordan, and Iraq came under the control of Britain and France. These British- and French-administered territories were called

  (A) demilitarized zones
  (B) spheres of influence
  (C) free-trade zones
  (D) nonaggression pacts
  (E) mandates

377. What was the name of the secret agreement by which Britain and France agreed to partition the Middle Eastern countries between them after World War I?

(A) Sykes-Picot Agreement
(B) Oslo Accords
(C) Balfour Declaration
(D) Molotov-Ribbentrop Pact
(E) Faisal-Weizmann Agreement

378. The Balfour Declaration

(A) was a British proposal to recognize a Jewish homeland in Palestine
(B) established the border between Jordan and Israel
(C) announced that the British would pull out of India
(D) determined the border between India and Pakistan
(E) demanded war reparations from the Ottoman Empire

379. Which of the following regions were targets of Russian imperialism in the 19th century?

(A) Africa and the Middle East
(B) Far East and the Pacific Islands
(C) North and South America
(D) the Caucasus and Central Asia
(E) South Asia

380. Besides oil and natural gas, the countries of the Caucasus and Central Asia are important to the United States, Russia, and Europe because

(A) of the pipelines that transport these vital resources
(B) of their abundant cotton supplies
(C) they all possess weapons of mass destruction
(D) they supply about 80 percent of the world's rice supply
(E) major terrorist groups have bases there

381. One of the main reasons why the British were able to establish control over India was

(A) Muslims and Hindus often clashed, weakening the central government
(B) the British defeated the Portuguese and drove them out of India
(C) the Mughal rulers invited the British to rule them
(D) geographically, Great Britain and India are very close to each other
(E) the Indians were won over by a promised access to British consumer goods

382. Initial British dominance of India was through

(A) willing Mughal rulers
(B) the British East India Company
(C) sepoys
(D) the British monarchy
(E) Muslim mercenaries

383. The underlying reason for the Sepoy Rebellion was

(A) India's opposition to Britain's salt monopoly
(B) Indian opposition to British attempts to impose British culture on them
(C) Indian soldiers' refusal to fight against the French
(D) Britain's violent suppression of a peaceful demonstration
(E) British export of Indian cows for slaughter to Britain

384. Which of the following was a result of the Sepoy Rebellion?

(A) India gained its independence.
(B) India became a protectorate of Britain.
(C) Britain began to rule India directly.
(D) The East India Company took over the rule of India.
(E) Indians were removed from all military service in British India.

385. All of the following can be considered benefits India derived from British colonial rule EXCEPT

(A) the British brought peace to the Indian subcontinent
(B) they introduced Western education to Indian elites
(C) the British brought legal reforms
(D) the British expanded India's infrastructure
(E) they brought economic prosperity

386. Which of the following statements best describes British economic policy in India?

(A) The British "deindustrialized" India by destroying native industries and forcing Indians to rely on British imported finished goods.
(B) The British "hyperindustrialized" India, making the country the most economically advanced in Asia.
(C) The British provided India with technological know-how so it could compete with other countries.
(D) Indian farmers produced more wheat and rice by learning British farming techniques.
(E) The British stirred resentment by raising taxes.

387. The British insistence that Indian farmers grow cash crops

(A) greatly benefited Indian farmers economically
(B) led to the invention of many new farming techniques
(C) benefited the British but led to famine in India
(D) benefited the British and the Indians
(E) allowed Britain to retain its global economic leadership

388. The main methods of opposition to British rule that Mohatma Gandhi used were

(A) terror and violence
(B) lectures and writing
(C) civil disobedience and nonviolence
(D) sabotage and conspiracies
(E) literature that criticized Britain in guarded ways

389. One result of Indian exposure to Western ideas was

(A) the bolstering of British power
(B) a move toward nationalism among educated Indians
(C) the destruction of the caste system and Hinduism
(D) the expansion of imperialism in India
(E) the eventual embrace of Marxism by India

390. The major lesson the Chinese learned from the Opium War was that

(A) opium was more popular than tea
(B) famines resulted because farmers were addicted to opium and therefore produced less food
(C) it had fallen behind the West in technological achievements
(D) Portugal was a strong naval power
(E) the Chinese could use opium to challenge the British

391. The most important long-term concession China had to make to Great Britain in the Treaty of Nanjing was to

(A) hand over most of its gold reserve
(B) allow Great Britain to set up a beer brewery in China
(C) hand over Hong Kong to Great Britain
(D) give up its whole navy to Great Britain
(E) make all other foreign countries remove themselves from Chinese trade

392. Foreign communities, especially Christian missionaries, were attacked during the

(A) Boxer Rebellion
(B) Taiping Rebellion
(C) Communist Revolution
(D) Cultural Revolution
(E) Self-Strengthening Movement

CHAPTER 14

Politics of the Extremes and World War I, 1870–1918

393. One reason Germany began to fear Russia from 1900 to 1914 was the

(A) Russian alliance with Austria
(B) Russian capture of Constantinople
(C) completion of a naval fleet matching Germany's in size
(D) rapid rate of industrialization
(E) Russian militarization of the Polish-German border

394. From 1900 to 1914 tensions arose between Britain and Germany because of all of the following EXCEPT

(A) bombastic threats of Wilhelm II
(B) a naval race
(C) colonial rivalries
(D) Germany's alliance with Russia
(E) increasing German investments in the Balkans

395. "All the remaining European culture-bearing peoples possess areas outside our continent where their languages and customs can take firm root and flourish. This fact, so painful to [our] national pride, also represents a great economic disadvantage."

"Our nation" in this passage was

(A) Russia
(B) Germany
(C) France
(D) Spain
(E) Italy

396. Austria-Hungary annexed Bosnia Herzegovina in 1908 in order to
  (A) block the creation of a greater Serbian kingdom
  (B) come to the aid of the Ottoman sultan
  (C) seal its alliance with Russia
  (D) enable the British navy to use Adriatic ports
  (E) facilitate the creation of a southern Slav state

397. By 1900 Europeans were importing all of the following EXCEPT
  (A) wool from Australia
  (B) beef from Argentina
  (C) oil from Saudi Arabia
  (D) sugar from the West Indies
  (E) cotton from India

398. "History shows me one way, and one way only, in which a state of civilization has been produced, namely, the struggle of race with race, and survival of the physically and mentally fitter races."

This passage represents the primary idea of
  (A) Social Darwinism
  (B) Marxism
  (C) positivism
  (D) Existentialism
  (E) utilitarianism

399. During the 19th century the Mediterranean Sea became a "British lake" because all of the following were controlled by the English EXCEPT
  (A) Egypt
  (B) Malta
  (C) Gibraltar
  (D) Sicily
  (E) Cyprus

400. Britain and France helped prop up the Ottoman Empire during the 19th century because
  (A) of increased religious toleration during the Victorian period
  (B) the Ottomans assisted them in keeping Greece from being independent
  (C) of fear that Russian power would penetrate into the Balkans
  (D) of personal regard for Abdul Hamid II
  (E) of pressure from Muslims at home

401. The primary reason for the Bolshevik success in taking over the government in November 1917 was

    (A) the overwhelming support the Bolsheviks had from the masses of the Russian people

    (B) the collapse of workers' and soldiers' soviets, which had been the backbone of the Provisional government support

    (C) the abdication of the czar and his son

    (D) the inability of the Provisional government to solve the overwhelming problems facing the Russian people

    (E) the support given to Lenin and the Bolsheviks by Western democracies that wished to keep Russia in the war

402. Trotsky's and Stalin's interpretations of Marxism differed most significantly in which of the following ways?

    (A) Stalin wanted to foster revolution in Western Europe while Trotsky wanted to develop the Soviet Union first.

    (B) Trotsky wanted to foster world revolution while Stalin wanted "to build Socialism in one country."

    (C) Stalin was a Bolshevik; Trotsky was a Menshevik.

    (D) Trotsky was a deviationist; Stalin followed the Communist Party line.

    (E) Stalin believed that Russia was too backward to support Communism; Trotsky believed the opposite.

403. Which slogan expresses the ideal of the Bolshevik Revolution of 1917?

    (A) Bread, Land, and Peace

    (B) Liberty, Equality, Fraternity

    (C) Nationalism, Democracy, The People's Livelihood

    (D) Russification

    (E) Lebensraum

404. At the heart of the Soviet Five-Year Plan was the idea that

    (A) Soviet foreign trade would improve if customers could sign five-year contracts

    (B) the Communist Party should let the state handle economic policy without interfering

    (C) central party-state control could replace capitalist self-regulation of economic resources

    (D) workers and farmers would be able to plan vacations more effectively if they had five-year work schedules

    (E) Soviet citizens should be allowed to own their own small stores and shops

405. Lenin had to adapt pure Marxist ideology to the situation in Russia because

    (A) workers in Russia played virtually no part in the activities of March 1917

    (B) the majority of Russians were peasants, and Marx said little about peasants' revolutionary potential

    (C) Marxism had taken on too much of a religious nature, and religion did not appeal to the atheistic masses in Russia

    (D) few revolutionary groups in Russia were acquainted with Marx's philosophy or plan of action

    (E) none of the above

406. Which of the following best characterizes the Russian Provisional government of March–November 1917?

    (A) a group of radical intellectuals committed to world revolution

    (B) monarchists who supported the czar

    (C) radical workers led by Communists

    (D) military commanders who wanted to install a dictatorship

    (E) middle-class and intellectual leaders who had little sympathy for workers and peasants

407. Which of the following best describes the essence of Lenin's New Economic Policy (NEP)?

    (A) mass opportunities for education

    (B) rapid industrialization and emphasis upon heavy industry

    (C) trade with Western nations

    (D) a significant resumption of private ownership

    (E) a huge increase in consumer products

408. The Soviet-controlled Comintern was

    (A) the name Stalin chose for the Communist Party

    (B) the policy of covertly financing subversive organizations in Western Europe and the United States

    (C) an organization that sought to coordinate revolutionary activities of the Communist Party abroad

    (D) a branch of the Soviet military dedicated to acquiring overseas colonies for the Soviet Union

    (E) an organization of international artists and writers who supported the Russian Revolution

409. Which of the following was Vladimir Lenin's contribution to Marxist theory?

(A) The sole determinant of value is human labor.

(B) The proletariat inevitably becomes conscious of its revolutionary mission.

(C) Capitalism resulted in a great increase in human capacity to produce economic goods.

(D) A Communist revolution must be led by a party of professional revolutionaries.

(E) The operations of capitalists will inevitably bring about the destruction of the capitalist system.

410. Which was the last major European country to adopt compulsory military service?

(A) Germany

(B) France

(C) Russia

(D) Britain

(E) Spain

411. "The Serbian Government must cooperate inside their country with the organs of the Imperial and Royal Government in the suppression of subversive movements directed against the integrity of the monarchy."

This requirement was part of the ultimatum issued in 1914 by

(A) Austria-Hungary

(B) Germany

(C) France

(D) Italy

(E) the Ottoman Empire

412. The most serious error in the Versailles Treaty that contributed to the breakout of the World War II was

(A) the reversal of Brest-Litovsk

(B) freedom for Estonia

(C) the harsh conditions imposed on Germany

(D) the establishment of Yugoslavia

(E) the failure to establish economic sanctions against the Soviet Union

413. Which of the following countries became independent as a result of World War I?

(A) Portugal
(B) Lithuania
(C) Egypt
(D) Austria
(E) Norway

414. Communists eliminated all internal and external opposition to their rule in Russia as early as which date?

(A) 1917
(B) 1918
(C) 1919
(D) 1921
(E) 1939

415. In 1917 Lenin offered the people of the Russian Empire

(A) Land, Bread, and Peace
(B) Blood, Sweat, and Tears
(C) Blood, Iron, and Guts
(D) Liberty, Equality, and Fraternity
(E) Life, Liberty, and Property

416. The principal difference between the Bolsheviks and Mensheviks was that

(A) Bolsheviks wanted a constitutional monarchy
(B) Mensheviks felt that Russia must develop as a bourgeois capitalist state
(C) Mensheviks were led by men who were more ruthless
(D) Bolsheviks made an alliance with the Cadets
(E) Mensheviks rejected Marxism

417. The theater of war on the western front 1914–1918 lay largely in

(A) Germany
(B) France
(C) Portugal
(D) Britain
(E) Netherlands

418. Popular opinion in Germany, Austria, and Russia largely reacted to the outbreak of war in 1914 with

(A) horror and aversion
(B) resigned acceptance
(C) great enthusiasm
(D) fear of defeat
(E) total indifference

419. All of the following were major figures in the Russian Revolution EXCEPT

(A) Czar Nicholas II
(B) Rasputin
(C) Lenin
(D) Czar Alexander II
(E) Alexander Kerensky

420. Trench warfare was established along the western front early in World War I because

(A) airplanes allowed most of the fighting to be done in the skies
(B) improvements in the rifle made snipers the principal combatants
(C) the terrain made it difficult to assemble large armies
(D) defensive weapons had gained the advantage over offensive ones
(E) night vision goggles could not detect them

421. "The three national designations—Serbs, Croats, and Slovenes are equal before the law throughout the territory of the Kingdom and everyone may use them freely upon all occasions of public life and in dealing with the authorities."

This statement refers to what country?

(A) Yugoslavia
(B) Czechoslovakia
(C) Poland
(D) Bulgaria
(E) Soviet Union

422. Russia was never a part of which of the following alliances?

(A) Triple Entente
(B) Triple Alliance
(C) Three Emperors League
(D) Allied Powers
(E) Holy Alliance

423. What is the social significance of women working in factories during World War I?

    (A) Due to the wartime shortage of male workers, only women could be supervisors.

    (B) Women were found to be more adept than men at close detail work.

    (C) Universal suffrage had been granted with the outbreak of war, and women used the vote as leverage for getting industrial jobs.

    (D) The vital contribution of women to the war effort helped in their liberation from narrow social roles.

    (E) Only women in those days would accept such tedious, menial work.

424. To break the deadlock of trench warfare, nations resorted to all of the following EXCEPT

    (A) the use of tanks

    (B) widespread use of poison gas

    (C) artillery barrages

    (D) unrestricted submarine warfare

    (E) increased dependence on cavalry

425. British promises and assistance to Arabs fighting in the Middle East were designed to

    (A) create their own independent countries

    (B) gain enough Arab goodwill so that opposition to a new Jewish state would be minimal

    (C) remove French and Russian influence from the region

    (D) assure the Arabs that an independent Jewish state would never come into existence

    (E) help the Allied war effort by denying Arab support to Turkey

426. Which of the following was NOT a provision of the Treaty of Versailles?

    (A) Germany accepted sole responsibility for starting World War I.

    (B) Austria was required to pay reparations to the Allies.

    (C) Germany was effectively disarmed.

    (D) The Rhineland was demilitarized.

    (E) Germany was to pay the cost of damage done to the property of Allied civilians.

427. Which of the following is the most accurate description of the fundamental difference behind what Woodrow Wilson expected from the treaty ending World War I and what the Allies wanted?

(A) The Allies wanted reparations from Germany; Wilson opposed them.

(B) Wilson was hampered by the need to negotiate a treaty that would pass the Senate, whereas the Allies had no political concerns.

(C) Wilson wanted autonomy and independence for various eastern European nations affected by the war, whereas the Allies had secretly agreed during the war to divide up these territories when they won the war.

(D) Establishment of the League of Nations was of less importance to Wilson than it was to the British and French representatives to Versailles.

(E) Wilson wanted a peace that would not lead to another war, whereas the Allies wanted revenge.

428. The British won a major propaganda victory at the start of World War I because of

(A) the sinking of the *Lusitania*

(B) the Zimmerman telegram

(C) German atrocities in Belgium

(D) the German destruction of major Parisian landmarks

(E) the Battle of the Marne

429. The mandate system, created by the League of Nations, was a form of colonialism where the colonial rulers were

(A) pledged to allow the inhabitants to establish self-rule immediately

(B) allowed to annex all former German colonies

(C) to appoint a provisional government immediately that was composed of the intellectual elites of those territories to rule their countries in the name of the League of Nations for a period of 30 years

(D) accountable for the well-being of the inhabitants with the ultimate goal of teaching them how to rule themselves

(E) responsible for maintaining indigenous cultures

430. The Austrian annexation of Bosnia in 1908 threatened the nationalist aspirations of which of the following countries?

(A) Turkey

(B) Romania

(C) Serbia

(D) France

(E) Bulgaria

431. All of the following were contributory causes of World War I EXCEPT

(A) imperialist rivalries
(B) alliances between all the great powers
(C) the arms race
(D) Bolshevism
(E) Balkan nationalism

432. The dismissal of Bismarck by Kaiser William II paved the way for an alliance between which of the following countries during World War I?

(A) France and Russia
(B) Germany and Italy
(C) Serbia and Russia
(D) Great Britain and Belgium
(E) Germany and Austria-Hungary

433. Which state existed in 1919 but NOT in 1914?

(A) Poland
(B) Denmark
(C) Belgium
(D) Croatia
(E) Bulgaria

434. The Schlieffen Plan indicated that the German General Staff

(A) did not expect to go to war with Russia
(B) expected a long, drawn-out war
(C) anticipated a war on two fronts
(D) did not expect Austria-Hungary to honor the Triple Alliance
(E) was relying heavily on Italy and the Ottoman Empire

435. France regained which of the following as part of the peace settlement after World War I?

(A) Alsace-Lorraine
(B) Burgundy
(C) Flanders
(D) the Rhineland
(E) the Ruhr

436. "The Allied and Associated Governments affirm and Germany accepts, the responsibility of Germany and her allies for causing all the loss and damage . . . as a consequence of the war."

Which of the following best states one purpose of this clause from the Treaty of Versailles?

(A) to give the League of Nations the power to impose economic and military sanctions

(B) to provide a basis for international disarmament talks

(C) to encourage independence for European colonies

(D) to include Germany in the peace negotiations

(E) to justify large reparations payments from Germany

437. Which of the following countries entered World War I last?

(A) Russia

(B) Germany

(C) France

(D) Serbia

(E) England

438. The two crises over Morocco in the early 20th century almost brought about war between

(A) England and France

(B) England and Morocco

(C) France and Germany

(D) Italy and Germany

(E) Italy and France

439. In 1915, Italy made the decision to

(A) enter the war on the side of the Central Powers

(B) enter the war on the side of the Entente Powers

(C) stay neutral

(D) wait until the United States entered the war

(E) hold a plebiscite on the question of whether to enter the war

440. President Wilson's Fourteen Points called for all of the following EXCEPT

(A) national self-determination

(B) the creation of a league of nations

(C) decolonization in Africa

(D) a peace without reparations

(E) the end of secret treaties between nations

441. The building of a large German navy in the first decade of the 20th century greatly antagonized

(A) Italy
(B) France
(C) Great Britain
(D) Russia
(E) the United States

442. Which of the following countries lost the most land as a result of fighting during World War I?

(A) Germany
(B) Austria
(C) Russia
(D) France
(E) the Ottoman Empire

443. Which of the following terms best reflects France's attitude toward Germany after World War I?

(A) revenge
(B) forgiveness
(C) indifference
(D) apathy
(E) fear

CHAPTER 15

The Interwar Years and World War II, 1918–1945

444. Hitler's primary reason for invading the Soviet Union in 1941 was

(A) to eliminate any possible resistance to German expansion in the Balkans and the Near East

(B) to block the westward expansion of Japan in Asia

(C) to knock the Soviet Union out of the war so that all of his forces could be focused against the French and the British

(D) to destroy Bolshevism and acquire *lebensraum* for German colonization

(E) to exterminate the Slavic population, which he believed to be a threat to German mastery of Europe

445. A significant British invention that helped turn the tide in the Battle of Britain against Germany was

(A) poison gas

(B) radar

(C) V-2 rockets

(D) Tiger tanks

(E) sonar

446. Which aspect of German strategy was employed during both World War I and World War II?

(A) a large-scale military push early in the war in the Balkans

(B) formation of an alliance with Japan

(C) violation of Belgium's neutrality in order to attack France

(D) respect for the rights of the United States on the sea

(E) invasion of North Africa to seize the Suez Canal

447. The chief argument between Truman and Stalin at Potsdam in July 1945 was over

(A) free elections in Eastern Europe
(B) the numbers of tanks Americans and the Soviet Union could keep in Europe
(C) whether Soviet Jews would be compensated for the Holocaust
(D) what to do with German prisoners of war
(E) whether or not the Soviet Union would join the United Nations

448. After Hitler occupied most of France, the remainder of the country became

(A) Communist France under Mendez France
(B) very prosperous
(C) Free France under Charles de Gaulle
(D) Republican France under Georges Clemenceau
(E) Vichy France under Marshall Henri Petain

449. Fighting on the eastern front turned in favor of the Soviets when

(A) German forces were beaten by the Red Army in Poland
(B) Allied forces came to the aid of Soviet troops in Iran
(C) German forces were surrounded and captured at the crucial Battle of Stalingrad
(D) German forces mutinied and abandoned the siege of Leningrad
(E) Hitler refused to send further supplies to the German troops besieging Moscow

450. Nazi occupation in Western Europe differed from that in the East because

(A) people in Western countries were glad to collaborate with the Germans
(B) Nazi occupation was more extremely brutal in the East because of Nazi racial ideology
(C) they introduced five-year plans in the East, but not in the West
(D) the Nazis treated captured American and British soldiers more humanely in the West than in the East
(E) Jews were lumped together with Slavic peoples in the East and so escaped the worst of the Holocaust there

451. Which statement expressed a defense used by some Nazi war criminals at their trials in an attempt to justify their actions during World War II?

(A) In a war, loss of lives cannot be avoided.

(B) The end justifies the means.

(C) A person should be held personally responsible for his or her own actions.

(D) One is not accountable for one's behavior when following orders.

(E) Those who hold power have the right to exercise it in any way they see fit.

452. Which of the following areas was conceded to Hitler at the Munich Conference of 1938?

(A) the Saarland

(B) the Rhineland

(C) Sudetenland

(D) Austria

(E) Poland

453. Which of the following was a major factor in German military victories from 1939 to 1940?

(A) overwhelming German technology and numerical superiority to the French and the English

(B) French insistence on continuing to fight, regardless of the cost

(C) Britain's campaign in Norway, which diverted British troops from Western Europe

(D) the German army's effective use of armor and air power in the blitzkrieg

(E) the German defeat of the Soviet army at Tannenberg in August 1939

454. The political and social values of the Vichy government in France during World War II are best described as

(A) democratic, socialistic, peaceful

(B) radically fascist, antichurch, anti-elitist

(C) conservative-authoritarian, corporatist, Catholic

(D) monarchist, nationalistic, antimilitary

(E) republican, liberal, expansionist

455. At Yalta in February 1945, the Big Three agreed to

(A) postpone dealing with the question of what to do concerning Germany

(B) a postwar division of Germany into British, American, Soviet, and French occupation zones

(C) a two-bloc division in Europe with the West under American domination and the East under Soviet control

(D) commence the distribution of American financial aid under the Marshall Plan

(E) distance themselves from the French, who under de Gaulle were making outlandish demands

456. The term "Phony War" refers to

(A) the French response to the German advance in 1940

(B) the way the British viewed the war in 1940

(C) the American attitude toward the war until the attack on Pearl Harbor

(D) the inability of Britain and France to come to the aid of the Poles

(E) the surprisingly little action on the western front following the fall of Poland

457. In the 1920s and 1930s Czechoslovakia differed from the other states in Eastern Europe by

(A) being a member of the League of Nations

(B) being a constitutional monarchy

(C) enjoying Soviet support

(D) being the only state to maintain a democratic form of government

(E) being the first to embrace fascism

458. When Churchill said, "Never have so many owed so much to so few," *few* referred to

(A) the American soldiers at Normandy

(B) the Royal Air Force

(C) the naval commanders at the Dunkirk evacuation

(D) British soldiers who liberated concentration camps

(E) the losses suffered by the Red Army in the Soviet Union

459. Operation Barbarossa occurred in

(A) China
(B) northern Africa
(C) the Soviet Union
(D) the Philippines
(E) Manchuria

460. At the Battle of El Alamein, which of the following countries was victorious?

(A) Germany
(B) the Soviet Union
(C) Britain
(D) America
(E) Japan

461. Which of the following countries was NOT present at the Munich Conference?

(A) England
(B) Germany
(C) Italy
(D) France
(E) the Soviet Union

462. After the Munich Conference, which of the following leaders proclaimed "peace in our time"?

(A) Churchill
(B) Chamberlain
(C) Franklin D. Roosevelt
(D) Stalin
(E) Hitler

463. The Allied strategy of "island-hopping" involved

(A) taking over all of the Pacific Islands one by one to push Japan back
(B) taking over the larger, heavily fortified islands in order to break the backs of the Japanese
(C) taking over the smaller islands in order to break the supply lines of the Japanese
(D) using the air force to wipe out the larger islands so that Allied soldiers could "hop" their way to Japan
(E) implementing the method Americans had envisioned to conquer Japan

464. After the division of Germany, Berlin was in the _____ sphere.
- (A) American
- (B) French
- (C) Soviet
- (D) British
- (E) Chinese

465. Which of the following leaders was one of three main players at the Potsdam Conference?
- (A) Winston Churchill
- (B) Hitler
- (C) Franklin D. Roosevelt
- (D) Clement Atlee
- (E) Charles de Gaulle

466. Which of the following statements in an accurate description of events?
- (A) The Soviet military leadership saved millions of lives during World War II.
- (B) The Maginot Line changed drastically between World War I and World War II.
- (C) V-J day came before V-E day.
- (D) The Battle of Midway and the Battle of Stalingrad were similar in that both marked turning points of World War II.
- (E) Military decoding work had little effect on the progress of the war.

467. Which of the following is considered a "low country"?
- (A) Sweden
- (B) Spain
- (C) Luxembourg
- (D) Portugal
- (E) Norway

CHAPTER 16

The Cold War and Beyond, 1945–Present

468. Which post–World War II leader is NOT paired with the country he led?

(A) MacMillan and England
(B) Tito and Italy
(C) Khrushchev and the Soviet Union
(D) de Gaulle and France
(E) Adenauer and West Germany

469. The collapse of the Fourth Republic and the rise of the Fifth Republic occurred in France over

(A) fear of renewed war with Germany
(B) economic collapse
(C) a breakdown in relations with the United States
(D) a Socialist welfare policy
(E) the independence movement in Algeria

470. The decision of the East German government to erect a wall dividing East Berlin and West Berlin

(A) was made in 1961 to halt the flow of refugees from East Germany
(B) recognized that Berlin was a city of spies whose movements needed to be restricted
(C) prevented the infiltration of Western spies into East Berlin
(D) occurred immediately following the outbreak of the Korean War to symbolize Communist disenchantment with the West
(E) was intended to illustrate that East Germany would never again unite with West Germany

471. Which Communist country successfully asserted its independence from Moscow's control soon after the end of World War II?

(A) Bulgaria
(B) Poland
(C) Yugoslavia
(D) Czechoslovakia
(E) Hungary

472. Under Clement Atlee's administration, the British government

(A) undertook a major housing program
(B) strongly supported British trade unions
(C) assumed ownership of certain major industries
(D) instituted a major program of welfare legislation
(E) all of the above

473. One of the most important causes of the Cold War between the Soviet Union and the United States after World War II was

(A) refusal of the Western powers to give the Soviet Union a role in postwar Germany
(B) rivalries with the Western European countries regarding the status of Germany
(C) the competition between rival political and economic systems
(D) border disputes in Scandinavia
(E) where to establish the border between Poland and Germany

474. The "Prague Spring" refers to

(A) a new agricultural program introduced by the Czechoslovak Communist leadership that led to the "green revolution" in Eastern Europe
(B) the unsuccessful liberalization program attempted by Alexander Dubcek
(C) a great drought in 1968
(D) cultural flowering of Czech literature in the immediate post–World War II era
(E) the increase in the number of Czech troops committed to the Warsaw Pact

475. The most serious post–World War II split in the worldwide Communist movement was

(A) the rupture of the Soviet-Chinese alliance
(B) the defection of Marshall Tito
(C) Cuba's objections to Soviet policy
(D) the Ceausescu regime in Romania
(E) the loss of Albania

476. The Marshall Plan

(A) would supply military assistance to any country threatened by Communism
(B) excluded the Soviet Union and Eastern Europe from participation
(C) was viewed by Western Europe as capitalist imperialism
(D) was not considered a success
(E) intended to rebuild European prosperity and stability

477. One of Gorbachev's key policies was *perestroika*, which meant

(A) significant restructuring of the centrally planned command economy
(B) the rapid creation of a free-market economy
(C) political rule by a three-person directorate
(D) abolishing the KGB and introducing free political elections
(E) at first, drastic political restructuring that Gorbachev later believed could be applied to society as a whole

478. During the Khrushchev era (1956–1964) the Soviet Union

(A) retreated from some Stalinist practices
(B) enjoyed great expansion in agricultural production
(C) sought to join NATO
(D) rapidly created a consumer economy
(E) held nationwide elections for the position of general secretary of the Communist Party

479. The most innovative Soviet postwar scientific achievement was its

(A) construction of the world's largest dam on the Volga River
(B) construction of the massive *gulag* network
(C) design and production of high-quality fighter planes
(D) launch of the world's first unmanned space satellite
(E) explosion of atomic and hydrogen bombs

480. Which of the following was NOT a result of the Polish and Hungarian disturbances in 1956?

(A) They demonstrated the hollowness of American political rhetoric.

(B) They demonstrated that Austrian neutrality would not be imitated in Eastern Europe.

(C) They demonstrated the limitations of independence within the Soviet bloc.

(D) They exposed the lack of military will on the part of the West to really help freedom-fighters in Eastern Europe.

(E) They brought an end to independent action in the Soviet bloc.

481. Between the death of Stalin and the rise of Gorbachev, the Soviet Union

(A) dismantled the KGB

(B) solved its agricultural problems

(C) experienced some liberalization along with increasing economic decline

(D) announced repression of revolts in the satellites

(E) all of the above

482. Khrushchev solidified his position as Stalin's successor with a speech to the 20th Communist Party Congress in 1956 in which he

(A) further glorified Stalin by revealing some of his additional achievements

(B) started a campaign to eliminate Stalin's influence by revealing his atrocities and reducing his prestige

(C) supported the Egyptian side in the Suez Crisis

(D) promised a rapid end to Communist control of Eastern Europe and China

(E) announced an end to the Cold War and the signing of a military alliance with America

483. As France's president, Charles de Gaulle's policy during the Cold War was to

(A) remain independent of both superpowers

(B) make France the leading member of NATO

(C) follow the American lead throughout

(D) form a close military and economic alliance with Britain and West Germany

(E) closely align France with the Warsaw Pact nations

484. The European Economic Community had its origins in an agreement about

(A) agricultural production
(B) coal and steel production
(C) railway operation
(D) river navigation
(E) a response to the report of the Club of Rome

485. All of the following are reactions to the development of nuclear weapons EXCEPT

(A) fear of "mutually assured destruction" (M.A.D.), which led to the suspension of nuclear war
(B) the proliferation of nuclear weapons
(C) the decline in the number of guerrilla wars with their dependence on traditional weapons
(D) modern war technology, which was confined to countries that can afford it, often with traumatic consequences to the national economies
(E) the space exploration programs of the Soviet Union and the United States, which included a consideration of the use of weapons technology

486. After the division of Germany, Berlin remained in _____-occupied territory.

(A) French
(B) American
(C) British
(D) United Nations
(E) Soviet

487. Which of the following countries is NOT a permanent member of the United Nations Security Council?

(A) the United States
(B) Germany
(C) France
(D) Russia
(E) China

488. The Truman Doctrine was made in response to threats of Communist advances in

(A) China and Vietnam
(B) Greece and Turkey
(C) West Germany and Italy
(D) France and Algeria
(E) Japan and North Korea

489. Which of the following world leaders described the Cold War division of Europe as an "Iron Curtain"?

(A) Reagan
(B) Churchill
(C) Stalin
(D) Khrushchev
(E) Gorbachev

490. Which of the following Communist countries accepted Marshall Plan aid?

(A) Czechoslovakia
(B) Albania
(C) Yugoslavia
(D) Bulgaria
(E) Poland

491. Which event, more than any other listed, caused Khrushchev to lose the support of the Soviet people?

(A) de-Stalinization
(B) the way in which the Hungarian Revolution was handled
(C) the Cuban missile crisis
(D) the Bay of Pigs invasion
(E) his crude mannerisms

492. The Brezhnev Doctrine addressed which of the following places?

(A) Communist countries in Southeast Asia
(B) NATO countries
(C) Soviet republics
(D) countries in the Soviet sphere of influence
(E) Latin America

493. All of the following were 20th-century artistic movements EXCEPT

(A) Bauhaus
(B) Dadaism
(C) impressionism
(D) cubism
(E) expressionism

494. Which statement best explains why many violent clashes have broken out between ethnic and religious groups in Central and Eastern Europe since the fall of Communism?

(A) The opening of Eastern Europe to a free-market economy has promoted ferocious competition, which has provoked ethnic hatred.
(B) Under Communism the different ethnic and religious groups were allowed complete freedom, but under the new governments they are repressed.
(C) The Eastern Europeans have simply imitated the growing nationalism in Russia.
(D) The Communist regimes suppressed or permitted only cultural expression of national ambitions, and now these ethnic differences have resurfaced.
(E) all of the above

495. Margaret Thatcher's popularity rose when she successfully prevented

(A) Japan from taking Taiwan
(B) Argentina from taking the Falklands
(C) China from taking Hong Kong
(D) India from taking Burma
(E) Mexico from taking El Salvador

496. Thatcherism stressed all of the following EXCEPT

(A) nationalization of industries
(B) destroying the power of labor unions
(C) sharp tax cuts
(D) reduced government spending
(E) close partnership with the United States

497. The Solidarity movement in Poland, which ultimately toppled the Communist government, was helped by what other Polish institution?

(A) the Polish parliament
(B) the peasantry
(C) the army
(D) the Catholic Church
(E) dissident Communist Party members

498. In mid-1991, war broke out in the former Yugoslavia when

(A) Croatia applied for NATO membership
(B) Bosnian Muslims attacked Serbs
(C) Serb armed forces carved out enclaves for Serb minorities in the republics of the former Yugoslavia
(D) Slovenia and Croatia massacred thousands of Serbs
(E) Croatian, Slovenian, and Bosnian forces attacked Serbia

499. In 1993 Czechoslovakia

(A) joined both the European Community and NATO
(B) split into the Czech Republic and Slovakia
(C) suffered a violent civil war
(D) allowed local autonomy for all ethnic minorities
(E) none of the above

500. Changes affecting women in Western Europe since the 1950s include

(A) greater participation in the labor force
(B) the achievement of wage equality with men
(C) a reduction in life expectancy
(D) increasing family size
(E) declining opportunities in higher education

ANSWERS

Chapter 1: Recovery and Expansion

1. (B) After the Hundred Years' War, England became involved in a civil war known as the Wars of the Roses. One reason for the civil war was nobles blaming each other for losing the Hundred Years' War. Option A is incorrect as the French found a new sense of purpose and unity after defeating the English in 1455. Option C is incorrect because cannons and firearms were just becoming widely used toward the end of the war. Option D is incorrect as the British Parliament could demand more concessions from the king, as the war went on so long. Option E is incorrect as the nobles of both sides bore the brunt of the fighting, and their reduced numbers helped end feudalism.

2. (D) The longbow was the most famous weapon of the Hundred Years' War. It was responsible for many of the English victories, particularly at the beginning of the war. Options A and C were used by both sides, which is why they are incorrect. Option B is incorrect, as it had not been developed yet. Option E is incorrect; though mace is a medieval weapon, it was more common in earlier centuries and not widely used in the war.

3. (A) Because of a shift in the climate at the beginning of the 14th century, harvests began to fall short during this time, leading to famines. Some historians believe that when the Black Death arrived, it affected an already weakened population in Europe. Option B is incorrect as the Renaissance is considered to have begun during the latter part of the 14th century at the earliest. Option C is incorrect as conflict was common in the 14th century, particularly since the Hundred Years' War had begun just 10 years earlier. Option D is incorrect as most historians date the end of the Dark Ages to about 1000 CE. Option E is incorrect as the Scientific Revolution would not begin for another 200 years.

4. (C) Fleas and the bacteria that they carry are the actual reason for the Black Death. Europeans at the time had no idea of the actual cause. Option A is incorrect because Jews were rumored to have poisoned wells and whole Jewish communities were destroyed. Option B is incorrect, as many believed that sin warranted self-flagellation, which would show repentance and perhaps move God to intervene. Option D is incorrect because many believed that breathing bad air could cause disease and fled to the country. Option E is incorrect as it was also proposed that a comet had brought poisonous material.

5. (A) Because of the reduced numbers of laborers, the Black Death had the effect of raising the wages of those who survived. Option B is incorrect as it is exactly the opposite of the correct option. Option C is incorrect because the economic disruptions of the Black Death destabilized feudalism and created social mobility in the general breakdown of order and custom. Option D is incorrect because the Hundred Years' War ended 90 years after the Black Death. Option E is incorrect because the Scientific Revolution began about 200 years after the Black Death.

6. (E) The kings of France and England taxed the great landed estates of the church, prompting the famous papal bull of 1302, directly prohibiting such taxes. King Philip of France resorted to arresting the pope, who promptly died. French influence among the cardinals elected a new pope who was dominated by Philip and took up residence in Avignon, France. Option A is incorrect as widespread use of and concern about indulgences did not seem to become a problem until the early 16th century, 200 years after the Avignon papacy. Option B is incorrect because the French seemed to be concerned only with controlling the church and being able to tax it, not whatever scandals may have been going on at the time. Option C is incorrect because the Medici will not become prominent until many years later. Option D is incorrect because this had been an issue earlier in England but not in France.

7. (A) The Avignon papacy was notorious for its splendor and wealth, using new taxes and "annates," or bishop taxes. Option B is incorrect because neither the pope nor the French seemed to be struck by a new piety at the time. Option C is incorrect because the church seemed to be losing respect and influence, not gaining it during this time. Option D is incorrect as new orders were later created during the Catholic Reformation but not during this time. Option E is incorrect as the Holy Roman Emperor seemed to be losing power and influence during the High Middle Ages and was in constant conflict with popes and others.

8. (E) After the College of Cardinals broke into rival camps and elected two popes, a church council was called at Constance to deal with the situation. They elected a third pope, who failed to get the other two to resign. The other options are incorrect as the council was concerned about all of them, and though the councils of this time made efforts to address these issues, the primary reason was to establish a unified church under one pope.

9. (D) In the end, the Conciliar Movement was a failure, and once a single pope was finally elected, he quickly moved to consolidate power for himself within the church. The reforms of the movement were forgotten until the Reformation. Options A, C, and E are incorrect because they will not take place until the Catholic Reformation. Option B is incorrect as reunification has never happened to this day.

10. (E) One of the causes of the Wars of the Roses was nobles faulting each other for English defeats at the end of the Hundred Years' War. Option A is incorrect as the wars had nothing to do with ideology, but with dynastic succession. Also, nobles often switched sides. Option B is incorrect because widespread conscription will not take place until the 19th century. Option C is incorrect because the Thirty Years' War will take place in central Europe almost 100 years later. Option D is incorrect because the Wars of the Roses ended with Henry VII becoming king, not Henry VIII.

11. (B) Noble families did the bulk of the fighting in the Wars of the Roses and many people died, continuing a social breakdown that allowed many peasants to move to towns, thereby helping to end feudalism. Option A is incorrect because the eventual king was Henry VII, who was a member of the House of Lancaster. Option C is incorrect because the Black Death had ended 110 years before this. Option D is incorrect because the private armies had made most of the trouble, and Henry VII outlawed them at the end of the wars. Option E is incorrect because the English Civil War was fought almost 200 years later for very different reasons.

12. (C) This was an agreement passed by French conciliar members who in effect created a locally controlled church in France. Parts of it were later withdrawn when the French and the pope reconciled. Options A, B, and D took place at least 100 years later and dealt with different issues. Option E is incorrect because it had nothing to do with the church.

13. (D) The king of England's power to tax was restricted by the Magna Carta, signed by King John in 1215. The French king was an absolute ruler. Option A is incorrect because both were Catholic. Option B is incorrect because both sides sought to suppress nobility in the face of civil war and/or centralizing tendencies. Option C is incorrect because both rulers governed people who had both endured the Hundred Years' War in France or the Wars of the Roses in England. Option E is incorrect, though the English Parliament was much stronger than the French Estates General.

14. (B) The people of Spain were very diverse and spoke dialects that were incomprehensible to people from other regions of the country. Option A is incorrect because the Catholic Church was the strongest unifying influence. Option C is incorrect as the Moors had been greatly weakened and were not known for being formidable at this time. Option D is incorrect because France never invaded Spain at this time. Option E is incorrect as it has nothing to do with Spanish unification and took place almost 100 years later.

15. (E) England had the only limited monarchy at the time, thanks to the Magna Carta. Options A, B, and C are incorrect as they had absolute monarchies. Option D is incorrect because the Netherlands was a decentralized republic.

16. (A) England was Catholic during the time of the medieval Crusades. Option B is incorrect as the *Reconquista* against the Moors was considered a Crusade. Option C is incorrect because a Crusade against the heretical Albigensians took place in southern France. Option D is incorrect because the main Crusades against the Turks were in the Holy Land. Option E is incorrect as there were Crusades to convert the last strongholds of paganism in Finland and northeastern Europe.

17. (D) Granada was the last stronghold of the Moors to be taken by the Christians, and the Moors were driven out in 1492. All other areas were north of this, and the Moors had been driven out during the previous centuries.

18. (A) After the Muslims and then the Jews were driven out of Spain, the Spanish Inquisition focused on watching any of the newly converted ex-Muslims and ex-Jews, to make sure they were not practicing their old religions on the sly. These converts were known as Moriscos and Marranos. Option B is incorrect as these were Protestants who will not exist until later and they were also in different countries. Option C is incorrect as Jews and Muslims had already been expelled. Option D is incorrect as there were no pagans in Spain at that time. Option E is incorrect as followers of Jan Hus were in Bohemia.

19. (B) The Inquisition served as the enforcement arm of the Catholic Church, and the Catholic Church served as the most powerful unifying force in Spain. Catholic zeal became a hallmark of "Spanishness." Option A is incorrect because the different regions of Spain were linguistically diverse. Option C is incorrect as the *Reconquista* was a very slow process and not all Spaniards hated or even remembered the Moors. Option D is incorrect because there were no foreign threats to Spain at the time. Option E is incorrect because Spain did not become a part of the Hapsburg Empire until the 16th century.

20. (B) The Holy Roman Empire over time became less centralized, not more. It gradually devolved into a confederation of principalities, with more control for local princes than for the Holy Roman Emperor. All other options are incorrect because they developed strong monarchies and more centralized government apparatuses, like bureaucracies, military structures, and tax collection systems.

21. (D) The Holy Roman Empire was mostly German speaking, but other factors prevented unification. Option A is incorrect because the German states had different sizes and governmental structures. Option B is incorrect because the emperor was elected, and the electors had an interest in selecting someone they could control, or at least work with. Option C is incorrect, because over time a strong tradition of local government evolved and the princes were loath to give up any of their power. Option E is incorrect because the Holy Roman Emperor often got into conflict with the pope and others and, therefore, had his attention diverted from making the German princes more subservient.

22. (B) Though there was plenty of religious conflict in the 16th century, none of it took place in Italy, which remained securely Catholic. However, Option A is incorrect because the pope was either in Avignon during the captivity or involved in some other aspect of the schism within the church and was too busy to unite Italy. Option C is incorrect because Florence, Milan, and Venice were indeed rivals and would not unite unless one conquered the others. Option D is incorrect as Italy was often invaded and divided up by foreigners, including, but not limited to the French, Germans, Normans, Muslims, and local nobles and princes. Option E is incorrect because the local merchant classes had no economic interest to see a united Italy.

23. (C) Italy sticks out into the Mediterranean and provides a key entry port into Europe from the south. It is also a gateway to the Mediterranean and the Holy Land and points east for pilgrims and other travelers. This allowed a certain amount of prosperity in Italy that was not always available to other parts of Europe. Option A is incorrect because the Muslims only conquered southern Italy and that was for a limited time. Option B is incorrect because Italy did not become a center of learning until the Renaissance. Option D is incorrect because Italy was indeed attacked by barbarians during the last centuries of the Roman Empire. Option E is incorrect because despite it being home to the Catholic Church, Italy was often attacked by Christian armies, including a Spanish/German army that sacked Rome in 1527.

24. (D) France was never a part of the Hapsburg Empire and was its main archrival for centuries. All the other options are incorrect because they were either part of the empire by blood or marriage alliances.

25. (A) The Spanish clearly looked at Columbus's ideas as a way to leapfrog the Portuguese, who were having success getting to the Indian Ocean by sailing around Africa. It looked for a time that the Portuguese were about to become the masters of the seas and dominate trade to Asia. Option B is incorrect because the Spanish did not know of the existence of America yet. Option C is incorrect because it was commonly known at the time that the world was round, and the clergy had no interest in proving it otherwise. Option D is incorrect because the Spanish had no knowledge of the existence of America at the time. Option E is incorrect because the English had expressed no such desire yet.

26. (C) The Spanish colonies, once they were established, had extractive economies, meaning silver, gold, and other raw materials were extracted for export and sale to others outside the empire. Option A is incorrect as Spanish America was known for the same religious intolerance that characterized Spain at the time. Option B is incorrect because the colonies were tightly controlled by Spain. Option D is incorrect because the Spanish tried to superimpose Spanish culture onto the natives. Option E is incorrect because native governments were usually destroyed by the Spanish and replaced by Spanish colonial administration.

27. (E) The *encomienda* system was a way for Spain to abuse native labor on estates in the New World. It bore a striking resemblance to European feudalism in that the natives had some rights and were only required to work for the landowner two days a week, reserving the other four workdays for their own land. All other options are incorrect because they refer to noneconomic institutions. Option C is also incorrect as it refers to the Cortes, or the parliament in Spain.

28. (B) The *peninsulares* were at the top of the social structure but were the smallest in number. However, they looked down at the other groups. *Peninsulares* were Spaniards in America who had actually come from Spain. All other options are incorrect because they were greater in number. Option A, creoles, were the Spanish descendants of the original Spanish settlers. Options C and D refer to the children of Africans and Spanish, and Indians and Spanish, respectively. Option E refers to Native American Indians.

Chapter 2: The Renaissance, 1350–1550

29. (C) For the first time since the fall of the western portion of the Roman Empire in AD 476 and the rise to prominence of the Christian Church, the leading role of this powerful institution was challenged by the Renaissance thinkers and artists. Beginning around the first half of the 14th century, these artists and thinkers emphasized individual achievement, as opposed to crediting God for their accomplishments. Many important works of art featured secular and even pagan themes, harking back to the ancient Greco-Roman civilizations for inspiration.

30. (B) As Ferdinand of Aragon and Isabella of Castile led the *Reconquista* of Spain from the Muslims, they received permission from the pope to hold an Inquisition against Jews and Muslims. Both groups were pressured to convert to Catholicism, forced into exile if they refused, or in some cases, killed.

31. (C) The question asks to compare cities at the center of specific historically significant eras. Florence was arguably the most important center of the Italian Renaissance, producing such luminaries as Sandro Botticelli, Michelangelo, Leonardo da Vinci, Donatello, and Machiavelli. Athens was the center of classical ancient Greek achievements in art, philosophy, mathematics, and science from 508 to 322 BC. Democracy was first practiced in Athens during this time. Socrates, Plato, and Pericles were among the famous philosophers born in Athens during this time.

32. (B) Neither country was part of the Holy Roman Empire. Poland did, however, experience more of the Renaissance influence from Italy than Russia did because of the factors listed in A, C, D, and E.

33. (D) Although the Renaissance was predicated on rediscovering the classical works of the Greeks and the Romans, humanist writers all over Europe began writing literary works and translating the Bible in the local, vernacular languages.

34. (D) Castiglione published a famous book in 1528 called *The Courtier* in which he described how a young man of the upper class was to become the ideal courtly gentleman, or "Renaissance man." He was expected to have a broad background in many academic subjects, and his spiritual, physical, and intellectual capabilities should be developed in school. Castiglione's concept of education was to produce refined, upper-class men of taste and sophistication—not compulsory mass education.

35. (A) The Hapsburg dynasty ruled over the Holy Roman Empire and Austria for almost 500 years beginning in 1438. The Tudors ruled England from 1485 to 1603, the Valois ruled France from 1358 to 1589, the Hohenzollerns ruled Prussia and then the German Empire from 1701 to 1918, the Piast dynasty was the first ruling dynasty of Poland, in power from 960 to 1370.

36. (C) Erasmus was not from Florence. He was a northern Renaissance writer from Amsterdam. All the rest were Florentine writers.

37. (A) Italian unification happened relatively late in European history—in 1861. Politically, one of the biggest problems that plagued the various Italian territories during the era of the Renaissance was the failure to unify under a centralized authority. As a result, Italy became the battleground of larger continental powers like France and Spain. Options B through E are major factors that contributed to the origins of the Renaissance in Italy.

38. (D) Except in the highly urbanized areas of northern Italy and Flanders, peasants constituted 85–90 percent of the total European population.

39. (B) The Renaissance was an artistic and cultural movement that overwhelmingly benefitted the elites in Europe. Patrons of the arts, such as the Medici from Florence, were wealthy merchant and banking families that commissioned works of art, sculptures, and buildings in large part to promote their greatness. Humanist writers found an audience only among the minority of the population that could actually read. Male merchants and nobles were the biggest benefactors of the Renaissance, while the overwhelming portion of the population, the peasants, hardly saw the benefits of formal education or cultural enrichment.

40. (B) One of the biggest problems plaguing the various Italian territories during the era of the Renaissance was the failure to unify under a centralized authority. As a result, Italy became the battleground of larger continental powers like France and Spain. To this point, Niccolò Machiavelli in the *Prince* urged the leaders of the various Italian states to put aside their differences and unify. Failing to do so, in 1527, Rome was sacked by troops of the Holy Roman Empire who were fighting against the French for supremacy on the Italian peninsula.

41. (C) The Ottoman attacks on the Byzantine Empire, culminating in the sacking of Constantinople and the end of the empire in 1453, resulted in Byzantine scholars moving to Italy, not the Holy Roman Empire. There was a greater cultural and intellectual affinity between Greek scholars and Italy, stemming from their common Greco-Roman past, than there was between the Greeks and the Germanic civilization in western Europe.

42. (A) Although Europeans during the Middle Ages and early Modern era primarily identified themselves by their religious affiliation, there was little understanding of nationalism or belonging to a nation. This is a notion that gains credence in Europe in the 19th century largely as a result of the French Revolution and the wars of Napoleon. Breaking the independent power of the nobility, the ability to raise taxes and create an army, and enlisting the support of the dominant Christian Church of the domain were all essential to building the authority of a monarch in Russia, France, and Spain.

43. (A) The Ottoman Empire began its conquest of the Balkans in 1345. In 1389 the empire defeated the Serbs at Kosovo Polje and in 1453, it took Constantinople, renamed it Istanbul, and brought to an end the Byzantine Empire.

44. (B) Around 1650 the landed aristocracy in Poland constituted about 8 percent of the country's population, the highest in Europe. This aristocracy prohibited the consolidation of the state along absolutist lines while also failing to create an effective constitutional or parliamentary government. Monarchy in Poland was elective, and upon election by the landed aristocrats, the king had to make significant concessions to them that prohibited his accumulation of power. This ultimately weakened the Polish state in relation to its absolutist neighbors, Russia, Prussia, and Austria, all of which contributed to the three partitions of Poland that totally dismembered that state by 1796.

45. (D) Sixteenth-century western European families were predominantly nuclear composed of a married couple and their children. Farther east, in Hungary and Muscovite Russia, taxation favored households that did encourage extended families. There several nuclear families often lived in the same household.

46. (E) The Medici family, particularly under Cosimo (1389–1464) and Lorenzo (1449–1492), were patrons to some of the most important Renaissance figures of the time: Filippo Brunelleschi, Donatello, Botticelli, Michelangelo, and Leonardo da Vinci.

47. (D) Botticelli's painting *La Primavera* (*The Spring*) features Venus celebrating the arrival of spring. Venus is associated with fertility, prosperity, and eternal youth. These are the values that were represented by the lifestyle of the Medici, the patrons of Botticelli. *The Birth of Venus* was a celebration of human desire, eroticism, physical desire, and passion once again embodied in the pagan goddess Venus.

48. (B) With the rise of the Islam in the seventh century, Arab armies looked to spread their control beyond the Arabian Peninsula. The first targets of Arab Islamic expansion were Middle Eastern and north African territories of the Byzantine Empire. Starting in the 11th century, a new threat to the Byzantine Empire came in the form of various Turkic tribes. Two of the most famous were the Seljuks and the Ottomans. By 1453 the Ottoman Turks sacked Constantinople, renamed it Istanbul, and destroyed the vestiges of the Byzantine Empire.

49. (A) Although Portugal did briefly come under the Spanish crown from 1580 to 1640, it was not part of Spain under Ferdinand and Isabella. Castile, Aragon, Grenada, and Catalonia were all incorporated into a unified Spain by them.

50. (E) Europe in the early Modern era consisted of three basic classes or estates: the clergy, the nobility, and the peasants. The royal families that were emerging in various European states were not considered a separate estate or class. The bourgeoisie, although rising in economic significance since the commercial revolution beginning in the 13th century, were still insignificant politically and not a separate estate. Finally, there was no proletariat until the Industrial Revolution in England in the 18th–19th centuries.

51. (B) The Hapsburg dynasty ruled over the Holy Roman Empire and Austria for almost 500 years beginning in 1438. The Valois dynasty ruled France from 1358 to 1589. The Carolingian dynasty ruled the Frankish kingdom that would ultimately become France and Germany from 800 to 888. The Hohenzollerns ruled Prussia and then the German Empire from 1701 to 1918, and the Stuart dynasty began with Robert II taking the throne as the king of Scots in 1371 and ended with the death of Anne of Great Britain in 1714.

52. (A) The purpose of the Treaty of Tordesillas was to divide the world between the two Catholic colonial powers: Spain and Portugal. It renegotiated the imaginary line of demarcation set by Pope Alexander VI in 1493 that ran north-south in the middle of the Atlantic Ocean. The treaty granted Spain most of South America (except Brazil) and points west (eventually including the Philippines) while Portugal was granted Africa and Asia (points east of the line of demarcation).

53. (D) Bartolome de las Casas wrote *A Short Account of the Destruction of the Indies* in 1542 (published in 1552) and sent it to Prince Philip II of Spain to inform him of the cruel treatment of Native Americans by the Spanish colonial authorities. The book was not written with the intent to destabilize the Spanish monarchy politically or criticize Catholic doctrine or practice, nor was it written for personal gain.

54. (B) The Crusades were launched in 1095 by Pope Urban II to ostensibly help the Byzantine emperor Alexis regain control of Jerusalem, which had fallen under Muslim rule since the seventh century. The First Crusade (1095–1099) was a military success for the Christian Crusaders, resulting in colonies being established in the Levant. Although ultimately the Muslims defeated the Christian Crusaders and these colonies were abandoned, it was the first time since Roman times that western Europeans had ventured beyond their boundaries in a concerted effort to colonize non-European territory.

55. (D) Japan at this time (16th century) largely isolated itself to the outside world of trade and foreign cultural contacts. The only European people that made any headway with the Japanese at this time were the Dutch, not the Portuguese. Japan was also not a prized destination for goods at this time. More sought after were the goods from China, the Spice Islands (Indonesia), and India.

56. (A) The high price of goods coming from the East was one of the most important reasons why the Portuguese and Spaniards looked for alternatives to the traditional overland trade routes between Europe and the Far East. By the end of the 16th century and the fall of the Mongol Empire, the Silk Road was no longer a viable and safe trade route. The Portuguese had begun using the Indian Ocean more to get to India and the Spice Islands while the Spaniards sailed west across the Atlantic hoping to reach the Spice Islands and India in the East.

57. (E) There was no "Germany" during the Age of Exploration. Germanic people and territories were part of the Holy Roman Empire during this time. Germany would not become an independent country until 1871.

58. (C) Sugarcane production and harvesting is very labor intensive, requiring many peasants to work on plantations. The demand for sugar increased greatly from the 16th century as global commercial connections increased and goods such as coffee, tea, and chocolate became more popular. Sugar became an important cash crop for colonial European powers such as Spain, France, and England.

59. (D) France's population in 1600 was approximately 20 million. In comparison, Spain's population was about 8 million, Russia's was 13–15 million, England's was 4.4 million, and Poland's was 8–10 million.

60. (A) Venice was practically the only city on the Italian peninsula that remained independent during the 16th century. Although Charles V did not possess Venice, the Venetian leadership was in an alliance with Charles against the growing Ottoman Turkish threat in the Mediterranean Sea.

61. (B) Along with mastering navigational technology, the Spanish and Portuguese also used military means to achieve their early domination of overseas exploration and colonization. The Portuguese militarily forced the Arabs out of the lucrative Indian Ocean trade while the Spaniards, with superior arms, were able to subjugate most of Latin America with a numerically inferior fighting force in comparison to the natives they encountered.

62. (A) Men of the middle class were typically not army officers. High-ranking positions in the military during this period of time were most often reserved for the nobility. With the rise of trade in Europe as a result of the commercial revolution, middle-class professions like bankers, lawyers, and shopkeepers grew substantially.

63. (D) The Columbian Exchange, named after Christopher Columbus, is the result of the contacts established between European explorers, colonists, merchants, and Native Americans in the Western Hemisphere and Africans. The significance of the Columbian Exchange is that it initiates the first truly global epoch of world history and signifies the growing importance of Europe and its eventual world dominance.

64. (C) From the period of the Renaissance until Italian unification in 1861, the Italian peninsula was the battlefield of greater powers such as Spain, France, and Austria. Because of its position in the Mediterranean, Italian merchants were in a favorable position to benefit from the commercial revolution in Europe as well as growing commercial relations with the Islamic world as a result of the Crusades.

65. (B) What distinguished the northern Renaissance from the Italian Renaissance was the emphasis on broad social reform based on Christian teachings in the north. Christian humanists believed the best way to achieve an ethical way of life was to combine the best elements of classical and Christian cultures.

Chapter 3: The Reformation, 1500–1600

66. (D) The sale of indulgences by the Catholic Church triggered the Protestant Reformation. The Council of Trent was convened to address the doctrines that the Protestants had challenged, including the issuing of indulgences. On this issue, the council did condemn "all base gain for securing indulgences," but the theory and correct practice of indulgences was reaffirmed.

67. (A) Fleeing the religious turmoil and anti-Protestant mood in France, the country of his birth, Calvin settled in Geneva in 1536.

68. (D) The selling of indulgences prompted Martin Luther to write his famous Ninety-Five Theses, which condemned the practice of selling indulgences and other papal abuses.

69. (B) In 1517 Luther issued his Ninety-Five Theses, condemning papal abuses and the selling of indulgences. In 1520, three of his best-known and most influential works were published: *On the Freedom of a Christian*, *To the Christian Nobility of the German Nation*, and *On the Babylonian Captivity of the Church*. In 1521 Luther was excommunicated by Pope Leo X. That same year, at the Diet of Worms, Luther refused to recant his writings in the Ninety-Five Theses. As a result, he was condemned by Emperor Charles V and subsequently given sanctity in a castle at Wartburg by Frederick III, elector of Saxony.

70. (B) John Knox was the leader of the Protestant Reformation in Scotland in the second half of the 16th century; therefore, he was Luther's contemporary. Wycliffe and Hus were active in the 14th and 15th centuries while Girolamo Savonarola, the firebrand preacher and opponent of the Medici and Pope Alexander VI, was active in the late 15th century.

71. (C) Henry VIII was not a supporter of Luther or any of the Protestant reformers. Henry's decision to break with the Catholic Church was in reaction to Pope Clement VII's refusal to grant Henry an annulment from his marriage to Catherine of Aragon, the aunt of Holy Roman Emperor Charles V.

72. (B) If the power of the Ottoman Empire threatened anybody in the Christian world, it was the Orthodox Church. Eastern Orthodoxy was the main faith of the people of the Balkans, who were conquered by the Turks by the 15th century. The authority of the Catholic Church in western Europe was challenged by the values promoted during the Renaissance, the scientific discoveries of the Scientific Revolution, and the growing authority of monarchs and their consolidation of nation-states.

73. (E) Princes, nobles, and feudal lords saw their power and independence severely curtailed when monarchs expanded their political power on a national scale. The best example of this was the 1650–1653 uprising of nobles in France, known as the rebellion of the Fronde.

74. (C) In 1559 Elizabeth and the Parliament reestablished the independence of the Church of England through two acts: the Act of Supremacy and the Act of Uniformity.

75. (B) It was not Martin Luther's intention to break away from the Catholic Church. By issuing his Ninety-Five Theses, he appealed to Pope Leo X to correct the abuse of indulgences. Facing growing opposition from the papacy and as a result of his excommunication from the Catholic Church, Luther decided a break was necessary. Henry VIII was actually named "Defender of the Faith" by Pope Leo X for his criticism of Martin Luther. Henry broke with Rome when the pope failed to issue him an annulment to his marriage to Catherine of Aragon.

76. (A) France, a staunchly Catholic country, was surrounded by Hapsburg possessions: to the east in the Holy Roman Empire, to the north—the Netherlands, and to the south—Spain. It was in France's foreign policy interests to fan religious discord in the Holy Roman Empire, even if that meant supporting the Protestants.

77. (E) Inspired by Luther's challenge to the Catholic Church, German peasants seized the opportunity to revolt against their oppressive social and economic conditions. Luther harshly condemned their rebellion and urged the secular authorities to ruthlessly crush the uprising.

78. (E) One of the biggest doctrinal differences between Luther and Calvin was the issue of predestination. Calvin held a pessimistic view of human nature and believed God knew in advance who was eligible for salvation. No amount of good earthly deeds could alter the outcome.

79. (D) The Peace of Augsburg was a victory for Lutherans because it officially recognized their right to exist as a Christian denomination. People who lived under a prince that declared himself Lutheran had to convert to his faith or move to territories ruled by Catholic princes.

80. (D) Erasmus and Luther were contemporaries and for a time, friends. Erasmus, as a preeminent humanist, was highly critical of the Catholic clerical hierarchy. One of his most famous works, *In Praise of Folly*, published eight years before Luther's Ninety-Five Theses, criticized the corruption and superstition of the Catholic Church hierarchy. Erasmus, however, did not approve of Luther's break with the Catholic Church.

81. (D) This quote is from Luther's Ninety-Five Theses, condemning the sale of indulgences to finance the construction of St. Peter's Basilica in Rome.

82. (A) The Peace of Augsburg of 1555 recognized the right of German princes in the Holy Roman Empire to openly declare themselves either Catholic or Lutheran but not Calvinist. This was a major victory for the Lutheran movement.

83. (C) In the 1550s John Knox brought Calvinism to Scotland, where Presbyterianism became the dominant Christian denomination. Other European countries with significant Calvinist appeal were the Netherlands, Switzerland, and France (Huguenots).

84. (D) In the first Act of Supremacy of 1534, the English Parliament declared Henry VIII the only leader of the Church of England.

85. (A) It was a central tenet of Martin Luther's teachings that Christians should live by the teachings of the Bible, not the pope. In this case Luther rejects the practice of fasting because there is no basis for it in the Bible.

86. (C) Luther rejected five of the seven sacraments. The two he approved were sacramental baptism and communion. Later other Protestants would dispute Luther's interpretation of these two sacraments, causing further splits in the Protestant movement.

87. (A) The struggle for retaining the feudal liberties against the centralizing tendencies of monarchs defined the political struggles emerging in Europe in the 16th–18th centuries. After 1648, as a result of the Thirty Years' War and the Treaty of Westphalia, the Holy Roman Empire nominally remained intact but political power was significantly devolved to the more than 300 princes and free cities that comprised the empire. In France, this struggle resulted in the consolidation of power in the hands of powerful monarchs like Louis XIV.

88. (D) King Henry IV of France issued the edict in 1598 granting religious tolerance to the Protestant Huguenots. Although the edict was not popular with Catholics and it was later renounced by Louis XIV, it did contribute to defusing the tensions that led to the religious wars in France in the 16th century.

89. (A) According to modern estimates, about a third of the population was lost as a result of the Thirty Years' War in Germany.

90. (C) The Peace of Augsburg recognized the right of German princes to officially identify themselves as Lutherans. Subjects living in their realm also needed to accept the Lutheran faith or move to Catholic-ruled areas. This was a defeat for Charles V. He abdicated the throne shortly afterward in 1556.

Chapter 4: The Rise of Sovereignty, 1600–1715

91. (E) In 1640 Charles I convened Parliament for the first time in 11 years because he needed to raise money to suppress a rebellion in Scotland. The Scots rose against attempts to impose the Anglican religion there. Option A is incorrect because England was not at war with France at this time. Option B is incorrect because Charles had absolutist tendencies and was far from open to the idea of even sharing power with Parliament. Option C is incorrect. Although Puritans in England suspected him of being sympathetic to Catholicism, there is no indication that he wanted to change his faith. Option D is incorrect as there was no interest on his part to wage war against Spain.

92. (A) The Dutch Republic was a leading banking center in Europe until the French Revolution. The Bank of Amsterdam, founded in 1609, accepted deposits from all over the world. The Dutch government guaranteed the safety of these deposits, which contributed to the popularity of the bank. During the 17th century, the Dutch dominated commercial shipping in Europe. They also expanded their trade beyond Europe. In 1619 they established the city of Batavia in Java; they were the only Europeans allowed by the Japanese to establish a presence in Japan for two centuries; and they established settlements in both North (Manhattan Island) and south (Brazil, Caracas, Curacao, Guiana) America. Options B, C, and E are incorrect because these industries didn't exist in Holland during this time, while Option D is incorrect because, although the Dutch were innovators in agricultural production, the economy rested on maritime trade, banking, and finance.

93. (E) The political struggles that defined England in the 17th century were a struggle between Stuart kings inclined to rule without the consent or limitations of Parliament and Parliament, which saw its place as an institution that shared power with the king. In 1688 the victory in this struggle went to Parliament. Option A is incorrect since it was Mary, a Stuart, who was married to William of Orange, who assumed the English throne as a result of the Glorious Revolution. Option B is incorrect because the United Kingdom achieved universal male suffrage in 1919. Option C is incorrect as the Anglican Church remained the dominant one in England after the Glorious Revolution. Discriminatory practices against the Catholics remained however. Option D is incorrect because the Glorious Revolution had little impact on the status of its colonies.

94. (E) The natural enemies of the consolidation of monarchial power were members of the nobility, who lost most of their feudal independence as a result. They also despised the upstart middle-class artisans and merchants who were becoming more and more prosperous with the expansion of commercial capitalism in western Europe. Monarchs needed money to build up strong armies and other state institutions as well as capable and educated bureaucrats for administering the realm in an efficient manner. For this they turned increasingly to the bourgeoisie. Option A is incorrect. Although serfdom in western Europe largely comes to an end by the 16th century, there is little connection between this and the rise of national states there. Option B is incorrect because the acquisition of foreign colonies could only happen after the consolidation of national states because larger national states could summon their financial resources to undertake a policy of colonization. Option C is incorrect because exactly the opposite needed to happen for the consolidation of the national state; that is, the power of the nobility had to be subordinated to that of the monarch or at least power needed to be shared between them. In cases where the feudal nobility remained strong (Poland, Holy Roman Empire), maintaining national unity was problematic. Option D is incorrect because the so-called barbarian invasions of western Europe largely ended by the 9th–10th centuries while the process of building national states began a few centuries later.

95. (B) Louis XIV never summoned the Estates General, which hadn't been brought together by a French king since 1615. Louis XIV did have the Palace of Versailles constructed, he did believe that his rule was based on divine right, he did support the development of art and culture, and he did continue the policies of his mentor, Cardinal Mazarin.

96. (B) Finance Minister Colbert did not establish a central bank in France. He did encourage the manufacture of silks, tapestries, glasswares, woolens, uniforms, and weapons for Louis XIV's army. He built roads and canals, created the French East India Company, and built up the navy to encourage overseas commerce and colonization.

97. (D) James I ruled 1603–1625, Charles I ruled 1625–1649, Charles II ruled 1660–1685, and James II ruled 1685–1688.

98. (B) William of Orange ruled as stadtholder over Holland when he was invited by English parliamentarians to depose James II and assume the throne by virtue of his marriage to Mary, the Protestant daughter of James.

99. (B) Richelieu's main goal was to strengthen the power of the state, and in 17th-century France this meant strengthening the power of the king. Richelieu did so by abolishing the Huguenots' rights, given to them in the Edict of Nantes, to have their own army and fortified cities and curtailing the freedoms of the nobility. Option A is incorrect. Richelieu served as first minister to King Louis XIII and had considerable influence on the king but becoming king was out of the question. Option C is incorrect. Although a cardinal, Richelieu's main concerns were not religious or even the promotion of the Catholic Church. Option D is incorrect. Richelieu's main foreign policy goal was to roll back the power of the Catholic Hapsburgs in Austria. To that end, Richelieu aligned France with Protestant Sweden in the Thirty Years' War. Option E is incorrect because England was not a priority for Richelieu's foreign policy.

100. (B) Many Huguenots fled France for England, Holland, Sweden, Switzerland, Prussia, Denmark, South Africa, and North America after Louis XIV's revocation of the Edict of Nantes in 1685. Option A is incorrect because it was very difficult for the Huguenots to launch an armed rebellion against Louis XIV since Cardinal Richelieu had revoked their military privileges earlier that century. Option C is incorrect because most Huguenots left France. Few remained in France. Eventually, the Huguenots were allowed to practice their faith openly in France. Option D is incorrect as the Huguenots chose to move to other countries more favorable to Protestant beliefs. Option E is incorrect. Although the St. Bartholomew's Day massacre was directed against the Huguenots by the Catholics, it took place in 1572 and not as a result of the revocation of the Edict of Nantes.

101. (D) Option A is incorrect as Charles I was the king of England that Cromwell's supporters fought in the civil war. Option B is incorrect because Parliament was on the side of the Roundheads, but its leader was Cromwell. Option C is incorrect; Henry VIII was the King of England (1509–1547). Option E is incorrect because John Pym was a leader of the Long Parliament and a prominent opponent of Charles I, but he wasn't the leader of the Roundheads.

102. (C) James II ignored the Test Act and appointed Catholics to positions of authority in the kingdom. He was openly sympathetic to Catholicism. In 1688 his Catholic wife gave birth to a son, which opened the way for a Catholic dynasty in England to emerge. Option A is incorrect; James II had good relations with France, fleeing to that country after he was deposed in 1689. Option B is incorrect because this is what ultimately happened with the support of English Protestants. Option D is incorrect because the Anglican Church had been the official church in the country during this time. Option E is incorrect because James already held the crown of both England and Ireland (as well as Scotland).

103. (C) The English Bill of Rights of 1689 set the limits of monarchial power as well as defined the rights of Parliament. Option A is incorrect because the Levellers were a political movement during the civil war that demanded constitutional reform and equal rights under the law. The Leveller movement was ended by the forces of Cromwell in 1649. Option B is incorrect as the Magna Carta dates to 1215. Option D is incorrect because the Long Parliament was convened by Charles I in 1640 to raise money for an army to suppress a rebellion in Scotland. Option E is incorrect since the pope had no role to play in English politics or the Anglican Church since 1534.

104. (C) Louis XIV required the nobles to live at Versailles to keep them away from politics and to keep watch over them. Option A is incorrect since the middle class, which was quite small at that time, showed no tendencies to rebel against the monarch. Option B is incorrect because the peasants were denied a voice in politics and were generally not considered worthy of enjoying the life at Versailles. Option D is incorrect because the clergy was also a trusted estate by Louis. Option E is incorrect because there were no sansculottes during Louis's time. They emerge as a powerful group during the radical phase of the French Revolution.

105. (A) Mercantilism was characterized by state regulation of trade in order to increase the state's power against its neighbors and rivals. Option B is incorrect because the merchants had little independence to initiate economic policy. Economic policy was usually determined by a finance minister intent on strengthening the state. Option C is incorrect because free trade was antithetical to the principles of mercantilism. Option D is incorrect because mercantilist theorists called for a favorable balance of trade, meaning an inflow of gold and silver. Option E is incorrect as labor was very immobile at the time.

106. (C) Gustavus Adolphus intervened in the Thirty Years' War in 1630 on the side of the Protestants, turning the tide of the war in favor of the latter. Option A is incorrect because Richelieu actually provided subsidies to the Swedish king as incentive to join the conflict against the Catholic forces of the Holy Roman Empire. Option B is incorrect because he was a belligerent on the side of the Protestants, not an intermediary. Option D is incorrect because he fought against all allies of the Catholic forces of the Holy Roman Empire. Option E is incorrect because this statement more resembles the policies of France's Cardinal Richelieu, who supported the Protestants financially and militarily in the Thirty Years' War in the hopes that they would weaken the Catholic Hapsburgs in the Holy Roman Empire and Spain.

107. (C) Poland. Approximately 8 percent of Poland's population was from the nobility, the highest percentage in Europe in the 18th century.

108. (D) The landed aristocracy prohibited the consolidation of the state along absolutist lines as well as the creation of an effective constitutional or parliamentary government. As in the Holy Roman Empire, Polish kings were elected at a time when some of the country's neighbors, namely Austria, Prussia, and Russia, were consolidating their states along solidly absolutist principles. Option A is incorrect because serfdom, far from being abolished, was strengthened in Poland during the 18th century. Option B is incorrect because Sweden was no longer a European military power after Charles XII died in battle in Norway in 1718. Option C is incorrect because Poland's real threats came from Russia, Austria, and Prussia. Option E is incorrect since there was no civil war in Poland between Catholics and Orthodox Slavs despite poor relations between Catholic Poles and Orthodox Ukrainians and Belorussians.

109. (A) All three countries bordered Russia in the west/northwest (Poland, Sweden) and south (Ottoman Empire), and all were considered to be European powers. Option B is incorrect as Holland, England, and the Holy Roman Empire were too preoccupied with other more important conflicts (English Civil War, the Thirty Years' War). Option C is incorrect mainly because Finland was not an independent state during that time. It was a part of Sweden from the 13th century until 1809, when it was annexed by Russia. Option D is incorrect mainly because Hungary was not an independent state at this time. It was divided between the Ottoman Turks and Austrian Hapsburgs. Option E is incorrect because England and France were preoccupied with other conflicts.

110. (B) Constitutional rule was not acceptable to absolutist rulers. All other options are essential characteristics of absolutist states.

111. (E) Ukraine and its capital city, Kiev, was the capital of the first Russian state (Kievan Rus'). From the mid-14th century until 1653, Ukraine was under the rule of the Polish-Lithuanian state. Option A is incorrect since Prussia was not a contender to control

Ukraine. Option B is incorrect because Belarus shared a similar fate to that of Ukraine; that is, it was contested by Poland-Lithuania and Russia. Option C is incorrect since Latvia was not an independent state until 1918. Option D is incorrect because Estonia was not an independent state until 1918, and Sweden never extended its control into Ukraine.

112. (B) The Time of Troubles ended in 1613 with the election of Mikhail Romanov as the new czar by the boyar council. Option A is incorrect because the Mongol occupation had ended in 1480. Option C is incorrect because the split that led to the separation of the "Old Believers" from the Russian Orthodox Church happened in 1666. Option D is incorrect because the opposite occurred; the Romanov dynasty began its 304 years of absolutist rule in Russia. Option E is incorrect because the Time of Troubles had little to do with the strengthening of serfdom in Russia. This was already taking place with a series of laws that were passed beginning in the 16th century.

Chapter 5: The Scientific Revolution During the 17th Century

113. (D) This theory is named after the ancient Greek astronomer Ptolemy (90–168). It is also known as the geocentric model of the universe. Options A and B are incorrect because Socrates and Plato were philosophers. Option C is incorrect because Diocletian was a Roman Emperor. Option E is incorrect because Hippocrates studied medicine, and the Hippocratic Oath is taken by health care professionals pledging to work ethically.

114. (B) Copernicus revealed his heliocentric model of the universe where the earth, and not the sun, was at the center of the universe, in his book, *On the Revolutions of the Celestial Spheres*, published in 1543. Options A and D are incorrect because Isaac Newton was responsible for both the theory of gravity and the development of calculus. Option C is incorrect because penicillin was discovered at the end of the 19th century and first used for medicinal purposes in the middle of the 20th century. Option E is incorrect because the periodic table of elements was developed by Russian scientist Dmitry Mendeleyev.

115. (C) In 1609, Galileo improved on earlier existing telescopes and was able to witness the changing positions of Jupiter's moons. Option A is incorrect. Although his understanding of mathematics was advanced, it wasn't a determining factor in confirming Copernicus's theory. Option B is incorrect because Copernicus's theory had nothing to do with the human anatomy. Option D is incorrect. Galileo claimed that the heliocentric theory didn't contradict biblical writings on the world and the earth, but he also didn't use those writings to confirm Copernicus's theory. Option E is incorrect because alchemy and astronomy are completely separate fields of study.

116. (B) The discoveries made by Copernicus, Brahe, Kepler, and Galileo advanced human understanding of the universe and directly challenged the established scientific orthodoxy of the Catholic Church. The trial of Galileo in 1633 by the Roman Inquisition best exemplifies the threat the Catholic Church felt as a result of these advances. Option A can be viewed as correct but not in Europe. Catholic missionaries like Matteo Ricci brought news of many scientific advances by European scientists to China in the 17th century but not about the heliocentric theory, since the official church still rejected the theory. Option C is incorrect because there was little collaboration between the church and the "scientific community" at that time. Option D is incorrect because this has never happened. Option E is incorrect because the Protestant Reformation was triggered by what was viewed as corruption in the church (sale of indulgences) by Martin Luther.

117. (E) Anton Lavoisier, known as the "father of modern chemistry," developed his theories in the 18th century. Medical advances included van Leeuwenhoek's observation of bacteria and microorganisms with a microscope and William Harvey's explanation of the circulatory system. Copernicus's heliocentric theory of the universe was a major advance in astronomy, while in physics, Isaac Newton discovered the laws of gravitational motion.

118. (D) Aristocratic men with an interest in science received subsidies from the English government to pursue their scientific interests. Option A is incorrect because the Royal Society of London had nothing to do with arts and culture. It was strictly limited to the pursuit of science. Option B is incorrect because although most people who received a government charter to pursue scientific study were nobles, the Royal Society did not ennoble men. Option C is incorrect because the organization had nothing to do with military affairs. Option E is incorrect because the Nobel Prize did not exist back then.

119. (A) A flu vaccine was not developed until the 20th century. Options B and D are closely related and are at the core of the Scientific Revolution. Option C may have been invented in the 16th century, but its first practical application was in the 17th century. In Option E, Edward Jenner developed the vaccine for smallpox in 1795.

120. (D) Galileo's defense of the heliocentric theory of the universe included arguments that the theory did not contradict scripture. Ultimately, he was ordered by the Roman Inquisition to refute the theory and his support of it. Option A is incorrect because scientists' primary concerns were questions of science and the universe. Option B is incorrect because, although most of the great scientists believed in the concept of a supreme being, resolving the problems between Christianity and Islam was not what they were concerned with. Option C is incorrect because mathematics was essential to the scientific advances of the age. Option E is incorrect because few governments actually funded scientific research in the 17th century.

121. (B) Copernicus addressing Pope Paul III in the introduction to his book *On the Revolutions of the Celestial Spheres* in which he describes his heliocentric theory of the universe. Options A and D are incorrect because Bacon and Descartes wrote more about the question of knowledge, and not astronomy. Option C is incorrect because Pope Urban was head of the Catholic Church during Galileo's time, not Copernicus's. Option E is incorrect because Servantes was a Spanish novelist and playwright.

122. (D) Option A is incorrect because Kepler's contributions were in astronomy and mathematics. Option B is incorrect because, although Leibniz did contribute original understandings of calculus, it was solely Newton that developed the theory of gravity. Option C is incorrect because Mendeleyev's biggest scientific contribution was the periodic table of elements. Option E is incorrect because Jenner developed a vaccine for smallpox.

123. (A) The use of reason, logic, and scientific inquiry were at the heart of the revolution in science. Philosophes of the Enlightenment believed these methods of thinking and inquiry could also be applied to government to improve how people are governed. Option B is incorrect because there was no confirmation of a supreme being during this time. Option C is incorrect because there was no correlation between separation of political power and the laws of nature. Option D is incorrect because the Scientific Revolution did have a major influence on the Enlightenment because the two movements shared the same emphasis on reason and logic.

Chapter 6: The Enlightenment: A Cultural Movement During the 18th Century

124. (D) Locke believed that people were born with certain "natural rights." These rights were life, liberty, and property. Option A is incorrect because Locke believed in a "social contract" between governed and government. The people would give up their "state of nature" to a government that they have chosen in order for that government to protect the rights of all. Government's biggest responsibility is to ensure the natural rights of its citizens. Option B is incorrect because this is Copernicus's theory. Option C is incorrect because, although the concept of universal suffrage and the welfare state are outgrowths of Enlightenment thinking, these were late 19th- and early 20th-century concepts, still premature for Locke's time. Option E is incorrect because this concept is closely related to Socialism or Communism.

125. (A) Hobbes, an Englishman, had limited appeal in his own country. His views were well received in absolutist countries in Europe, albeit not well publicized, since the Bible and religion had little influence on his work. Option B is incorrect because Locke was a much bigger influence on the philosophy behind the American Revolution than Hobbes's support for absolutism. Option C is incorrect because he didn't have much faith in people to participate in a democratic government. Option D is incorrect because his work had nothing in common with the works of Karl Marx, the originator of the concept of "scientific Socialism." Option E is incorrect because libertarians believe in a small role for government in society and the economy, whereas Hobbes was an advocate of absolutist rule.

126. (B) In *The Social Contract* (1762), Rousseau wrote that the "general will" or a set of common interests that citizens possess or should possess serve as the foundation for a government's legitimacy. Option A is incorrect because Locke never discussed the concept of the general will in his works. Option C is incorrect because Montesquieu's emphasis was more on the separation of power in a government. Option D is incorrect because although Voltaire's writings spanned many topics, from censorship to government, he never wrote about general will. Option E is incorrect because Kant was a German philosopher whose works focused primarily on the human intellect and the place of reason in human thought.

127. (C) Voltaire admired absolutist monarchs such as Louis XIV of France and Frederick the Great of Prussia for their promotion of art, literature, and science. Voltaire cared less about political liberty and more about a leader who was an "enlightened despot," who promoted progress while reigning in the power of official churches. Option A is incorrect for a number of reasons but primarily because a representative government, elected by men and women, was a progressive idea even beyond Voltaire's imagination. Option B is incorrect because Voltaire rejected any political power that rested on divine explanations as superstitious and regressive. Option D is incorrect because neither Voltaire nor any of the major Enlightenment philosophes called for a direct form of democracy. Option E is incorrect because none of the early Enlightenment thinkers were radical enough in their views to advocate a dictatorship of the lowest class elements in society.

128. (C) In his famous work, *The Spirit of Laws*, Montesquieu believed political power in France should be divided between the king and parliaments, provincial estates, organized nobility, chartered towns, and even the church. He admired England's government as a model of separation of powers. Option A is incorrect. Montesquieu was a great admirer of England's political system, particularly after the victory of the parliamentary side in the English Civil War. Option B is incorrect because Montesquieu opposed despotism, even if it was enlightened, on the grounds that a despot accumulated too much political power. Option D is incorrect because like most Enlightenment thinkers of his time, Montesquieu believed the right to own private property was an essential prerequisite of a free society.

129. (A) Montesquieu admired England because he believed that England's political system was the most effective combination of monarchy (king), aristocracy (lords), and democracy (commons). Options B and E are incorrect as Montesquieu was a prominent supporter of separation of political power, but France and Russia were solidly absolutist. Most of his written works were subjected to censorship by the French authorities. Option C is incorrect as Prussia was ruled in an absolutist manner. Option D is incorrect as Spain was an absolutist country in decline in the 18th century.

130. (D) Rousseau believed that people could attain the "general will" by creating laws that they would live by together. Therefore, the social contract was between the people themselves. Option A is incorrect because Rousseau advocated popular sovereignty over monarchy and religious toleration instead of an official church. This is why Option C is incorrect as well. Option B is incorrect because he saw the "government"—magistrates and governing officials—as carrying out the policies developed by the people. Option E is incorrect because Rousseau's main concept in *The Social Contract* is the general will, and the general will is meant to include all people, regardless of class background.

131. (A) The center of the Enlightenment was Paris, France, where philosophes and educated elites from France and other European countries gathered in salons to exchange ideas. France was also the home of the most influential Enlightenment thinkers: Voltaire, Rousseau, Montesquieu, and Diderot. Option B is incorrect. Although England could boast of John Locke, Adam Smith, David Ricardo, and others, England was not a gathering place of Enlightenment thinkers. Option C is incorrect because Austria was not a gathering place for Enlightenment thinkers. Option D is incorrect. Although Voltaire for a time lived in Potsdam at the invitation of Fredrick the Great, not many other thinkers were attracted to Prussia like Paris. Option E is incorrect. Enlightenment ideas reached Russia in the late 18th century under Catherine the Great, who corresponded with Diderot and Voltaire. But Russia did not attract the Enlightenment thinkers from the West.

132. (C) The peasantry, the largest segment of the Third Estate, bore the majority of the tax burden in France prior to the outbreak of the revolution in 1789. This was one of the causes of the French Revolution. The landed nobility of the Second Estate, the clergy of the First Estate, and the monarchy were all exempt from paying taxes.

133. (A) Rene Descartes is alternately known as the "father of rationalism" and the "father of modern philosophy."

134. (C) Mary Wollstonecraft's most influential work was *Vindication of the Rights of Woman*, published in 1792.

135. (B) Voltaire denounced the Catholic Church primarily because he felt that it was a bulwark against progress and "enlightenment." Voltaire was a harsh critic of censorship, and the Catholic Church's *Index of Forbidden Books* banned many of the great works of western art, science, philosophy, and literature. Option A is incorrect because Voltaire admired Great Britain as among the freest countries in the world. Option C is incorrect because Voltaire carried on correspondence with Catherine, referring to her as "the star of the North." Option D is incorrect because, as a leading thinker in the Enlightenment, Voltaire was a major supporter of science and scientific inquiry. Option E is incorrect because at the invitation of Fredrick (the Great), Voltaire moved to Potsdam. There was a strong mutual admiration between the two.

136. (A) Although being reform minded, enlightened despots did not surrender to limits on their political powers as absolute monarchs. Options B through E are incorrect as all are characteristic reforms of enlightened despots.

137. (D) Enlightened despots curbed the power of the church, but they did not "abolish" any religions. The other options are reforms implemented by Joseph II of Austria, Frederick the Great of Prussia, and Catherine the Great of Russia.

138. (A) Maria Theresa wanted to minimize the harmful effects of serfdom on peasants from a humanitarian perspective but also for the purposes of freeing up more males for military conscription. She didn't abolish serfdom completely, for fear of offending the landed aristocracy, but minimized the harsher aspects of it. The other options are all characteristic of Maria Theresa and her rule.

139. (B) As an enlightened despot, Joseph II believed that far-reaching reforms were the responsibility of the monarch and the state. Enlightened despots were not to be subjected to elections. All other options are reforms of Joseph II.

140. (D) One of Maria Theresa's main goals while in power was to prevent the dissolution of the monarchy. To that end, her administration broke the control of territorial nobles in their diets. The Bohemian and Austrian provinces were welded together (the kingdom of Bohemia losing its constitutional charter in 1749). Under Joseph II, regional diets and aristocratic self-government fared even worse. Unlike his mother, Joseph also applied his centralizing policies in Hungary. He made German the official administrative language in a country made up of Poles, Czechs, Magyars, Slovenes, and others.

141. (B) With the "Germanization" of the Slavic and Magyar population of the Austrian Empire, nationalism among the Czechs, Poles, and Hungarians grew to become a threat to the empire in the next century. Option A is incorrect because the Austrian War of Succession (1740–1748) took place prior to Joseph II's reign (1765–1790). Option C is incorrect because both Prussia and Austria increasingly saw themselves as the leaders of the German world in Europe. Talk of unification would have been antithetical to their desire to be the leaders. Option D is incorrect. Although it was during Joseph II's rule that the first partition of Poland, with Austria's participation, took place, this had nothing to do with Joseph's "Germanization" policy. Option E is incorrect because making the German language the main administrative language of the Austrian Empire was not opposed by the German-speaking Prussians.

142. (B) The Junkers were the commanders of the Prussian army and, therefore, could not be antagonized by reforms that would break their hold on their serfs. This is the reason why Option A is incorrect. Option C is incorrect because the number of serfs on crown lands was only about 25 percent of all serfs. Option D is incorrect because although Frederick was an enlightened despot and did move to alleviate serfdom, moral considerations had less to do with abolishing it on crown lands than appeasing the Junkers.

143. (A) Frederick was anything but a mediocre leader with limited intelligence and ambition. His talents and intelligence were recognized by no less of a luminary than Voltaire. All other options accurately describe Frederick's rule.

144. (A) The Pugachev Rebellion, a peasant rebellion led by Emelian Pugachev, had to be suppressed violently by the Russian army under Catherine in 1774. It was the largest peasant revolt in European history and it shook Catherine. Less than 20 years later, the French Revolution broke out. Both of these revolts led to Catherine curtailing her reforms and becoming more politically conservative. Option B is incorrect as the wars against the Ottoman Turks and the partitions of Poland led to the strengthening and expansion of the Russian state but had little effect on reforms. Options C and D are incorrect because neither Catherine's social life nor the American Revolution had an impact on her reform efforts.

145. (C) Russian forces under Catherine defeated the Turks twice and took full control of the Crimean peninsula by 1792. Russia also benefited from the three partitions of Poland, expanding its borders westward. Option A is incorrect because Russia's expansion into Central Asia took place in the 19th century. Option B is incorrect because the Crimean War was fought from 1853 to 1856 and Russia lost to the Turks, who were supported by the British and French. Option D is incorrect because there was no such attempt on the part of Russia to enter into an alliance with China. Option E is incorrect because it was Peter the Great who defeated the Swedes in the Great Northern War.

146. (D) Joseph II of Austria went further than any other European monarch up to the French Revolution in granting equal civil rights to Jews. He allowed Jews to obtain noble status, but with that he also made them equal in service to the king, which meant they had to serve in the military. Options A and E are incorrect because neither ruler was known to be an enlightened despot. Louis XVI's failure to enact any substantial reforms contributed to the outbreak of revolution in France in 1789, while Philip II (1527–1598) was an extremely conservative Catholic ruler of Spain who intensified the work of the Inquisition. As to Options B and C, neither Maria Theresa nor Frederick the Great implemented any reforms that specifically dealt with the Jews.

147. (B) In response to the largest peasant rebellion in European history, Catherine strengthened and expanded serfdom into the Ukrainian territories of the Russian Empire. Option A is incorrect because the opposite occurred. Options C, D, and E never occurred.

148. (A) Ultimately, enlightened despots needed the support of the nobility, which they never fully received because the monarchs looked to further undercut the nobles' power. Once the enlightened despots were gone in Russia and Prussia, for example, the power of the nobles, at least over their serfs, returned. Option B is incorrect because while enlightened despotism may have introduced the concept that reform comes from the state, no provisions were made to create a welfare state and enlightened despots were thoroughly opposed to any sort of democratic limitations to their power. Option C is incorrect because the attempt to return to absolute rule was more in response to the upheavals resulting from the French Revolution than to the changes brought by enlightened despotism. Option D is incorrect because the opposite occurred. Political power was more centralized as a result of enlightened despotism.

149. (E) All options are correct. By the end of the 19th century, limited suffrage was achieved in Germany and France. In Option B, Italy achieved national unification in 1861 while Germany achieved the same in 1865. In Option C, the Poles unsuccessfully revolted against Russian rule in 1830 and again in 1863. The Serbs and Greeks were able to achieve their independence from the Ottoman Turks in 1832 and 1867, respectively. In Option D, limited monarchy became the standard in most major European countries except Russia, which remained an absolute monarchy until 1905.

150. (C) Great Britain only formed a permanent standing army in the beginning of the 20th century.

151. (A) Since the home of the Enlightenment was France and most aristocrats in Europe preferred speaking French, French was the "lingua franca" of Europe during the 18th century. Option B is incorrect because German was largely confined to the German-speaking territories of the Holy Roman Empire and Prussia. Option C is incorrect because English will become the dominant international language thanks to the extent of British imperialism, but not as yet during the Enlightenment. Option D is incorrect because Italian was largely limited to the Italian peninsula, and Option E is incorrect because French superseded Spanish in Europe.

152. (A) The officer corps in European armies in the 18th century came largely from the landed aristocracy. Option B is incorrect because middle-class males rarely attained positions of leadership in militaries. Option C is incorrect because, unlike in the 15th and 16th centuries, mercenaries were no longer used because of their questionable reliability. Option D is incorrect because the peasants almost always comprised the rank-and-file soldiers, and Option E was rarely if ever the case.

153. (D) Until the Industrial Revolution in Europe, which began in Great Britain in the mid-18th century and in the 19th century in most other western European states, the peasants made up the overwhelming majority of the population. For example, on the eve of the French Revolution, peasants constituted about 76 percent of the population. But the farther east one went in Europe (Poland, Russia), the peasant population approached 90 percent.

154. (A) The nobility in all European countries except Poland rarely exceeded 5 percent of the population. Poland had the largest percentage of nobles with 8 percent.

Chapter 7: Social Transformation and State-Building in the 18th Century

155. (D) Dutch banks did charge interest on loans but much lower than French or English banks. All of the other options are true and are all factors that contributed to the Dutch Republic's prosperity during the 17th century.

156. (E) Holland, which was one of the provinces that eventually comprised the Dutch Republic, gained its independence from Spain in 1648 as a result of the Thirty Years' War and the Peace of Westphalia. This was the culmination of 80 years of rebellion by the Dutch against Spanish rule. The other options were contributing factors to the success of the Dutch Republic during the 17th century.

157. (A) The Navigation Acts were a series of laws the English Parliament passed that prohibited foreign trade with its colonial possessions. These acts primarily targeted the supremacy of Dutch commercial shipping, which had dominated trade on the Iberian Peninsula in 1647, the Mediterranean, the Baltic, and even with English colonies. The result was three wars between the English and the Dutch from 1652 to 1674 during which the English annexed New Amsterdam and renamed it New York.

158. (A) Tensions between Parliament and Charles I began in 1628 when Parliament forced Charles to agree to the Petition of Right, which stipulated that he must gain the consent of Parliament before he could raise new taxes. In response, Charles refused to call Parliament into session between 1629 and 1640. When Charles tried to bring Anglican reforms to Presbyterian Scotland, the Scots revolted. To raise money to fight the war, Charles called Parliament into session, which then brought the conflict between the monarch and Parliament to a head.

159. (D) Prior to the outbreak of the English Civil War, Charles attempted to raise taxes without the consent of Parliament. This attempt was to raise "ship money." This tax was intended to finance a modern navy by taxing everyone, not just residents of coastal towns. In 1640 Charles reluctantly convened Parliament because he needed money to put down a rebellion in Scotland. The Parliament used the Scottish rebellion to press its demands against Charles.

160. (A) Captured by Oliver Cromwell's forces while trying to flee to Scotland, Charles I was tried by a much smaller Parliament of about 53 members, convicted of treason, and sentenced to death by beheading. Option B is incorrect because the Tudor line ended with the death of Queen Elizabeth in 1603. James VI of Scotland assumed the English throne unopposed. In Option C, the execution of Charles I did lead to the abolition of the monarchy and the establishment of a republic (the English Commonwealth). But the republic was short-lived; it ended with Cromwell's death, and the military reestablished the monarchy by inviting back Charles I's eldest son. Neither Options D nor E occurred as a result of Charles's execution, as Cromwell's forces crushed any remnants of opposition from those two nations.

161. (B) The execution of Charles I, a Stuart with Scottish roots, turned public opinion in Scotland strongly against Cromwell's new government. Cromwell sent his forces to Scotland in 1650 to pacify the Scots; therefore, Option A is incorrect. For Option C, although Scotland had been plagued by lack of unity on the question of fighting English occupation throughout its history, the problem was not between nobles and peasants, but instead the nobles and barons and burgesses. Option D did not happen.

162. (D) After executing Charles I in 1649, Oliver Cromwell declared England to be a republic and named the country the Commonwealth. But his domestic policies led to growing opposition to his republic, and he disbanded the Rump Parliament in 1653, naming himself "Lord Protector." Option A is incorrect because all forms of monarchy were abolished by the "Rump Parliament" and the Council of State shortly after the execution of Charles I. Although Cromwell was a strict Puritan who saw himself as "God's agent," his rule cannot be considered a theocracy, rendering Option B incorrect. Option C is incorrect as Cromwell's republic may have begun as something resembling a parliamentary republic, but by 1653, he abolished this institution when opposition to his domestic economic policies grew. Option E is incorrect because something closer to the opposite occurred: by force, Cromwell created the foundation of what would ultimately become Great Britain.

163. (C) Although Cromwell did enter into a secret alliance with France against Spain, it cannot be said that his government relied on France for its survival. In Option A, landowners and merchants in the Rump Parliament did increasingly oppose Cromwell's taxation policies that were intended to fund his wars against the Spaniards. This led to its disbanding in 1653. In Option B, the majority of England's population did reject the more extreme Puritan-inspired policies of Cromwell's government, like the ban on sports, theaters, and pubs, and the transformation of feast days in honor of saints to fast days, among other things. In Option D, Cromwell's brutal military campaign in Ireland (1649–1650) that led to the occupation of that country by British forces resulted in him being one of the most hated figures in Irish history. In Option E, Cromwell alienated many republicans and religious radicals by dissolving the Rump Parliament and taking on the title of "Lord Protector" for life.

164. (D) After an initial "honeymoon" period of mutual understanding between Charles II and the Parliament, relations began to deteriorate when Charles exhibited his admiration for French King Louis XIV and openly declared his support for the principle of religious toleration. Parliament interpreted this as his way of promoting Catholicism in England. Parliament also feared the ascension to power of his younger brother and heir James, who had publicly announced his conversion to Catholicism in 1668.

165. (A) The Cavaliers were the Royalist supporters of King Charles I, and Roundheads was the nickname given to the Parliamentary forces that opposed the king in the English Civil War.

166. (D) The English Civil War had been largely triggered by the struggle between the Stuart monarchs who favored royal absolutism and Parliament, which favored a power-sharing arrangement between itself and the king. In 1688 and 1689 the conflict had been resolved when James II abdicated and William of Orange and Mary accepted the throne from Parliament on agreement that they would share power. Option A is incorrect because the opposite occurred. Option B is incorrect as this took place in 1707 in the Act of Union by the Parliaments of England and Scotland. Option C is incorrect because if this would have happened, the anti-British uprising in the American colonies may not have taken place. Option E is incorrect because the Industrial Revolution, beginning around 1750, contributed more than any other single factor to England's rise to supremacy in Europe. After the unification of Germany in 1871, England's dominant position in Europe was significantly challenged.

167. (A) Louis considered religious unity necessary to the strength of France and his royal authority. To that end, in 1685 Louis revoked the Edict of Nantes. As a result, many Huguenots left France for Holland, Germany, and America. Option B is incorrect because the First and Second Estates continued to enjoy tax-free status until the French Revolution. Option C is incorrect because as an absolute ruler, Louis was not interested in the Estates General or any other institution limiting his power. The first part of Option D is generally correct but the second part—the monarch answering to the pope—is incorrect. Once again, as absolute monarch, Louis was convinced of his absolute authority to rule given to him by the good graces of God and not a temporal authority even in the form of the leader of the Catholic Church.

168. (A) In 1685 Louis XIV revoked the Edict of Nantes, which was issued by Henry IV in 1598 as a means to end the religious wars that engulfed France in the 16th century. The edict provided the right to Huguenots to practice their brand of Christianity in the towns where they predominated and to extend them the same rights as Catholics. Option B is incorrect because the English Bill of Rights, passed by the English Parliament in 1689, reaffirmed the Declaration of Right presented to William and Mary inviting them to rule England. The Bill of Rights defined the power of the monarch and the rights of Parliament to share in administering the state. Option C is incorrect because the Ninety-Five Theses was Martin Luther's list of grievances against abuses of the Catholic pope. In Option D, the Edict of Fontainebleau *is* the revocation of the Edict of Nantes. It is the wrong option because the question states: this statement was most likely issued *as a result of* the Edict of Nantes. Option E is incorrect because the Peace of Augsburg of 1555 put an end to the war between an alliance of Lutheran princes and free German cities known as the League of Shmalkald and the Catholic forces of Holy Roman Emperor Charles V. Incidentally, the

Peace of Augsburg was a victory for Protestants, as it recognized for the first time the right of each state and free city within the empire to choose Catholicism or Lutheranism as its faith.

169. (C) Colbert actually lowered internal tariffs in a large portion of the country by creating an internal free-trade zone the size of England called the Five Great Farms. The remaining options are all measures Colbert undertook to strengthen the French economy so that Louis XIV could reorganize and enlarge his army, construct Versailles, and accommodate the growing bureaucracy necessary to help administer the growing state.

170. (C) Louis XIV ruled longer than any other monarch in European history (1643–1715). From 1643 to 1661, Cardinal Mazarin ruled in his name, with Louis taking personal control of France at the age of 23. During his rule Louis consolidated political power in his hands by subordinating the nobility to his authority, building up a powerful army bent on expansion, revoking the rights of the Huguenots, exhibiting the glory and grandeur of his rule by constructing Versailles outside of Paris, and following mercantilist economic policies to finance his imperial ambitions. Although Henry IV (Option A) can be seen as the monarch that lays the foundation for absolute rule in France (he never once summoned the Estates General), this option is incorrect because his Edict of Nantes gave Huguenots the right to hold about 100 fortified towns defended by their own forces and allowed for mixed chambers of Huguenot and Catholic superior law courts. Louis XIII, Option B, was a monarch that continued the process of consolidating absolute rule, but the option is incorrect because Louis XIV brings absolutism in France to its peak. The two monarchs in Options D and E presided over the decline (Louis XV) and end (Louis XVI) of royal absolutism in France.

171. (A) Charles II, the last Hapsburg ruler of Spain, reigned from 1665 to 1700. He had no legitimate heir to the throne but did stipulate in his will that all Spanish territories should go to the grandson of Louis XIV of France. In the event Louis refused in his grandson's name, the entire inheritance would go to the son of the Hapsburg emperor in Vienna, thus pitting the French against the Hapsburgs and everyone else in Europe opposed to the rise of French power.

172. (B) Philip V, the grandson of France's Louis XIV, was allowed to keep the throne in Spain as a result of the Peace of Utrecht, but he was forced to renounce his line of succession in the French line of succession. Option A is incorrect because, although the Hapsburgs gained the former Spanish possessions of Milan, Naples, Sicily, and the Netherlands, they did not gain control over Spain proper, which went to Philip V. Option C is incorrect because what was eventually to become part of a unified Italy in 1861 was transferred to Austrian control. Option D is incorrect because close to the opposite occurred: the British added to their North American possessions largely at the expense of France.

173. (B) The United Provinces, also known as the Netherlands and Low Countries, were a personal union comprised of the kingdoms of the Netherlands, Belgium, the grand duchy of Luxemburg, a good portion of northern France, and a small part of western Germany. Option A is incorrect because it corresponds to largely eastern German lands. Option C is incorrect as it corresponds to the future United Kingdom, which is separated from mainland Europe by the English Channel. Option D is incorrect because these territories comprise Spain proper on the Iberian Peninsula. Option E is incorrect because the United Provinces was comprised of more than just Belgium and the Netherlands.

174. (A) In 17th-century Europe, the justification of political authority largely rested on the theory of divine right of kings, whereby the king was the political embodiment of God's ultimate representative on earth. As such, his power was absolute and not to be challenged by any persons or institutions, like a parliament. Option B is incorrect because since the Protestant Reformation and the rise of the nation-state, papal power declined while secular power increased. Whereas in the Middle Ages, papal authority could claim to be God's representative on earth, this began to change with the rise of absolute monarchy. Option C is incorrect as the rights of subjects were to become an issue during the Enlightenment, beginning in the 18th century. Option D is incorrect because, although the papacy would have liked to have this type of power over secular authority, with the rise of absolutism, spiritual power took a back seat to secular authority. Option E is incorrect as this theory more resembles the Chinese theory of the Mandate of Heaven and the dynastic cycle.

175. (C) In 1609 the Dutch established the Bank of Amsterdam, which became the most important and most reliable financial institution in all of Europe. Deposits were guaranteed by the Dutch government, and the bank attracted capital from all parts of Europe, making it possible to make loans for various purposes. Ultimately, in the 18th and 19th centuries, London becomes the financial center of Europe by virtue of Great Britain's leading role in the Industrial Revolution.

176. (D) The events in England of 1688 were known as the Glorious Revolution because English constitutionalism and parliamentary government triumphed over an overbearing monarchy. At the same time, after 1688, membership in Parliament became more exclusive: an act of 1710 required members of the House of Commons to possess private incomes at such a level that only a few thousand people could legally qualify. This income had to come from ownership of land, indicating the aristocratic and oligarchic nature of British government during this period.

177. (B) These discriminatory policies targeted Ireland for fear that Ireland would foment a pro-Catholic uprising against the English and to prevent it from entering any potentially anti-English alliances. Option A is incorrect as England and Scotland would soon sign the Act of Union in 1707, joining the two countries in the United Kingdom. Options C and D are incorrect as England would not have the right to impose these policies on sovereign states. Option E is incorrect as there were hardly any Catholics in Wales.

178. (B) Anglo-Dutch forces seized Gibraltar in 1704, and the British retained possession of it as a result of the Treaty of Utrecht in 1713. Option A is incorrect as Jamaica became a British colony in 1655 when the British captured it from Spain. Option C is incorrect as Manhattan became an English possession in 1674 when the Dutch ceded the island to them. Option D is incorrect as the French forfeited their claims to Canada to the British in 1763 as a result of the Treaty of Paris that ended the Seven Years' War. Option E is incorrect as India became a direct possession of the British crown in 1858 in response to the failed Sepoy uprising against the rule of the British East India Company.

179. (C) In 1701 the Act of Settlement stipulated that no Catholic could be king of England in response to the pro-Catholic sentiments of James II, who was deposed in 1688 by the English Parliament, and William of Orange, chosen to replace James. Option A is incorrect as the Solemn League and Covenant, passed by Parliament during the English Civil War in 1642, called for Presbyterianism to be the united faith of England, Scotland, and Ireland. Parliament passed the act to gain the support of the Scots against pro-Charles I Royalist forces. Option B is incorrect as the Triennial Act was passed in 1641 requiring Charles to call Parliament into session for a 50-day period at least once every three years. Option D is incorrect as the Petition of Right of 1628 called for Charles I to honor four specific constitutional principles: no taxation without Parliament's consent; no imprisonment without just cause; no forced billeting of soldiers; and no martial law in time of peace. Option E is incorrect as the English Bill of Rights, enacted in 1689, confirmed the principle of power-sharing between the English monarch and the Parliament. The king could not raise taxes or an army without the consent of Parliament, and no subject could be arrested and detained without due process. William III (Orange) had to accept these principles prior to the throne being offered to him.

180. (C) John Churchill, also known as the Duke of Marlborough, was a distinguished military leader and pro-Royalist in his political beliefs. But he was born in 1650, after the English Civil War, making it impossible for him to participate. Because of his father's staunch pro-Royalist sentiments, young John rose quickly through the ranks of King James II's military. All the others were leaders of the opposition to Charles II. Thomas Grey (Option A) was one of the military leaders of the Parliamentary forces and later signed Charles I's death warrant. John Pym (Option B) and John Hampden (Option D) were moderately well-to-do gentry and leaders of the Long Parliamentary opposition to Charles. Oliver Cromwell (Option E) emerged as the most popular leader of the anti-Royalist forces, known as the Roundheads.

181. (A) France became the "model" absolutist state in western Europe, with the origins of absolute rule beginning with Henry IV, peaking during the reign of Louis XIV, and ending with the beginning of the French Revolution. Option B is incorrect as Holland in the 17th century, better known as the Dutch Republic, was governed by the States General, an institution that gathered delegates from seven provinces that comprised the country and the king. Option C is incorrect because Italy, as a unified state, only came into existence in the 19th century. Option D is incorrect as Poland's monarchy was an elected position that kept it weak in relations to the strong aristocracy. Option E is incorrect as the outcome of the Glorious Revolution in 1689 confirmed the principle of shared power between Parliament and king.

182. (C) In England, the principle of shared power was confirmed during the Glorious Revolution, when Dutch King William III was offered the English throne as long as he agreed with the English Bill of Rights, which called for parliamentary consent on most important administrative issues. In Holland, for much of the 17th century, the republican forces in favor of a power-sharing arrangement between the king and the States General dominated the political landscape. After a brief interlude during the reign of William III where monarchial power was supreme, the republican forces won out after his death in 1702.

183. (B) The three partitions of Poland at the end of the 18th century at the hands of Russia, Prussia, and Austria put an end to that state until 1918. Option A is incorrect because the exact opposite occurred. Option C is incorrect because Poland was partitioned between Russia, Prussia, and Austria. Option D should have Prussia, not Hungary. Option E is incorrect as Lithuania was also partitioned away as a result of its union with Poland.

184. (E) The Polish aristocracy in the 17th century comprised about 8 percent of the country's population, the highest proportion in Europe.

185. (A) The Pragmatic Sanction of 1713, issued by Austrian Hapsburg Emperor Charles VI, called on every diet in the empire and the various archdukes of the Hapsburg family to agree to the family's territory as indivisible and to recognize only one heir to the throne. The situation that prompted this edict was the absence of a male heir to succeed Charles VI.

186. (A) Spending on the military was typically the largest expenditure (excluding payment of debt) that the 18th-century state incurred. Option B, spending on royal palaces, although costly, did not match expenditures on the military. The remaining options are not correct because 18th-century governments typically spent very little on education, anything that could be identified with welfare programs, or even infrastructure projects. Such government programs were not a mainstay feature of European nations until the 20th century.

187. (D) The Polish aristocracy, being the largest in Europe, was keen on preserving its substantial liberties from a strong absolute monarch. The aristocracy was able to control the power of the monarch by making that position an elected one. As a result, foreign influence became pervasive, and as Poland's absolutist neighbors Austria, Prussia, and especially Russia became more powerful, Poland's position weakened. This ultimately led to the three partitions of Poland that culminated with the elimination of the Polish state in 1796.

188. (C) As a result of a succession controversy that grew into a period in Russian history known as the Time of Troubles (1598–1613), some of the country's neighbors decided to take advantage of the chaos and militarily intervene. One of those countries was Poland, which invaded and occupied Moscow in 1610 and briefly put one of its own, Vladislav, on the Russian throne. Option A is incorrect because France under Napoleon briefly and unsuccessfully occupied Moscow in 1812, two centuries after the Poles did. Options B and D are incorrect as both Sweden and the Ottoman Empire fought wars against Russia but neither occupied Moscow. Option E is incorrect because Russia and Holland never fought a war against one another.

189. (A) This quote is a 17th-century account of the Polish king Jan Sobieski's victory over Ottoman Turkish forces at Vienna in 1683. Fighting along with Sobieski's Polish forces were Austrian and German troops. This was the second and last failed Ottoman attempt to conquer Vienna, the capital of the Austrian Empire.

190. (C) Written constitutions became a central demand of Enlightenment thinkers of the 18th and 19th centuries to limit the power of monarchs and to define the rights of citizens; therefore, constitutions were antithetical to absolute rule. The other options were necessary characteristics of absolute rule.

191. (B) In the 17th century, the measure of wealth was in land ownership (Option C), not one's possession of cash or capital, which was becoming more commonplace but not yet a dominating factor as it would be in industrial Europe after the 19th century. Options A, D, and E were signs of high social status in Europe during the 17th century.

192. (C) Although the rise and expansion of Prussia in large measure was due to its powerful and disciplined military (Option D), this military power was based on land, not on sea. Options A, B, D, and E are factors in the rise and expansion of Prussia during the 17th and 18th centuries.

193. (B) Peter's construction of the city bearing his name (completed in 1703) was meant to be his "window on the West," symbolically reorienting his policies toward western Europe, away from Moscow, which was located southeast of St. Petersburg. Option A is incorrect as Peter incorporated Baltic territories formerly belonging to Sweden as a result of the Treaty of Nystad, which ended the Great Northern War (1700–1721). Option C is incorrect as the cost of governing in Moscow had nothing to do with the decision to move the capital to St. Petersburg. Option D is incorrect. Although Peter's focus was to learn from the West to reform Russia, this did not stop Russian future expansion eastward. It was in the 19th century when the Russian Empire expanded farther southward into the Caucasus and eastward into the Central Asian Turkestan region, sparking an imperial competition with Great Britain. Option E is incorrect as Kiev had ceased to be Russia's capital since the 13th century.

194. (C) In the 18th century, although Russia made substantial territorial gains against both the Ottoman Empire (Option B) in southern Ukraine, the northern Caucasus, and the Crimean Peninsula, and Sweden (Option E) in the Baltic region as a result of the Treaty of Nystad, most of its gains were at the expense of Poland. During the three partitions of Poland between Russia, Prussia, and Austria, Russia regained control over Belarus, most of the Ukraine, and Lithuania. Option D is incorrect as Russian did not expand at the expense of Prussian territory.

195. (C) The Medici dynasty's rule over Tuscany ended with the death of Gian Gastone de Medici in 1737 when there was no male heir to succeed him and with Austrian occupation that same year. Also, the Medici did not rule over a unified Italy. Instead they ruled over only the province of Tuscany, whereas all of the other dynastic families listed in the other options ruled independent states.

196. (D) Poland's aristocracy, like in the Holy Roman Empire, was successful in preventing the centralization of political authority in the person of a strong monarch or in the institution of parliament. Monarchy in Poland was an elected position and although there was a central diet, it was too weak to make any decision affecting Poland as a whole, largely because of the infamous liberum veto, which allowed any member of the diet to stop an action if one person opposed that action. Instead, the aristocracy met in 50 to 60 regional diets, which prevented the unity of the country and allowed rising powers like Russia, Prussia, and Austria to gain substantial influence within the fractured Polish state.

197. (A) The Treaty of Karlowitz (1699) cemented the Austrian Hapsburg victory over the Ottoman Turks in the Austro-Ottoman War of 1683–1697. Besides significant territorial losses in central Europe, the Ottoman loss is viewed as the beginning of the decline of Ottoman power in east and central Europe. Option B is incorrect as the Union of Lublin of 1569 created a united Polish-Lithuanian state. Option C is incorrect as the Treaty of Kuchuk Kainarji of 1774 followed the Russian victory over the Ottoman Turks in the Russo-Turkish War of 1768–1774. Option D is incorrect as the Treaty of Utrecht of 1713 helped bring an end to the War of the Spanish Succession (1701–1714). Option E is incorrect as the Treaty of Rastatt (1714), a prelude to the Treaty of Utrecht, ended hostilities between France and Austria during the War of the Spanish Succession.

198. (A) The ethnic majority of the Austrian Hapsburg Empire was the Slavic people. They were comprised of Poles, Serbs, Czechs, Slovaks, Slovenes, and Croats. Option B, although seemingly the obvious choice, is incorrect as the Austrian and other ethnically Germanic people were outnumbered by the more numerous Slavs. Option C is incorrect as while there were Italians part of the emerging Austrian Empire, they were not very numerous. Option D is incorrect as the Magyars (Hungarians) grew in number and ultimately co-ruled the empire after 1867 but did not comprise the mathematical majority in the Austrian and Austro-Hungarian Empire. Option E is incorrect as the ethnically Turkic populations were largely part of the Ottoman Empire and the northern Caucasus region of the emerging Russian Empire.

199. (D) The origins of the Prussian state are in Brandenburg, which came to be ruled by the Hohenzollern dynasty in 1415. In 1609 the dynasty inherited lands in the Rhine valley in western Germany, and nine years later they received the duchy of Prussia in northeast Germany bordering the Baltic Sea. The growth and consolidation of the Prussian state continued under Frederick William (1640–1688) and his son, Frederick III (1688–1713), who became the first king of Prussia.

200. (E) The Prussian state did not expand as a result of military conflict with the Dutch Republic, or Holland. All other options demonstrate an example of Prussian expansion and German unification. In Option A, Prussia's victory over the French in 1870 directly led to the creation of the German Empire. In Option B, most of Prussia's wars resulting in territorial expansion came at the expense of the Austrians. In the Austrian Wars of Succession (1740–1748) and the Seven Years' War (1756–1763), Prussia gained control of all of Silesia. A century later, the Prussians defeated Austria in the Austro-Prussian War (1866) and annexed pro-Austrian German states as well as all of Schleswig-Holstein. In Option C, both Prussia and Austria went to war with Denmark over the duchies of Schleswig and Holstein. The result was a Danish defeat and dual administration of the duchies, Schleswig to Austria and Holstein to Prussia. This set the stage for the Austro-Prussian War of 1866 described in Option B. In Option D, as a result of the partitions of Poland between Russia, Austria, and Prussia, the latter acquired almost 20 percent of divided Poland. These territorial acquisitions helped unify Brandenburg with eastern Prussian lands.

201. (B) As a result of its defeat in the Great Northern War (1700–1721) at the hands of Russia and the subsequent Peace of Nystad that confirmed the loss of Estonia, Latvia, and southeast Finland, Sweden lost its empire and its status as the dominant Baltic Sea power.

Option A is incorrect as the Thirty Years' War (1618–1648) contributed to the rise of Sweden's power in Europe. The Treaty of Westphalia (1648), which ended the war, confirmed Swedish control over western Pomerania and the former bishoprics of Bremen and Verdun on the North Sea. Option C is incorrect as the Swedes did not take part in the War of the Spanish Succession (1700–1714). Option D is incorrect as Sweden had the fortune of being ruled by a succession of capable monarchs: Gustavus Adolphus (1611–1632), Queen Christina (1632–1654), and Charles XII (1697–1718). Option E is incorrect as the Seven Years' War (1756–1763) and Sweden's participation in it (known as the Pomeranian War, 1757–1762) took place after Sweden's defeat in the Great Northern War.

202. (A) In return for aiding the Hapsburg Holy Roman Emperor in the War of the Spanish Succession, Frederick III of Prussia (Frederick I) became known as King Frederick I of Prussia. Option B is incorrect as the king of Prussia during the Seven Years' War (1756–1763) was Frederick II (Frederick the Great). Option C is incorrect as the French Revolution broke out in 1789. Options D and E are incorrect as the English Civil War and the Fronde Rebellion in France preceded Frederick I's ascendancy to the Prussian throne by a half a century.

203. (E) All of the options are factors that contributed to the consolidation of absolutist rule in Russia by Peter the Great. In Option A, Peter's creation of the Table of Ranks gave him control over the status of individuals in Russia, control that he didn't have when rank and status were based on heredity. In Option B, the construction of St. Petersburg, similar to the construction of Versailles by French king Louis XIV, was done to gather important nobles to live in one place under the watchful eye of the monarch. Both Peter and Louis also had bad childhood experiences with political intrigues in their respective capital cities, which had an impact on their decisions to construct new glorious cities. In Option C, the abolition of the position of patriarch by Peter and its replacement with a committee of bishops known as the Holy Synod, chaired by a civilian official known as the Procurator, was Peter's way of gaining administrative control of the powerful Russian Orthodox Church. Finally, in Option D, Peter's strengthening of serfdom was a sort of concession to the Russian nobility for their loss of hereditary status, since they now had more administrative control over their peasants than they did before Peter's reign.

204. (A) Kiev, the capital of Ukraine, had been the capital and center of the first Russian state, known as Kievan Rus'. After the Mongol invasions, Kiev was destroyed in 1240. In the 14th century, Ukraine came under Lithuanian control. After the Treaty of Lublin in 1569, which officially unified Poland and Lithuania into a unified state, Ukraine came under Polish control. In 1648, Cossack leader Boghdan Khmelnitsky led an uprising of Orthodox Slavs against Polish rule that became successful after he asked for help from Russian czar Alexei I. This resulted in parts of Ukraine becoming reintegrated into the Russian Empire. Finally, as a result of the three partitions of Poland in the late 18th century, most of Ukraine had been reincorporated into the Russian Empire.

205. (B) The Time of Troubles (1598–1613) saw the Russian state threatened with disintegration as a succession crisis triggered the biggest crisis in Russian history since the Mongol conquest and occupation. During the Time of Troubles, boyars fought amongst themselves, the lower classes revolted against their growing bondage, and foreign armies occupied Moscow. It was this situation that led many to conclude that czarist absolutism was necessary to restore order and unity to the Russian state.

206. (C) The Battle of Kosovo (also known as the Battle of Kosovo Polje) in 1389 was an important one from the standpoint of the Serbs because Kosovo was the cradle of Serbian civilization and the location of its oldest Christian Orthodox monasteries. The Serb loss in this battle resulted in occupation by the Ottoman Turks that would last close to 500 years.

207. (B) The non-Muslim people of the Ottoman Empire were organized according to the millet system, which gave them limited community autonomy to regulate their own issues within the context of the Ottoman administration. The first and largest millet was Orthodox Christian. Armenian Christian, Jewish, and other millets were also created. Option A is incorrect as a vizier was akin to a prime minister in the Ottoman government, second only to the sultan in political power. Option C is incorrect as the Janissaries were the elite fighting force of the Ottoman Empire created by Sultan Murad I in the 14th century. It was comprised of Christian boys conscripted from conquered territories. Option D is incorrect as the harem was defined as the women's quarters in a Muslim household. The Ottoman imperial harem contained the households of the sultan's mother, his wives, his concubines, his sisters, and the female servants of the women. Option E is incorrect as the Divan was the Ottoman imperial council, presided over by the grand vizier.

208. (D) Suleiman the Magnificent ruled the Ottoman Empire from 1520 to 1566, making him the longest ruling sultan in Ottoman history. His legal and educational reforms, promotion of culture, and expansion of the empire resulted in the "golden age" of Ottoman history. Option A is incorrect as there was no Ottoman ruler by that name and title. Option B is incorrect as Bayezid II, who ruled prior to Suleiman, was viewed as an effective and religiously tolerant ruler but his achievements are significantly less than Suleiman's. Option C is incorrect as Vlad the Impaler (Vlad III, Prince of Wallachia) was a Romanian prince who fought against Ottoman expansion into Wallachia. Option E is incorrect as Mustafa Kemal Ataturk was the founder and first president of post-Ottoman Turkey.

209. (C) It had been a foreign policy goal of Russia's since Peter the Great's rule to have unhindered naval access to the Black Sea and ultimately through the straits and into the Mediterranean. Control of Constantinople was a goal for Russian nationalists and pan-Slavs who felt an affinity to the city that was the center of Byzantine Christian Orthodoxy. Option A is incorrect as the Ottoman Empire gained no Polish territory as a result of the partitions of that country. Option B is incorrect as the Ottoman Turks were too weak to protect the Turkic people living in the Caucasus during Russia's conquest of that area in the 19th century. Option D is incorrect as the Ottoman rulers were not known to destroy any Orthodox churches in Istanbul, formerly Constantinople. Option E is incorrect as oil was not yet an important source of energy as it would become in the 20th and 21st centuries.

210. (B) During Peter the Great's rule (1689–1725), Russia was at war for all but two years. The country's main foes were formidable: the Ottoman Turks to the south, who were blocking Russia's access to the Black Sea, and Sweden, which controlled the entire eastern shore of the Baltic Sea. To defeat the two militarily, Peter had to create a navy from scratch, invite foreign military experts to train his army, and reorganize his governing bureaucracy among other reforms he undertook.

211. (B) Under Peter the Great, the nobility was forced to serve the state: virtually all landowning and serf-owning aristocrats were required to serve in the army or civil administration. The bureaucracy was increased to accommodate the growth in service requirements. Options A, C, and D reflect the condition of the Russian nobility under Peter the Great.

212. (A) The Battle of Poltava of 1709 ended with the entire Swedish army under Charles XII destroyed. The Swedish king was able to escape to Ottoman Turkey, and Peter the Great's forces went on to conquer Livonia (Latvia) and eastern Finland. Option B is incorrect as the Battle of Kosovo (1389) was fought mainly by the Serbs against the Ottoman Turks. Option C is incorrect as the Battle of Kursk was fought in 1943 on the eastern front during World War II between the Soviet Red Army and the Nazi Wehrmacht and is known as the largest tank battle in history. Option D is incorrect as there was no Battle of Stockholm during the Great Northern War, although Russian troops did reach near the city. Option E is incorrect as the Battle of Narva in 1700 was a crushing victory for Charles XII's Swedish forces over the Russians. However, Charles failed to deliver the final victory over Peter as he turned to secure his interests in Poland.

Chapter 8: The French Revolution and the Rise of Napoleon, 1789–1799

213. (C) Liberty, equality, fraternity first appeared during the French Revolution. In December 1790 Robespierre advocated in a speech to the National Guards that the words "The French People and Liberty, Equality, Fraternity" be written on uniforms and flags, but his proposal was rejected. Nonetheless, the slogan was associated with the revolution until it was discarded during the empire.

214. (A) The nobility, through the Parliament of Paris, forced the summoning of the Estates General for the first time since 1614. The revolution began as a challenge by the nobility against the absolute authority of the king. Option B is incorrect as the Catholic clergy comprised one of the two privileged estates and was part of the official church of France. Option C is incorrect as the British and Dutch had nothing to do with the outbreak of the French Revolution. Later they will end up fighting against the French revolutionaries. Option D is incorrect. The key here is the word *initial* in the question. Although the nobility initially set off the revolution, for most of its progression, the middle class undoubtedly led it through all of its stages. Option E is incorrect because the Haitian slaves rose up against their masters as a result of the French Revolution. They were not the cause of it.

215. (C) The last time the Estates General was assembled was 1614. Option A is incorrect as that year is best known for the issuing of the Magna Carta in England. Option B is incorrect as there is no particular significance associated with that year. Option D is incorrect as that is the year best known for the death of Louis XIV. Option E is incorrect as this is when Louis XVI promised to call the Estates General in May 1789.

216. (B) Delegates to the Estates General from the Third Estate formed the National Assembly in June 1789 with the intent to create a constitution for France. When they were locked out of the meeting place of the Estates General, the delegates moved to a tennis court nearby and pledged to not disband until a constitution was established. This oath was a rejection of the absolutist nature of the French state (Option A). Option C is incorrect because the overwhelming majority of those pledging the oath were members of the Third Estate, while the clergy comprised the First Estate. Option D is incorrect because, although the French Revolution will enter a more radical phase characterized by the period known as the "Reign of Terror," this was not the original intention of those delegates pledging allegiance to the Tennis Court Oath. Option E is incorrect because the Tennis Court Oath had nothing to do with the reinstatement of the Edict of Nantes. The goal in the oath was to create a constitution. Religious reforms were dealt with in later measures.

217. (B) When convened, the Estates General voted by estate. Usually, the First Estate, made up of clergy, and the Second Estate, comprised of the nobility, outvoted the Third Estate, which included the rest of the French population, by a 2–1 margin. Delegates from the Third Estate to the Estates General in 1789 proposed altering the system to a one person/one vote procedure but the idea was rejected, prompting the delegates from the Third Estate to declare themselves in favor of a constitution.

218. (A) It is debatable whether the reformers who created the Declaration of the Rights of Man and Citizen had females in mind when producing this historic document. There is no explicit mention of women or women's rights anywhere in the document. Although progressive in its nature, it apparently didn't go far enough for Olympe de Gouges, who believed that the declaration was not being applied to women. This prompted her to write in 1791 her own manifesto for women's rights, the Declaration of the Rights of Woman and Citizen.

219. (E) Militant members of the Third Estate went to the Bastille to procure weapons to defend themselves from what they felt was an imminent attack from the royal forces. They were denied entry by the prison guards, who then fired at the demonstrators when they pushed forward into the prison yard. Almost 100 people were killed in the violence, the first of its magnitude in the French Revolution. This has been acknowledged as the beginning of the French Revolution.

220. (A) Louis and the National Assembly were brought to Paris by radical women and elements of the newly formed prorevolutionary National Guard. The move signified an increased distrust for the ruling family by the radicalized supporters of the revolution.

221. (D) In the context of the French Revolution, émigrés were nobles and aristocrats that opposed the revolution and fled France. Many organized opposition to the revolution from countries like Austria. Because this is a French word meaning "to migrate out," Options A, B, C, and E are incorrect.

222. (B) In response to the Declaration of Pillnitz in which Austrian king Leopold declared his intention to use military force in conjunction with other European powers to restore order in France, the National Assembly voted to declare war on Austria on April 20, 1792.

To add to the internal instability caused by the revolution, France now faced a new challenge—foreign intervention. Soon afterward, France would find itself at war with Great Britain, Option C, and Holland, Option E, but this is after the National Assembly's declaration of war. Italy, Option A, did not exist as a country during the French Revolution, and Russia, Option D, will eventually go to war with France, but not before Napoleon Bonaparte's accession to power.

223. (E) This answer is correct because it is the one exception to all of the other accurate options. There was no evidence of mass desertions that adversely affected the fighting ability of the anti-French coalition.

224. (C) This answer is best illustrated in Maximilien Robespierre's February 1794 speech, On Virtue and Terror. In the speech, virtue, which is defined as love of country, its laws, and equality, is the "fundamental principle of democratic or popular government," i.e., virtue is the "general will."

225. (E) Lemaire is a French Canadian hockey player and former coach of the New Jersey Devils. All the other options refer to real French statesmen who proposed various reforms of the French financial system.

226. (D) The first constitution was produced in 1791, only to be abrogated the following year. The Committee of Public Safety produced a republican constitution in 1793 that provided for universal male suffrage, but it was suspended indefinitely and never implemented. The post-Jacobin National Convention produced a third constitution, the Constitution of the Year III, which went into effect in 1795. Finally, in 1799, Napoleon Bonaparte created a new constitution, the fourth since 1789. It created the veneer of power-sharing.

227. (A) Urban workers suffered the most from the rise in food prices because they relied on the peasants in the countryside to provide food to the cities. Peasants horded food rather than sell it for depreciating prices.

228. (C) In 1788 the French government devoted about 25 percent of its annual expenditures to maintain the armed forces. Military expenditures contributed most to the debt of all countries in Europe. Besides maintaining current armies and navies, another significant portion of the public debt came from the cost of past wars. Option A is incorrect because the upkeep of the royal court only accounted for 5 percent of public expenditures in France in 1788. Option E on its own is incorrect, although it is part of the bigger correct Option C.

229. (C) The bourgeoisie, or middle class, was part of the Third Estate. This was the wealthiest, best educated, and most active driving force behind the French Revolution. Options A and B are incorrect because the First Estate was exclusively comprised of the clergy while the Second Estate was exclusively the aristocracy.

230. (C) The guillotine became the main method of execution during the radical phase of the French Revolution. Among its most notable victims were Louis XVI; his wife, Marie Antoinette; and Maximilien Robespierre.

231. (E) On August 4, 1789, a small group of liberal noblemen in the National Assembly surrendered their hunting rights, their rights in manorial courts, and feudal and seigneurial privileges in general. This paved the way for the Declaration of the Rights of Man and Citizen, issued less than three weeks later, which enshrined the principles of the rule of law, equal citizenship, and collective sovereignty of the people. Option A is incorrect. The declaration to abolish feudalism paved the way for the Declaration of the Rights of Man, which in turn directly led to the formation of the French Constitution of 1791. Option B is incorrect because the decision to execute Louis XVI came during his January 1793 trial. Option C is incorrect because the storming of the Tuileries by working-class Parisians happened spontaneously in August 1792. Option D is incorrect because the National Assembly declared war on Austria on April 20, 1792.

232. (A) The Civil Constitution of the Clergy of 1790 stipulated a number of points that brought the church under state authority. Among these points were: all clergy received salaries from the state; the church was prohibited from acknowledging any papal authority without government permission; and parish priests and bishops were to be elected by the voting-eligible citizenry, including non-Catholics.

233. (D) The Vatican condemned the Civil Constitution of the Clergy as an infringement on the rightful duties of the Catholic Church. As a result, relations between the French revolutionaries and the pro-Vatican and "refractory" elements of the French Catholic Church were hostile. All other options were measures taken by the revolutionary government against the Catholic Church.

234. (B) Under the Constitution of 1791, the king had to share power with a newly established Legislative Assembly whose members were to be indirectly elected. Option A did not happen until the execution of Louis XVI in January 1793. Option C is incorrect because the franchise was increased, but not to all citizens. Options D and E were not part of the constitution.

235. (C) Robespierre presided over the period of the French Revolution known as the "Reign of Terror." During this radical phase of the revolution, Robespierre attempted to eliminate real and perceived enemies of the revolution. About 40,000 people were executed during this time. But by July 1794 Robespierre was executed by members of the Committee of Public Safety who felt Robespierre had lost the right to lead the revolution.

236. (A) Robespierre, arguably the leader of the Jacobins, had called for universal suffrage in 1789. The Jacobins were also strongly in favor of not only executing Louis XVI for treason but abolishing monarchy as a form of government in France. As radical as the Jacobins were, they generally did not seriously pursue policies that could be described as feminist or socialist as described in Options B and C. Although the Jacobins did believe that the revolution in France could only succeed if it was spread throughout Europe, they stopped with the continent. Finally, although the Jacobins did abolish slavery in Haiti in 1794, they stopped short of granting the colony independence.

237. (C) Maximilien Robespierre was the leader who advocated the use of terror to promote the virtuous goals of the revolution.

238. (C) European countries remembered the expansionist goals of the French king Louis XIV and welcomed the instability that detracted the country from pursuing an active foreign policy on the continent. On the other hand, with the radicalization of the revolution, the fear among the conservative monarchs was that the "contagion" of the revolution would spread to their countries and threaten the political order there.

239. (B) The sansculottes (so named because they did not wear upper-class breeches), the French working class in a pre-industrial age, helped radicalize the revolution with their militancy and their demands for equality, direct democracy, a vigorous pursuit of revolutionary war against France's conservative enemies, and sworn opposition to the monarchy.

240. (A) Throughout the revolution, the bourgeoisie provided the intellectual leadership. It was the bourgeois representatives to the National Assembly that drew up the Declaration of the Rights of Man and Citizen, the Civil Constitution of the Clergy, and the Constitution of 1791. The more radicalized elements of the bourgeoisie, like Marat, Danton, St. Just, and Robespierre, led the radical phase of the revolution. After the initial desire to convene the Estates General and a handful of nobles agreeing to "abolish feudalism," the nobility opposed the revolution. This is why Option B is incorrect. Option C is incorrect because the sansculottes were arguably the "muscle" of the radical phase of the revolution. Option D is incorrect because the royal family opposed the revolution.

241. (D) Paris was the capital of France and the center of the revolutionary upheaval. The royal family was returned to Paris from Versailles in October 1789.

242. (B) The Committee of Public Safety was successful in all of the options except bringing political violence to an end. Political violence reached its peak in 1793–1794, when approximately 40,000 people were killed for political reasons.

243. (A) The Haitian Revolution, inspired by the upheavals in France, led to the abolition of slavery on the island as well as independence. It was the second country in the Western Hemisphere to successfully establish its independence.

244. (B) The Legislative Assembly was established as a result of the Constitution of 1791; the September Massacres occurred in September of 1792; the execution of Louis XVI took place in January 1793; the Committee of Public Safety was created in April 1793 by the National Convention. Option A is incorrect because France declared war on Austria before the Reign of Terror. Option C is incorrect because the storming of the Tuileries came after the Tennis Court Oath but before France's declaration of war on the Dutch Republic and Great Britain and the execution of Robespierre. Option D is incorrect because Necker was fired first and then came the formation of the Jacobin clubs followed by the rise and fall of the Directory.

245. (B) The Directory became increasingly unpopular from the political Left and Right in France from the time it came to power in 1795. Pro-Royalists who rallied around the dead king's brother, Louis XVIII, had supported his intentions to reinstate the Old Regime. On the Left, the Directory crushed an uprising known as the Conspiracy of Equals, a group that sympathized with the Jacobins and called for the abolition of private property. When the results of the elections in the spring of 1797 favored the pro-Royalist forces, the government annulled the election results. That September, the Directory called on Napoleon and his army to support the rule of the Directory. From this point until Napoleon's coup against the Directory in 1799, the army was the backbone of the Directory's ineffective rule.

246. (B) The peasants comprised about 90 percent of France's population in 1789. Option A is incorrect as the sansculottes, who were largely shopkeepers, tradespeople, artisans, and factory workers primarily in Paris, were politically significant from 1792 to 1794 but numerically small. Option C is incorrect as the bourgeoisie were the driving force intellectually behind the uprising of the Third Estate but numerically inferior to the peasants. Option D is incorrect as the French governing bureaucracy came largely from the First Estate (less than 1 percent of the total population) or the bourgeoisie from the Third Estate who were numerically inferior to the peasantry. Option E is incorrect as the clergy belonged to the separate Second Estate.

247. (E) All of the events listed contributed to the radicalization of the French Revolution. In Option A, the Jacobins feared that Austria would intervene militarily in France to crush the revolution. Therefore, they favored a preemptive strike against Austria and spreading the revolution militarily throughout Europe. In Option B, the September Massacres of 1792 continued the chaotic violence unleashed by radicalized soldiers and workers in Paris a month earlier in the storming of the Tuileries royal palace, with more than 1,000 refractory priests and other counterrevolutionaries dragged from the prisons and massacred. In Option C, Louis XVI's execution for treason in 1793 brought an end to the Bourbon monarchy and resulted in the radical Committee of Public Safety coming to power with Maximilien Robespierre emerging as its leader. In Option D, the storming of the Tuileries resulted in the capture and arrest of King Louis XVI and his family. He was later convicted of treason and executed.

248. (B) Although Napoleon Bonaparte was a strong supporter of the Jacobins who were the most vocal supporters of executing Louis XVI, he did not vote on whether to execute the king. Napoleon normalized relations with the Catholic Church in Rome and French Catholics, Option A, and convinced many of the nobles who had fled France and actively opposed the revolution that they were needed in the country but that the clock would not be turned back to pre-1789 conditions, Option C. Napoleon's military prowess was undisputable from his early victories in France's revolutionary wars and this fact, coupled with his intelligence, his desire to preserve the gains of the revolution, and his goal to make France (and himself) bask in power and glory contributed to his extreme popularity during this period, Options D and E.

249. (D) About 70 percent of the 40,000 or so victims of the Reign of Terror were peasants and working people. Option A is incorrect as the nobles and clergy comprised about 8 percent and 6 percent of the total victims. Option B is incorrect as 14 percent of the victims were from the bourgeoisie. Option C is incorrect because the question implies the domestic victims of the political terror unleashed by the Committee of Public Safety, the government in control of France during the Reign of Terror.

Chapter 9: The Fall of Napoleon and the Post-Napoleonic Era, 1800–1848

250. (C) By late 1799 the Directory had lost the support of most of France. It had become unpopular both with the Left and the Right. More and more it relied on the army and Bonaparte for its existence. In November 1799, Napoleon, Abbe Sieyes, and their followers orchestrated a coup. In the Directory's place they proclaimed a new form of government called the Consulate, with Napoleon as First Consul.

251. (A) The Dutch Republic was not part of the Quadruple Alliance, which was an alliance of countries that were responsible for the final defeat of Napoleon at Waterloo.

252. (E) Napoleon had favored quick, decisive battles as well as living off the occupied country's own supplies. Given the vast expanses of Russia, Czar Alexander I could afford to retreat deep into the Russian heartland, overexposing Napoleon's supply lines. Napoleon reached Moscow in September 1812, but the city was desolate and soon to be in flames. Shortly afterward, Napoleon began his disastrous retreat, which eventually cost him more than 500,000 men.

253. (C) Napoleon Bonaparte was born in Corsica in 1769 into a family of minor nobles.

254. (C) The code did not grant privileges to any groups, especially the aristocracy, as this would have run counter to the ideals of the French Revolution. Napoleon was a strong supporter of the French Revolution because without the revolution, he, as a Corsican from minor nobility, would have never risen to ranks as high as he did in the French Army and, later, in French politics. The Napoleonic Code reflects the revolutionary ideals that he supported.

255. (C) The Continental System was an economic embargo of British trade devised by Napoleon and imposed on his satellites and allies with the intention of weakening Great Britain economically. The Continental System was ultimately a failure for a number of reasons. First, the British carried on substantial commerce with its overseas colonies, so the loss of continental European trade did not significantly impact the health of the British economy. Second, the Continental System caused wide-scale resentment toward Napoleon and his regime among the occupied countries as well as allies such as Russia. Third, the Continental System financially wrecked some of the European commercial bourgeoisie who were heavily dependent on overseas trade.

256. (A) Napoleon's forces lost more than 500,000 men in their retreat from Moscow, as bitterly cold winter conditions and determined Russian forces pursued the Grand Armee westward out of Russia and into Europe.

257. (C) The major powers at the Congress of Vienna wanted to prevent any attempts by France to spread its influence beyond its borders. To that end, the Congress implemented a series of measures to contain France. Among those measures were to revive the Dutch Republic and transform it into the kingdom of Holland, adding to that country Belgium.

The Italian kingdom of Piedmont was restored and strengthened by adding the defunct Republic of Genoa to it. All Bonapartes that were put in power by Napoleon, including Napoleon himself, were forced to leave, replaced by the former monarchs or their offspring.

258. (D) In 1815, Parliament, dominated by the gentry, passed the Corn Laws, which raised the protective tariff to the benefit of landlords and their farmers.

259. (A) Upon inheriting the throne from his brother, Alexander I, Nicholas I put down the Decembrist Revolt of officers in the Russian military in 1825. It was the first manifestation of a modern revolutionary movement in Russia as well as the first and only military-led uprising against civilian authority in that country's history. As a result of the Decembrist Revolt, the leaders were either executed or exiled to Siberia, and Nicholas I strengthened autocratic rule in Russia.

260. (D) After Napoleon's defeat at Waterloo in 1815, he demanded political asylum in Great Britain. However, the decision was made to send him into exile on the island of St. Helena, far from the European mainland.

261. (B) Russia formally withdrew from the Continental System in 1810 and resumed commercial relations with Great Britain. This angered Napoleon and convinced him that an invasion of his former ally was necessary to teach Alexander I a lesson.

262. (A) The Congress of Vienna made no attempt to reconstitute the Holy Roman Empire, which was dissolved by Napoleon in 1804. There were 39 German states that emerged from the ashes of the Napoleonic Wars, and the Congress of Vienna confirmed this state of affairs in the German world. The two most powerful, Prussia and Austria, would compete with each other for dominance over the others.

263. (C) Ever since the Third Partition of Poland in 1795, Poles pinned their hopes on revolutionary France to gain their state back. Napoleon created the Duchy of Warsaw in 1807, and many Poles fought in the Grand Armee. More than 90,000 fought in Napoleon's Russian campaign.

264. (E) Austrian Foreign Minister Klemens von Metternich, along with British Foreign Secretary Lord Castlereagh, primarily feared growing expansion and influence in European affairs, but Metternich also worried about a stronger and bigger Prussia. Czar Alexander I of Russia wanted to undo the partitions of Poland and bring that country under Russian control. To do that he would need the permission of Prussia. Prussia agreed, if Russia would support its claim to the entire Kingdom of Saxony. News of a secret pact between France, Britain, and Austria to go to war against Prussia and Russia if necessary over the Polish-Saxon question led Alexander I to back down and compromise, accepting a reduced Poland called "Congress Poland," and Prussia received two-fifths of Saxony while the rest remained to the Saxon king.

265. (A) Louis David was the only artist listed not part of the Romantic movement. He was of the French neoclassical style.

266. (C) Liberals generally favored constitutional monarchy and the more moderate phase of the revolution. Conservatives opposed the revolution from the outset and favored the old order prior to 1789. Republicans favored the radical Jacobin phase of the French Revolution. They favored the abolition of monarchy.

267. (D) Metternich led the way in trying to organize collective security arrangements with the leading powers of Europe to stamp out any manifestations of revolutionary challenges to the post–Congress of Vienna order. His closest allies became Russia and Prussia, with France occasionally on board and Britain rarely wanting to commit itself to collective security agreements on the continent.

268. (A) Initially Britain was willing to counter any resurgence of French expansionism on the continent but reserved the right to act independently according to its own national interests—not bound by collective security agreements. For example, the British refused to entertain the proposal of an international naval organization that would combat the slave trade and the Barbary pirates. The British also rejected the principles of collective security devised by Metternich at the Congress of Troppau.

269. (B) It was a policy of Russia since the times of Peter the Great to gain more influence in the Ottoman Empire through the Christian Orthodox population (Greeks, Serbs, Bulgarians, Romanians, and Slavic Macedonians). By failing to support Alexander Ypsilanti's Greek uprising against Ottoman rule in 1821, Alexander I chose instead to support Metternich's policy of defense against revolutionary uprisings.

270. (C) At the Congress of Verona, the French government under Louis XVIII requested permission to send troops to Spain to restore Ferdinand VII to the throne. With the exception of Great Britain, Congress members Austria, Russia, and Prussia gave France the green light to intervene, which it did, installing Ferdinand back to power.

271. (B) In 1876, Serbia declared war on the Ottoman Empire and proclaimed unification with Bosnia, whose population was predominantly Slavic and Christian Orthodox. Serbian expectations were that Bosnia would be united with Serbia proper, but instead, the leading Powers at the Treaty of Berlin decided to cede it to Austria-Hungary. Option A is incorrect as Croatia's population, although linguistically and racially related to the Serbs, was Catholic and already part of the Austro-Hungarian Empire. Option C is incorrect as Kosovo remained part of the Ottoman Empire until 1913, when it was reunited with Serbia. Option D is incorrect as Slovenia had a negligible Serbian population and had already been part of the Austro-Hungarian Empire. Option E is incorrect as Montenegro had never been part of the Austro-Hungarian Empire.

272. (A) In 1825 the legislative chambers voted to compensate émigrés who lost land in the first French Revolution "perpetually," totaling 30 million francs a year. In addition, Catholic education was growing in public schools, thanks to the efforts of the clergy. As a result, strong opposition developed from those forces who saw in these moves an attempt to restore the old regime.

273. (C) First, the fact that it was the Marquis de Lafayette, hero of two revolutions and a supporter of constitutional monarchy in France that offered to broker the stalemate between the conflicting sides lent credence to the compromise that was proposed. Lafayette called on all sides to support the Duke of Orleans, who had served in the Republican army in 1792 but was also a distant relative of the Bourbons. He was accepted by both sides and became Louis Philippe, king of France until 1848.

274. (D) Russian Czar Nicholas I intended to send troops to crush the Belgian uprising against Dutch rule in 1830 but was distracted by an uprising in Poland against Russian rule. Neither the British nor French came to the support of the Poles, who were defeated by the Russians. Congress Poland was abolished along with its constitution and fully incorporated into the Russian Empire. Meanwhile, events in Belgium led to its independence in 1831, agreed upon by France and Great Britain. It had become too late for Russia to intervene.

275. (A) Revolutions in France and Belgium sparked an uprising in Poland against Russian rule. This uprising failed when Czar Nicholas I sent troops to crush the rebellion. Congress Poland was abolished along with its constitution and fully incorporated into the Russian Empire. The Polish Catholic Church was allowed to operate. Ukraine and Belarus had been reincorporated into Russia during the partitions of Poland in the 18th century, long before the 1830 uprising.

276. (C) In *The Eighteenth Brumaire of Louis Bonaparte*, written in 1852, Karl Marx referred to the June Days, also known as the June Insurrection, as "the most colossal event in the history of European civil wars." In his analysis, the crushing of the proletarian insurrection was an example of the ruthless struggle of the bourgeoisie against the assertion of the interests of the proletariat class.

277. (B) The Reform Act, passed by Parliament in 1832, introduced significant changes to the British electoral system to reflect the transformations brought on by the Industrial Revolution. For example, in addition to increasing the number of males who could vote from 500,000 to more than 800,000, the Reform Act redistributed suffrage rights by region and class. As a result, more seats in Parliament were made for industrial towns where middle-class factory owners, businessmen, doctors, lawyers, and bankers lived at the expense of seats for smaller older towns.

278. (D) Liberals were generally middle-class businessmen and professionals: lawyers, doctors, and bankers. They supported representative government, freedom of speech and the press, and religious tolerance, but they opposed extending democratic rights to all, fearing the possibility of mob rule. They supported laissez-faire economics and opposed the formation of labor unions.

279. (A) Karl Marx rejected Utopian Socialism for being based on idealism rather than a materialist approach to studying history and economics.

280. (B) According to Engels's *Socialism: Utopian and Scientific*, published in 1880, his explanation for why his and Marx's version of Socialism is scientific can be summarized in the following passage: "The materialist conception of history starts from the proposition that the production of the means to support human life and, next to production, the exchange of things produced, is the basis of all social structure; that in every society that has appeared in history, the manner in which wealth is distributed and society divided into classes or orders is dependent upon what is produced, how it is produced, and how the products are exchanged. From this point of view, the final causes of all social changes and political revolutions are to be sought, not in men's brains, not in men's better insights into eternal truth and justice, but in changes in the modes of production and exchange. They are to be sought, not in the *philosophy*, but in the *economics* of each particular epoch."

281. (C) The repeal of the Corn Laws of 1846 symbolized the ascendancy of industrial interests over agricultural. The Corn Laws placed high protective tariffs on grain imports, hurting the British working class. To prevent uprisings of the workers, industrialists were forced to raise wages, keeping the cost of production up, resulting in more expensive products that hurt their exports. By repealing the Corn Laws, the British became dependent on its industries for its economic power and imports of agricultural supplies.

282. (A) In 1848, following the June Days in France, the Constituent Assembly decided to create a strong executive to be elected by universal male suffrage. The elections were held in December of that year, and Louis Napoleon Bonaparte, the nephew of the great Napoleon, won the election in a landslide.

283. (D) In the tumultuous 19th century, the British populace largely avoided revolution because of the factors mentioned in Options A, B, C, and E but not D. Universal suffrage and extensive social welfare programs would not be a reality in Great Britain until the 20th century.

Chapter 10: The Second Industrial Revolution, 1820–1900

284. (B) A series of successful inventions in the textile industry such as John Kay's flying shuttle, the spinning jenny, and Richard Arkwright's water frame required many workers to operate them and large buildings where these large machines could be gathered. This led to the establishment of the first factories.

285. (C) The colonial empire that Britain built in Latin America and India, and later in Africa, along with its dominant position in the slave trade provided an important market for British goods. Option A is incorrect because the British guarded their industrial production from outsiders as long as they could. Options B and D are incorrect because at the outset of the Industrial Revolution, British factory owners were setting up factories exclusively in Britain. Wages were low enough in Britain so that there wasn't a need to establish factories and export jobs to the colonies. Option E is incorrect because Britain had an abundance of coal and iron for its industrialization.

286. (D) Although Britain's supply of key natural resources like iron and coal were abundant, the country was not diverse in the resources that it possessed. All of the other options are factors that contributed to the Industrial Revolution in Britain.

287. (D) The goal of the enclosure movement was not to collectivize land. Collectivization of agricultural land was an important policy of Joseph Stalin and the Soviet Communist Party of the late 1920s–1930s. If anything, the enclosure movement was the complete opposite of collectivization. The hundreds of enclosure acts passed by a British Parliament dominated by large landowners in the 17th and 18th centuries fenced in open fields in villages and divided the common land in proportion to one's property in the open fields.

288. (A) Charles Townshend introduced to England the four-crop rotation that he learned from Dutch farmers when he was Britain's ambassador to that country. The four-crop rotation (wheat, barley, a root crop, and clover) replaced the three-field system in which two fields were used to grow and one would remain fallow so as to not drain the soil of all of its nutrients. Option C is incorrect. Although he also was known to use abundant manure in fertilizing his own fields upon return to England, he is not known as the pioneer of this agricultural practice. Neither is he associated with the agricultural innovations mentioned in Options D and E.

289. (D) The putting-out system is where the merchant provided (put out) raw materials to several cottage workers, who processed the raw materials in their homes and returned the finished products to the merchant. Although the putting-out system, like the factory system that eventually replaced it, ended up producing a variety of goods, both types of production began largely with textile-based finished goods.

290. (A) The first large factories in the British Industrial Revolution were in the cotton textile industry. A series of successful inventions in the textile industry, such as John Kay's flying shuttle, the spinning jenny, and Richard Arkwright's water frame, required many workers to operate them and large buildings to accommodate these large machines. This led to the establishment of the first factories.

291. (A) As a result of these inventions, cotton production was 10 times higher in 1790 than it was in 1770. Option B is incorrect because the opposite occurred. With the invention of new technology that sped up the production of textile-based products, factories were established to accommodate the new production reality. In Option C, the new inventions did give rise to a new type of energy source, but the solution was not yet oil, it was steam. In Option D, the inventions that led to increased production in textile-based products may have had some distant effect on the production of faster ships, but the link is not as strong as in Option A.

292. (A) Cotton-based clothing became much cheaper and more affordable for the masses. Prior to the Industrial Revolution, only the wealthy could afford the comfort and cleanliness of underwear because it was made from expensive linen cloth. Option B is incorrect because, with few exceptions, Great Britain had a steady supply of cotton from its North American colonies or India. Option C is incorrect because the opposite took place: India's textile industry (not industry in the modern sense) was destroyed by the innovations in textile production developed in Great Britain. Option D is incorrect because the opposite was true: working conditions in the textile factories were terrible, with the exploitation of child labor a common occurrence. Option E is incorrect because a new source of energy, steam, was developed.

293. (D) As a result of Watt's steam engine, inventors and engineers could devise and implement all kinds of power equipment to aid people in their work.

294. (E) The development of the railroad and railroad transportation in Britain in the 19th century was revolutionary for the factors listed in Options A through D. The opposite of Option E actually occurred. Because coal replaced wood as the main energy source for steam engines, the expansion of the network of railroads in Britain and other industrializing nations led to the growth of coal production.

295. (C) The effect of the rapid increase in population in Britain from 1780 to 1851 is a controversial topic among historians, and no consensus has been found among them. On the one hand, while the British economy rose fourfold, the world population more than doubled and the average per person consumption rose only by 75 percent. On the other hand, historians argue that the rapid population growth was actually helpful because it facilitated industrial expansion because of a larger industrial workforce.

296. (B) List believed that, in the case of the German states and other industrializing nations, protective tariffs were essential to support the development of domestic industries against more developed economies. He was critical of Britain's free-trade policies because he felt that this was Britain's way to reduce everyone else to dependency on it.

297. (E) The Luddites, active in England between 1811 and 1816, were named after Ned Ludd, a mythical figure who supposedly led the movement. The Luddites, who blamed unemployment on the mechanization of the textile industry, broke into factories and smashed power looms and wide weaving frames. Ultimately, the "movement" fizzled out on its own.

298. (C) The standard of living of British workers did not rise from 1792 to 1820. The Napoleonic Wars took a toll on the economies of the continental countries, and the British working class was not immune. Only after 1820, and especially after 1840, did real wages rise significantly, but so did the hours in the average worker's week.

299. (B) The Factory Act of 1833 limited the factory workday for children ages 9–13 to 8 hours and that of adolescents ages 14–18 to 12 hours. The act did not specify domestic labor or work in small businesses. Concerns for the environment, equal wages for women, and workman's compensation were not addressed by the act.

300. (A) In *The Conditions of the Working Class in England in 1844*, Friedrich Engels blamed industrial capitalism for the extreme misery of the English proletariat's miserable living and working conditions. Engels, Karl Marx's longtime friend and ally, had managed to see firsthand the plight of the working class in Manchester. Marx and Engels recognized the productive capacity of capitalism and the progressive nature of it compared to feudalism, but neither lauded the system nor defended its exploitative nature, as Options B and C state. Option D is incorrect because both Marx and Engels believed capitalism was a higher stage of development than the agriculturally dominated economy of feudalism. Option E is incorrect because it best resembles the actions of the Luddites.

301. (A) The Mines Act, passed by the British Parliament in 1842, prohibited underground work for all women as well as for boys under the age of 10. Option B is incorrect because women had been working in coal mines long before the Mines Act. Options C and D are incorrect as there were no provisions made for work in mines during summer break or after school nor was there any mention of quotas. Option E is incorrect because the act has nothing to do with the effects of the advent of oil and its impact on the coal industry.

302. (D) The Combination Acts, first passed by the British Parliament in 1799, outlawed labor unions and strikes. Parliament repealed the acts in 1824 in the face of widespread working-class opposition to them.

303. (A) The Crystal Palace Exhibition, also known as the Great Exhibition, was organized by members of the Royal Society of the Arts. The purpose of this exhibition was for Great Britain to demonstrate its industrial leadership, not for skilled artisans to stave off industrialization of their craft, as Option D states. Option B is incorrect because crystal was not the focus of this exhibition. Option C is incorrect because although the bourgeoisie may have used the exhibition as an opportunity to "show off" their wealth, that was not the main idea behind the exhibition. Although all nations were encouraged to participate, in 1851, Great Britain was clearly the world's industrial leader, rendering Option E incorrect.

304. (D) The Zollverein was a tariff union between the various German states first implemented in 1834. The Zollverein facilitated trade among member German states by allowing goods to move tariff-free while erecting a single tariff against other nations. Besides helping develop the economies of the German Zollverein members, this economic union was seen as a significant step toward the creation of a unified German state in 1871.

305. (B) There was a drop in the number of deaths from famines, epidemics, and war. Major diseases such as plague and smallpox declined noticeably. Option A is incorrect as that time period witnessed conflicts on an international scale such as the Seven Years' War (1756–1763), the French Revolution and the Napoleonic Wars that followed (1789–1815), and several smaller conflicts. Option C is incorrect as immigration from Latin America and Africa to Europe was negligible. Option D is incorrect as the use of contraceptives was not widespread until the 20th century.

306. (C) Ireland's population doubled between 1781 and 1845. But as a result of the devastating potato famine that struck Ireland between 1845 and 1851, more than one million died of starvation and disease while almost two million migrated to the United States. All of the other countries listed experienced population growth.

307. (C) In 1800 Great Britain had one major city, London, with a population of one million, and six cities with a population of between 50,000 and 100,000. Fifty years later, London's population had soared to 2.3 million, while nine other cities had populations of more than 100,000.

308. (D) Rotterdam is located in Holland, not England. All of the other cities listed were major English industrial cities.

309. (A) Edwin Chadwick, an urban reformer, published the *Report* in 1842. In it, he concluded that serious diseases and illnesses were caused by pollution, poor sanitary conditions, and overcrowded living conditions. He called for sanitary reforms including efficient sewers and improvements in the supply of clean water. Six years later the National Board of Health was created.

310. (C) Factory workers comprised the working class, or in Marxist terminology, the proletariat.

311. (E) The Chartist movement was a working-class movement that got its name from the "People's Charter," which was an 1838 campaign for parliamentary reform of the political inequities arising from the Reform Act of 1832. The most important demand of the Chartists was universal male suffrage. The Chartists presented Parliament with three signed petitions with their demands between 1839 and 1848; one of them had more than three million signatures in 1842. All of them were rejected. After the final rejection in 1848, the movement ended.

Chapter 11: The Rise of New Ideologies in the 19th Century

312. (D) The importance of the subconscious was first emphasized by Sigmund Freud, the pioneering psychoanalyst. It is in the field of social science. Romanticism is generally an artistic movement. Option A is incorrect because moods and expressions are at the center of Romanticism. Option B is essentially the same as Option A. Option C is incorrect because customs that cannot be classified or analyzed describes behaviors based on unscientific feelings and moods, the hallmark of Romanticism. Nationalism, the subject of many Romantic paintings and other works of art, is often based on the peculiar customs of national identity. Option E is incorrect as Romantics saw emotion at the very center of what they were trying to appeal to.

313. (A) Jacques-Louis David was a painter of the neoclassical style, which preceded Romanticism. He is famous for paintings such as *The Death of Marat*. Eugene Delacroix, Option B, was a leader of the French Romantic school of painting. Lord Byron, Option C, and William Wordsworth, Option D, were both English Romantic poets. Option E, Victor Hugo, was a French Romantic writer of books such as *Les Miserables*.

314. (D) Nationalism posed a major challenge to the unity of the Ottoman Empire as the Serbs and Greeks were the first among the Christian Europeans to fight for their independence from the Muslim Turks. The same nationalist challenges to the Austrian Empire were felt as the non-German populations in that country (Magyars, Romanians, Czechs, Slovaks, Serbs, Croatians, and Slovenes) demanded more political autonomy. The Poles challenged Russian rule twice in the 19th century, until they finally gained their independence in 1918. Option A is incorrect because although German unification was motivated by nationalist ideas, Germany was largely a unitary state, overwhelmingly dominated by ethnic Germans, with only about 5 percent of the population ethnically Polish. Italian unification was the unification of ethnically Italian states. Option B is incorrect as multi-ethnic states did not proliferate in the 19th century. Option C is incorrect as the growth of nationalism did not lead to an overall strengthening of the Catholic Church in Europe. Finally, Option E is incorrect because although the multi-ethnic states fought on opposite sides in World War I, this happened in the 20th century, not the 19th.

315. (D) The general theme of Metternich's congresses, starting from the Congress of Vienna, was to create a system of reliable order and stability in Europe. Each of these succeeding congresses aimed to do just that. Option A is incorrect as the congresses made no demands on how its participants ran their respective governments, and many of the participating nations were tyrannies of one sort or another. Option B is incorrect as France was admitted as a full member at Aix-la-Chapelle and did not have to make regular payments. Option C is incorrect as this was mostly done at the Congress of Vienna. Option E is incorrect because the Great Powers had no general interest in expanding the political powers of lower classes.

316. (A) The British refused to take part in the interventions of the Quintuple Alliance to which it belonged. Option B is incorrect as Britain did not belong to the Holy Alliance. Option C is incorrect as Britain did not assist revolutionary forces at any time during the 19th century. Option D is incorrect as Britain did have a stake in maintaining peace in Europe at this time. Option E is incorrect as the British at no time made any claim to territory in Europe.

317. (B) Stability and preservation of the old social order was much more important to Alexander I than anything else, including sympathy for the Greeks. Option A is incorrect as Russia continued to play a major role in Balkan politics for at least the next century. Option C is incorrect as Russia probably did not fear the Ottoman Empire at that time. Option D is incorrect as no such action on the part of the Ottomans ever occurred. Option E is incorrect because the Greek rebels continued to appeal to Russia for assistance and eventually got it.

318. (C) The Congress of Verona was called in part to deal with the Spanish question, and permission was eventually given, over British objections, to the French to return Ferdinand VII to the Spanish throne. Option A is incorrect as the result of the Congress of Aix-la-Chapelle was to end the occupation of France by the allies, and to admit France as a member of the now renamed Quintuple Alliance. Option B is incorrect as the result of the Congress of Troppau was to deal with revolutionaries in Naples and other places. Option D is incorrect because the July Ordinances were Charles X's new laws attempting to greatly restrict civil liberties in France in 1830. Option E is incorrect as the Congress of Vienna was convened to deal with the situation in Europe immediately after the fall of Napoleon.

319. (D) The Decembrist Revolt was a rebellion of Russian officers demanding more constitutional rights and modernization from the government. Nicholas I ruthlessly cracked down on them. Options A through C have nothing to do with Russia and did not occur in 1825. Option E occurred in 1861.

320. (B) The rebellion in Greece created a movement called philhellenism, where popular support was aroused in the west for Greek independence, based in part on the view that Greece was the foundation of western civilization. Russians traditionally sympathized with and aided their Christian brethren in the Balkans, like the Greeks, Serbs, and Bulgarians who fought against Muslim Turkish occupation. Option A is incorrect as no such offers were made. Option C is incorrect as he did not study at the Sorbonne, and this would hardly have been enough reason to get involved in a war. Option D is incorrect as there was no famine caused by the Turks. Option E is incorrect as there were no known coal deposits in Greece and the Industrial Revolution was just getting under way at that point.

321. (A) One of the first laws made by Charles X was to compensate émigrés during the French Revolution. It led to protests that Charles X attempted to put down, which then led to the Revolution of 1830 and his abdication. Option B is incorrect as the protestors defying the ban were a part of the revolution, not the issue that sparked it. Option C is incorrect because it happened later in the 19th century. Option D is incorrect as what might happen in Belgium would probably not be a cause of a revolution in France. Option E is incorrect as it did not happen.

322. (C) Louis Philippe had Republican sympathies during the French Revolution, but was also a Bourbon, though more removed from the line of succession than Charles X. He was therefore acceptable to Republicans, Liberals, and Royalists. Option A is incorrect as it simply did not happen. Option B is incorrect as Louis Philippe never had that position. Option D is incorrect because Louis Philippe had actually been friendly with Charles X in the years leading up to 1830 and even been acting as regent for the grandson that Charles hoped would succeed him. Option E is incorrect as Louis Philippe had never fought in America.

323. (D) During 1830, Poland erupted in rebellion against Russia. While Russia, Prussia, and Austria would have liked to have seen the Belgian rebellion put down, they were too focused on crushing the Polish rebellion. Therefore, they went along with the British and French policy of noninterference.

324. (A) Though Poland officially had a constitution, Russian authorities continually disregarded it. The resulting Polish rebellion was brutally crushed by Russia, and Poland became an official province of the Russian Empire. Option B is incorrect as Poland did not become independent until after World War I. Option C is incorrect as Russia simply annulled Poland's constitution. Option D is incorrect as Russia never officially disallowed Catholicism in Poland. Option E is incorrect as Poland was completely incorporated into Russia, with not even nominal autonomy.

325. (D) The Industrial Revolution became entrenched in France by 1848, and with it, Socialist ideas. Many of the leaders of the rebellion were Socialists, though the Revolution of 1848 did not produce a Socialist government. Option A is incorrect because though 3,000 were killed, which is less than other rebellions in 1830 and 1848, and is not particularly unique. Options B and C are incorrect as both choices never happened. Option E is incorrect because this occurred many times before and after 1848.

326. (C) Though both revolutions depended on working-class support, the bourgeoisie only wanted civil liberties and a voice for itself in the government, which could be satisfied be granting suffrage to people with property. When these were granted, the bourgeoisie abandoned the workers and refused to support their demands. Option A is incorrect as both revolutions led to monarchies, and these were often popularly supported. Option B is incorrect as the Catholic Church often reclaimed previously eliminated rights and privileges after 1848. Option D is incorrect as no noble property was confiscated. Option E is incorrect as the French Republican calendar was not revived except during a brief time during the Paris Commune of 1871.

327. (C) Karl Marx did extensive writing about the Revolution of 1848 in France, such as *The Eighteenth Brumaire of Louis Napoleon*. Options A, B, and D refer to people who died before 1848. Otto von Bismarck was the father of German unification but was not known for his writings, of which there are not very many.

328. (D) All Frenchmen would consider themselves patriotic and this was never in question. Since the other options were considered and debated by various revolutionary figures, these options are incorrect. Eventually, a dictatorship under Louis Napoleon was created.

329. (B) The Reform Act of 1832 expanded the franchise to include most of the middle class. Option A is incorrect as the law had nothing to do with the army. Option C is incorrect as the House of Lords continues to this day. Option D is incorrect as there has never even been a William IV. Option E is incorrect as universal suffrage will not occur in Britain until later in the 19th century.

330. (D) Liberalism was a belief in individualism, free trade and commercial development, and constitutionalism. This would benefit the bourgeoisie most, as it would protect and develop business under a strong legal footing. Options A and B are incorrect as peasant and worker representation were not usually included among liberal demands. Options C and E are incorrect because these classes were already represented in the old order.

331. (A) Karl Marx is the founder of "scientific Socialism," which argues Socialism is the eventual result of proletarian revolution. All other choices are incorrect because they are men who tried to propose or create workers' communes of various types as model communities, without proposing how society as a whole might adopt such forms of Socialism as their dominant economic model.

332. (B) Karl Marx put forward a reasoned argument, based on the philosophy of the dialectic developed by Georg Hegel, for how Socialism was inevitable. Other Socialists were "utopian," meaning they proposed Socialist schemes but no clear way of how to move society to them. Option A is incorrect because such a philosophy does not describe natural phenomena and, therefore, cannot be proven with the scientific method. Option C is incorrect as Charles Darwin said nothing about Socialism. Options D and E are also incorrect.

333. (C) Bourgeois industrialists would favor the repeal of the protective Corn Laws, as this would mean cheaper food for workers, and, therefore, the industrialists could pay workers lower wages. Option A is incorrect because though British agricultural production declined, it was not destroyed. Option B is incorrect because British farmers did not abandon corn for other crops. Option D is incorrect as the repeal is the removal of a protective tariff, not the creation of one. Option E is incorrect because the price of corn decreased after 1846.

334. (D) Blanc's ideas amounted to Utopian Socialism, where production would take place in small communes. He foresaw it as the future basic unit of the economy. Option A is incorrect because laissez-faire economics is exactly the opposite of these communal workshops. Option B is incorrect because workshops never became commonplace; they were merely experiments, which generally did not work. Option C is incorrect because the workshops were never meant for prisons, but for general production. Option E is incorrect as workshops were supposed to be examples of local control of production, not top-down economic planning.

335. (A) The Second Republic was proclaimed in 1848 with elections based on universal suffrage for men. Option B is incorrect because women were officially excluded, though there were many women's political clubs. Option C is incorrect because, though François-Vincent Raspail was elected, he was hardly the first Socialist-leaning politician. The first official Socialist will not be elected until more than 30 years later. Option D is incorrect because while Louis Napoleon is elected, he was Napoleon's nephew not his son. Option E is incorrect as conservatives won a majority, thanks to support from the peasants.

336. (D) Though the British eventually attained universal suffrage and an extensive social welfare system, it will not be until the 20th century that these take place. All other options are incorrect as they did occur during the 1800s.

Chapter 12: Nationalism and State-Building, 1848–1900

337. (E) Nationalists believed in the importance and unique characteristics of different nationalities and that they should be respected and allowed to flourish, usually in their national homelands. All other choices contradict this ideal or have nothing to do with it. Option A is clearly incorrect as part of national pride is having your own national language, not giving it up for a common one. Option B is incorrect as nationalists may or may not believe in human rights. Options C and D are incorrect as nationalism officially has nothing to do with Socialism, free trade, or economics in general.

338. (D) The goal of Metternich's Concert of Europe was to preserve peace, the social order, and national boundaries as drawn up at the Congress of Vienna, unless the parties agreed to the change. While there were wars in the 18th century in Europe, the only conflict to take place between member countries that resulted in the forced transfer of territory within Europe was the Franco-Prussian War. It shattered the ideal of peace and stability within Europe and inaugurated the new German nation, which would threaten European stability for 80 years. This would dramatically change the balance of power in Europe. Option A is incorrect because though the Crimean War was between member countries of the Concert of Europe, no major land swaps between them occurred. It did not substantially change the balance of power. Option C presumably refers to the war of Denmark against Prussia and Austria. It resulted in minor transfers of territory and did not greatly change things. Option E was primarily an Italian matter and did not have much bearing on the balance of power in Europe.

339. (E) Nationalists traditionally valued the unique traits of their nations and often had idealized visions of their countries. A romanticized national ideal was often at the heart of their movements. It is hard to ascribe ideological aspects to the early nationalist movements. Therefore, all other options, which do have political, economic, or social agendas, cannot accurately characterize nationalism of the period.

340. (B) Nationalists were frequently conservatives who harkened back to an idealized time of order and national purity. Conservatives could appeal to the more negative side of nationalism, that which saw anything foreign as evil and distrusted anything alien. Options A and D are incorrect as Socialists and radicals often saw themselves through the lens of class-consciousness, which transcends national borders. Option C is incorrect as liberals were more interested in practical reforms of society, not romanticized notions of nationhood. Option E is incorrect because religious zealots were more interested in religious ideals, which would also cross borders.

341. (C) This term was created by Johann Herder, who suggested that each nation had its own nature and national talents. Options A and B are both incorrect as while *Volksgeist* could lead to unification movements, it does not refer to specific German or Italian unification movements. Option D is incorrect as the German car that sounds like the term in the question is a Volkswagen. Option E is incorrect as the term has nothing to do with war reparations.

342. (C) There had been a rebellion in Naples in July 1820. The Troppau Protocol was designed and used in that rebellion.

343. (C) Russia had intervened, along with Britain and France, in the cause of Greek independence in 1821. Options A, B, and D are incorrect as these countries had nothing to do with the war. Option E is incorrect as it was the Ottoman Empire that the Greeks were fighting to free themselves from.

344. (C) The Ottoman Empire had been in decline for centuries before it finally collapsed after World War I. However, much European diplomacy had to do with whether to hasten that decline or to try to stop it. Austria-Hungary and the United Kingdom sought to preserve it, whereas other powers sought to speed its demise. Option A is incorrect because Austria was not considered eastern. Option B is incorrect as the Russian Empire was not in decline yet. Option D is incorrect because it is certainly in the east, but not in the eastern end of Europe. Option E is to the west of Europe.

345. (C) The Greek rebellion had substantial support from Britain, France, and Russia, and as such, they insisted that the new government be a monarchy. A Bavarian prince assumed the throne of the newly independent Greece. Option A is incorrect as it would have made Greece the most progressive state in the world, something neither the Greeks nor Great Powers desired. Option B is incorrect as Socialism was still a very immature idea, supported by few in western Europe, let alone Greece. Option D is incorrect because it might have been possible but was disallowed by the Great Powers. Option E is incorrect because the revolutionaries wanted a functioning unified country and were more linguistically united than in classical Greece.

346. (A) Most of Poland had been occupied by Russia, and therefore the Poles sought independence from that empire. Option B is incorrect as France did not even have a land border with Poland. Options C, D, and E are incorrect because they were closer to Russia but did not occupy most Polish land.

347. (B) The Decembrist Revolt took place in 1825, at the beginning of the reign of Nicholas I. The rebellious officers were trying to have Constantine, the brother of dead Czar Alexander, become czar instead of the rightful heir, Nicholas. They failed. The other options represent czars that ruled at other times.

348. (B) The southern, or Austrian Netherlands were united with the Dutch Republic at the Congress of Vienna. This created an uneasy situation where the Catholic south was forced to unite with the Protestant north. Economic issues also played a role in the Belgian independence struggle, which it won from the Netherlands in 1830. The other options are incorrect because they did not rule Belgium.

349. (C) Louis Blanc came up with the idea of "social workshops," which he had a chance to put into practice in the Revolution of 1848. However, the government was not really ready for such a scheme, and they were not executed well. Eventually the "national workshops" were ended, and he was blamed for the failure and discontent that was created when they were closed. Options A, D, and E are incorrect as Charles X, Louis Philippe, and Louis XVIII left the throne of France before the workshops were created. Option B is incorrect because the workshops were disbanded before Louis Napoleon assumed the throne.

350. (C) The national workshops were created by the provisional government to alleviate the unemployment problem in Paris. They were hated by the rest of the country, though, because of the taxes necessary to fund them. When the workshops were dissolved by the government in June, rebellion broke out in Paris—the so-called "June Days." Option A is incorrect as Louis Philippe had been overthrown in February. Option B is incorrect as Louis Napoleon's coup did not happen until 1851. Option D is incorrect because it occurred in May. Option E is incorrect as it had no bearing on the uprising of the working class in June and may not have happened at all.

351. (C) Nicholas I and Russia came to the aid of Austria in suppressing the Hungarian rebellion. Option A is incorrect as Napoleon III had just become president of France and did not take part in an Austrian affair. Option B is incorrect because Kaiser Wilhelm was a rival of Frederick Joseph and would not have assisted him. Option D is incorrect as Louis Philippe had abdicated. Option E is incorrect as Elizabeth II was not alive in the 19th century.

352. (E) This quote makes reference to "class antagonism," or class struggle, and makes reference to a future society with free development for all, instead of the old bourgeois one. Therefore, it most closely follows the philosophy of Karl Marx. Option A is incorrect because de Tocqueville never expresses Socialist sentiments like this. Option B is incorrect because Locke made many statements supporting the protection of private property, which contradicts the sentiment expressed. Option C is incorrect as Rousseau never discussed details of class antagonisms or made predictions of future societies. Option D is incorrect because Burke was a conservative and would never say such a quote.

353. (E) The Austrian chancellor Metternich led the Congress of Vienna, which created a system of stability for Europe after the Napoleonic Wars. Metternich's goals were stability and the maintenance of a conservative status quo. The system that was set up followed Metternich's goals for Europe. Options A, C, and D are incorrect because while these were figures who were present, they were not as dominant as Metternich. Option B is incorrect because the entire conference was composed of representatives of countries that had defeated Napoleon I, and he was in exile.

354. (C) The Frankfurt Parliament of 1848 was an attempt to create a constitution for a united Germany, with a kaiser as a constitutional monarch. It failed and was crushed by Austria and Prussia. Option A is incorrect because it was a response to revolutionary events in Europe in 1848, not Prussia. Option B is incorrect because the Zollverein was created many years before. Option D is incorrect because the Frankfort Parliament was a way to create a united German state, not a confederation of cities. Option E is incorrect, because though Prussia and Austria were rivals for German leadership, there was no conflict at the time and organizers were more influenced by other European events.

355. (D) The first Zionist Congress was held in 1897, just a year after the publication of Herzl's book. Option A is incorrect as Jews had been immigrating to the United States before the book was published. Option B is incorrect as the Ottoman Empire never declared that Jews could not go to Palestine. Option C is incorrect as there were not nearly enough Jews to declare a state, even if they wanted to. Option E is incorrect because Jews from Arab countries did not move to Palestine until after the declaration of the state of Israel in 1948.

356. (D) Pogroms, or organized riots against Jews, sponsored by the government took place in Russia. All other options are incorrect as no such actions occurred there.

357. (B) Bismarck came from a Junker family. Junkers were Prussian nobles.

358. (D) France lost the Franco-Prussian War in 1870, and Louis Napoleon was captured by the Germans. He was officially deposed, and the French Third Republic was born. He spent the rest of his life in England. Options A and B are incorrect as they occurred a number of years before this. Option C was not significant enough to make Napoleon III lose his throne. Option E, the Dreyfus Affair, occurred more than 20 years after Louis Napoleon was captured by the Germans and deposed.

359. (A) All other choices had greater reason to fear a united Prussian-dominated Germany than Russia. Option B is incorrect as Prussia was Austria's greatest rival. Option C is incorrect because the German states were united against the maneuverings of Napoleon III between 1866 and 1870. Option D is incorrect because Hanover was forcibly annexed by Prussia as part of German unification. Option E is incorrect because of Danish hatred of Germany following their loss in the Wars of Schleswig.

360. (C) The Austrian Empire gave way to the dual monarchy of Austria-Hungary, mid-century. It was a way to preserve the peace between the two largest components of the Austrian Empire. Hungarian nobles agreed to the compromise that created the Austro-Hungarian Empire. Option A is incorrect because England and Scotland were a united kingdom. Option B is incorrect because it never existed; they were both united in the new German nation. Option D is incorrect because it only existed as the United Kingdom of the Netherlands for 15 years, until the Belgian rebellion of 1830. Option E is incorrect because Poland had a king that operated under the Russian emperor, until Poland was completely absorbed by Russia in 1830.

361. (B) Most schools of the time did not offer religious instruction but left it to whatever church the family belonged. Option A is incorrect because often military training was included in schools, particularly for boys. Options C, D, and E are incorrect because there was a belief that an educated citizenry would be both productive and less likely to succumb to poverty and being tyrannized by a despot.

362. (C) This is a quote from the Emancipation Reform of 1861 in Russia, the last country to free its serfs. Option A is incorrect as the pope did not make laws for serfs or anyone else. Options B, D, and E are incorrect as they were in power after the serfs had been freed in their countries.

363. (C) Bismarck saw that adult male suffrage would lead to peasants outvoting urban workers. Bismarck was most afraid of Socialists and saw this as a strategic way to block their election. Option A is incorrect because Bismarck was at heart a conservative man. Option B is incorrect because all men did not have the right to vote in England at this time. Option D is incorrect because the emperor said no such thing, nor would anybody expect him to. Option E is incorrect because there were no such demonstrations.

364. (C) No feminists of the 19th century would have dreamed about military service for women. Indeed, conscription for men was just becoming more common. Option A is incorrect because women could not own property before the women's rights movement. Options B and D are incorrect because there were unequal qualifications and standards regarding divorce and adultery for men and women. Option E is incorrect as reproductive rights were not a subject for feminist agitation until the 20th century.

365. (A) Anarchists, those who reject government as an enslaver of men, became notorious for their violence. While not all anarchists justified violence, anarchists were responsible for a number of attacks against government officials in Europe. Option B is incorrect because anarchists considered Communists to be favoring a government of workers that would ultimately become as repressive as the capitalist order now in existence. Options C, D, and E are incorrect as they suggest support for the government and its forces and actions.

Chapter 13: Mass Politics and Imperialism in Africa and Asia, 1860–1914

366. (D) Britain was interested in maintaining good communication and sea routes to India, as well as the prime agricultural land in southern Africa. Accordingly, Britain conquered the majority of southern Africa. Option A is incorrect as the French were more dominant in western Africa. Option B is incorrect as Italy was more active in Ethiopia and Libya. Option C is incorrect as there were few Spanish regions of Africa. Option E is incorrect as Belgium controlled only the Congo in central Africa.

367. (B) The idea of Social Darwinism is that certain races are superior to others and, therefore, justified in conquering others. As a result the white man should shoulder the burden of teaching a superior culture to the lesser races. Option A is incorrect as it refers to free-market capitalism, which should not consider race in its pure form. Option C is incorrect because those who believe in the "white man's burden" would not respect native traditions. Options D and E are ideologies of the 19th century that would regard racism and cultural superiority as primitive and ignorant.

368. (A) North Africa is populated by Arabs, who live predominantly in the Middle East. It is also mostly desert, like much of the Middle East. This contradicts Options C and E. Option B is incorrect because Britain, France, and Italy conquered northern Africa. Option D is incorrect because they are quite undeveloped and have few natural resources, though Libya has oil reserves.

369. (A) There were slaves for colonial plantations and natural resources for the taking that Europeans greatly prized. The contacts in Africa were strictly to get these products during the 17th and 18th centuries. Option B is incorrect because there was no health care given to Africans during this time. Option C is incorrect because there were few industrial improvements to bring to Africa. Option D is incorrect as Europeans had no respect for tribal culture. Option E is incorrect because Europeans at the time had no idea about the advancement of Islam into Africa, and they might not care.

370. (B) The job of missionaries is to spread religion. Therefore, they tried to do this in Africa as much as possible. Option A is incorrect because missionaries had no slaves. Option C is incorrect as missionaries had no particular interest in tribal culture, though they might have learned some along the way. Option D is incorrect as missionaries have no reason to study rivers. Option E is incorrect because there was no great demand for ivory icons, and missionaries had no great interest fancy materials for icons.

371. (C) Unbridled competition for Africa could lead to war between European powers. The Berlin Conference was set up to establish rules for the conquest and competition for Africa by the Europeans; therefore, Option B is incorrect. Option A is incorrect as Leopold was given the area around the Congo River. Option D is wrong as the participants discussed the whole continent, not just the Congo. Option E is incorrect, as the conference had nothing to do with specific European conflicts.

372. (E) King Leopold of Belgium took over the Congo as his almost personal dominion, ruling it with a particularly cruel administration. Millions died from disease, maltreatment, and harsh working conditions on rubber plantations and other enterprises. Options A and C were countries colonized by Britain. Option B was a Portuguese colony. Option D was colonized by Germany and later France.

373. (D) The Suez Canal connects the Mediterranean Sea to the Red Sea by creating a shipping channel between the Sinai Peninsula and Africa. Therefore, ships did not have to go around all of Africa to go from Europe to the Indian Ocean. Options A and E are incorrect as they apply to the Panama Canal, which bisects the Panamanian isthmus at its narrowest point. Option B is incorrect because while there are oil refineries adjacent to the canal, they are not of particular strategic importance and were not the main reason for the canal's construction. Option C is incorrect because revenue from the canal goes to the Egyptian government.

374. (C) Because of external debts, the Egyptian leadership sold their shares in the canal to Britain. However, the majority of the shares were still owned by French business interests. Options A and E are incorrect as they had nothing to do with the creation or operation of the canal. Option D is incorrect because it did not even exist at the time.

375. (C) Although oil had been discovered and produced in large quantities in the United States and Russia prior to 1908, its discovery in Persia in 1908 by the British Anglo-Persian Oil Company opened the way to even more discoveries of petroleum in Iraq, Bahrain, and Saudi Arabia in the period between the World Wars. The increasing popularity of gasoline-powered cars created a growing demand for oil that continues to this day, making the Middle East much more important than ever before.

376. (E) The League of Nations designated Palestine, Syria, Lebanon, Jordan, and Iraq to become "mandates" of the British and French, which meant the two European powers divided and administered them. Prior to the end of World War I, these territories were part of the Ottoman Empire. Option A is incorrect because they had military forces in them. Option B is incorrect because they were directly administered by outsiders, without much local autonomy. Option C is incorrect because a mandate is a political not an economic term. Option D is incorrect because a mandate refers to administration of territory, not a treaty between nations.

377. (A) The Sykes-Picot Agreement was created after World War I to carve up the Middle Eastern territories of the Ottoman Empire between Britain and France. Option B is incorrect as this was a peace process developed between Israel and the Palestinians in 1991. Option C is incorrect as this was a statement of support for a Jewish homeland in Israel by the British in 1917. Option D is incorrect as this was a nonaggression pact between Germany and the Soviet Union before World War II. Option E is incorrect as this refers to a short-term agreement on Arab-Jewish cooperation in the Middle East in 1919.

378. (A) The Balfour Declaration of 1917 was the official statement of support for Jewish emigration to British Mandate Palestine and the establishment of a Jewish homeland there. Option B is incorrect as Israel and Jordan did not exist. Option C is incorrect because that announcement would not happen until 1947. Option D is incorrect as that did not happen until the partition of British India in 1948. Option E is incorrect as such a demand never happened.

379. (D) These areas were conquered and added to the Russian Empire in the first half of the century. Option A is incorrect as Russia has never had any border or presence in these areas. Option B is incorrect as Russia has never had a presence in the Pacific Islands. Option D is incorrect because though Russia held northwestern North America for a time, it never got close to South America. Option E is incorrect as the Russian Empire never got farther south than Central Asia.

380. (A) The issue of pipelines has become of major importance as there are significant deposits of oil and gas particularly in Kazakhstan and Azerbaijan, and how these supplies will get to Europe and elsewhere has major strategic implications. Option B is incorrect because though there is much cotton production there, there are other areas where cotton production is much greater. Options C, D, and E are factually incorrect.

381. (A) Britain practiced a policy called "divide and rule," which took advantage of Muslim-Hindu tensions. It may have led to the eventual partition of India and Pakistan. Option B is incorrect because the Portuguese had been driven out of India long before the British were able to establish control over it. Option C is incorrect because no Mughals had invited anyone from the outside into India. Option D is absurd as India and Great Britain are thousands of miles apart. Option E is incorrect as British consumer goods were not greatly available in the mid-19th century. This is in addition to the Indians having no desire or ability to pay for such things at the time.

382. (B) The British East India Company had actually ruled India, not the British government itself. The British government took over India directly after 1857. Option A is incorrect because the Mughal Empire had already declined before British rule came to India. Option C is incorrect because the sepoys, or Indian soldiers working for the British, had been trained after the British East India Company arrived and controlled India. Option D is incorrect because the British East India Company had conquered India initially. Option E is incorrect because there was no such thing in the conflict as Muslim mercenaries.

383. (B) There was resentment and rumors among Indians about efforts, real or imagined, to convert Indians to Anglican Christianity. This was made worse by the tallow controversy, when Indian sepoy troops thought they were being ordered to tear open with their mouths gun cartridges made with cow or pig tallow—offensive to both Hindus and Muslims. Option A is incorrect as there was no salt monopoly. Option C is incorrect because there were no French in India at the time. Option D is incorrect because mass violence began with the sepoys. Option E is incorrect as no such export took place.

384. (C) When the Sepoy Rebellion was over, the British government decided that the British East India Company had mismanaged India and assumed direct control over British India. Option A is incorrect because India will not become independent until 1947. Option B is incorrect because India became a British territory, not a protectorate. Option D is incorrect because it was the end of the British East India Company, not the beginning. Option E is incorrect because though there was some military reorganization, after the rebellion, Indians continued to be used by the British army.

385. (E) Though a small, educated middle class emerged in British India, the living conditions for the majority of Indians declined. The reasons for this are debated by historians. Option A is incorrect because there was a time of overall peace, particularly after the Sepoy Rebellion of 1857. Option B is incorrect as a new class of educated Indian elites began to grow. Option C is incorrect as the British tried to eliminate archaic Indian practices. Option D is incorrect as the British built roads and railroads in India.

386. (A) There were was a great sphere of domestic industry that existed in India prior to the arrival of the British. This was greatly destroyed by a classic imperialist economic policy that required India to become a market for British manufactured goods. Option B is incorrect as British India became less economically advanced as time went on. Option C is incorrect because any technological improvements to India were done to allow more British economic exploitation. Option D is incorrect as there were more frequent famines during the British colonial period. Option E is incorrect because taxes were actually lower during this time than during the Mogul Empire.

387. (C) British India continued to export agricultural products, including foodstuffs, during famines. This was a direct result of British policies encouraging these exports to other countries such as China as payment for other goods. Option A is incorrect as Indian farmers did worse economically under the British. Option B is incorrect as Indian agriculture continued to be backward. Option D is incorrect as Indian agriculture did not prosper under the British. Option E is incorrect as Britain continued its economic decline relative to Germany and the United States.

388. (C) Gandhi is known as a founder in the use of nonviolent opposition, and his use of it in India has become a model in other struggles. Options A and D are incorrect as they are the exact opposite of nonviolence, and Gandhi opposed such tactics as counterproductive. Options B and E are incorrect because though Gandhi did write, writing was not the main technique that he used.

389. (B) Indians were inspired by and read about nationalist struggles in Europe and elsewhere during the 19th century. If anything, this encouraged opposition to British rule. Option A is incorrect as the British became more resented over time, not less. Option C is incorrect because, although modified and less rigid, the caste system still exists today in India, particularly in the more rural regions. Hinduism is still the predominant religion of the country, with around 85 percent of the population identifying themselves as Hindu. Option D is incorrect because imperialism stayed the same through this period, or even became less coercive over time. Option E is incorrect because Marxism was never fully embraced by Indians.

390. (C) The Opium War was humiliating for the Chinese, and they finally realized how far behind the West they had fallen. Option A is incorrect because though opium was appealing, it was never more popular than tea. Option B is incorrect because there were no opium-caused famines. Option D is incorrect as Portugal was never a major player in China. Option E is incorrect because there was no way for China to use opium against the British.

391. (C) Hong Kong became a British colony for the next 99 years. This was a major embarrassment for the Chinese until the lease ran out. Options A and B did not occur. Option D did not occur as China continued to have a classic, though distinctly unmodern navy, which make no threat to Britain. Option E is wrong because it would just hurt locals more than it would help China.

392. (A) The Boxers were particularly interested in freeing China from foreigners. To that end, Christian missionaries were often attacked as representatives of a totally alien religion. Option B is wrong as it was an internal rebellion sponsored by a strange religious cult. Option C is incorrect as the Communist Revolution would not happen until 1948. Option D is incorrect because it will not happen until the 1960s. Option E is incorrect because it was confined to improving defense industries.

Chapter 14: Politics of the Extremes and World War I, 1870–1918

393. (D) The Germans were alarmed at what they saw as the rapid modernization of their eastern neighbor and thought it was just a matter of time before Russia eclipsed Germany as the most advanced economy in Europe. Therefore, they felt war was inevitable and that it would be better for the Germans if it came sooner rather than later. Option A is incorrect because Russia and Austria were rivals, not allies. Option B never happened. Option C is incorrect because the Russian fleet was nowhere near the size of the German fleet. Option E is incorrect because no militarization of the border had gone on, and officially there was no German-Polish border, as Poland was mostly within the Russian Empire.

394. (D) There was no alliance between Germany and Russia at this time. Russia was allied with Britain and France. Option A is incorrect because Wilhelm was known for his bombastic style. Option B is incorrect because it is true that Germany had dreams of creating a navy to match Britain's. Option C is incorrect because there were colonial rivalries among all the powers of Europe. Option E is incorrect because there was increasing German involvement in the Balkans, particularly the proposed rail link between Germany and Baghdad.

395. (B) "Our nation" in the passage refers to Germany. It arrived late to the game of imperialism and had to take the less desirable of colonies, but this passage shows the attitude of Germany in the late 19th-century to early 20th-century period of wanting to surpass more established European powers. Option A is incorrect as Russia had no plans or ability to create overseas imperialism as it had an enormous empire that was connected to it. Options C and D are incorrect because both had already created enormous overseas empires. Option E is incorrect because Italy had already created some colonies in Africa.

396. (A) With the creation of a new independent Bulgaria, and the coming to power of Serbian nationalists in Serbia, the Austro-Hungarians were afraid of a new power to their south. They, therefore, preemptively annexed Bosnia-Herzegovina in 1908 and almost started a major war. Option B is incorrect because the Austro-Hungarians had no particular use for the Ottoman sultan. Option C is incorrect because Austria-Hungary had a rivalry, not an alliance with Russia. Option D is incorrect because Austria-Hungary was not an ally of Britain. Option E is incorrect because the Austro-Hungarians feared Slavs and would not want another Slav state on its borders.

397. (C) Oil will not be discovered in the Arabian Peninsula until the 1920s. All other options represent importing of goods that had been going on since at least the early 1800s, if not before.

398. (A) Social Darwinism is the theory, derived from biological Darwinism, that groups and individuals compete against each other and the strongest and most fit survive. This was eventually taken to include racial groups. Option B is incorrect because Marxism was an economic and political theory that ascribed racial and national conflict as illegitimate and masking class struggle. Options C, D, and E are incorrect because they represent philosophies concerned with either the point of existence or how to perceive sensory experiences.

399. (D) Sicily was incorporated into the new Italian state in the mid-19th century. All other options are incorrect because the British had put them under British rule in one way or another in the 19th century. Gibraltar is British to this day.

400. (C) It was fear of Russian expansion southward into the Balkans that kept Britain and France involved in the reinforcement of the declining Ottoman Empire in the 19th century, even going so far as to fight Russia in the Crimean War. Russia was seen as the main threat to the Balkans and Mediterranean until later, when the threat of Germany became much greater. Option A is incorrect because while Britain was becoming more religiously tolerant, this had nothing to do with diplomacy in the Balkans or Asia Minor. Option B is incorrect because if anything the British sympathized with the Greeks. Option D is incorrect because personal regard for individual leaders had very little to do with diplomacy during this period. Option E is incorrect because there were few if any Muslims in Britain at the time.

401. (D) The main problems of Russia during the war were food shortages, the collapse of the Russian war effort against Germany, and the lack of land for peasants. People demanded "Peace, Land, and Bread," a popular slogan of the time. Option A is incorrect because the majority of Russians were still peasants and therefore supported the agrarian socialist-oriented Revolutionary Party (SR), not the Bolsheviks. Option B is incorrect because it was the soviets who were gaining power during this time at the expense of the Provisional government. Option C is incorrect because the czar had already abdicated in March. Option E is incorrect because the Western democracies had supported the Provisional government and Lenin had promised to take Russia out of the war.

402. (B) Trotsky (and Lenin) feared that if the Communist Revolution did not break out in Western Europe, Russia would find itself isolated and surrounded by hostile capitalist regimes. Therefore, Trotsky favored organized support of workers' parties to create revolution abroad. Stalin believed this was impractical and wanted to oppose Trotsky politically in the ensuing power struggle, anyway. Option A is incorrect because it is exactly the opposite of Option B. Option C is incorrect as both were Bolsheviks. Option D is incorrect as there was no party line; both leaders were endeavoring to make the party policy and that's what they were arguing about. Option E is incorrect because both believed that Russia would support Communism.

403. (A) These were the main demands of Russians in the summer and fall of 1917. Option B is incorrect as it is the slogan of the French Revolution. Option C is incorrect because it is not any slogan, and is not a particularly good one, either. Option D is also not a slogan, but a czarist policy. Option E is the Nazi policy of expansion.

404. (C) The Soviet Five-Year Plan was the method by which the Soviet Union embarked on a centrally planned economy. It was believed it would be more efficient than the supposed anarchy and duplication of capitalism. It was an exact plan for economic development over five years. Option A is incorrect as no such belief existed. Option B is incorrect because the Communist Party ran the state and was not separate from it. Option D is incorrect because vacations had nothing to do with the five-year intervals. Option E is incorrect because under the Soviet Five-Year Plans, all economic resources were owned by the state.

405. (B) Marx theorized that it was necessary for a society to reach industrial capitalism for the circumstances to be right for a Socialist Revolution. Lenin had to come up with a way to explain how it was acceptable to create a Socialist Revolution in a country that was still predominantly rural. Option A is incorrect because urban workers helped overthrow the czar in 1917. Option C is incorrect as Marxism is clearly not religious, and the Russian masses were anything but atheistic. Option D is incorrect as there were many revolutionary groups in Russia who were either Marxist or well acquainted with Karl Marx.

406. (E) The Provisional government was what Karl Marx would call a bourgeois government, which supported civil liberties and private property. As such, workers and peasants were not represented. Option A is the exact opposite of Option E and is, therefore, incorrect. Option B is incorrect because monarchists would not overthrow the czar. Option C is incorrect as this will not happen until November 1917. Option D is not correct as constitutional democrats ran the government.

407. (D) The NEP was Lenin's policy for the Russian economy to step back on recovery by allowing a small amount of private industry, while the government retained the "commanding heights" of heavy industrial production. It lasted throughout the 1920s. Option A is incorrect because it addresses education, not economic policy. Option B is incorrect as it most closely follows the policy in the Soviet Union in the 1930s. Option C is incorrect because the Soviet Union was pretty much isolated during the 1920s. Option E is incorrect because there was never a policy to greatly increase consumer products during Soviet times.

408. (C) The Comintern (Communist International) was an organization that coordinated the activities of the Communist Party worldwide. The goal was to promote international proletarian revolutions, but in reality it became a foreign policy tool of the Communist Party of the Soviet Union. Option A is incorrect because the name of the Communist Party never changed from the one that Lenin gave it. Option B is incorrect because Comintern was not a secret organization. Option D is incorrect because the Soviet military never desired to acquire official colonies. Option E is incorrect because Comintern was not an organization of artists.

409. (D) Lenin believed that the only way a Communist Revolution would be successful would be if professional revolutionaries in a single unified party with clear structure, aims, and an official newspaper worked to bring it about. It was a much more specific plan than anything specified by Karl Marx. All other options were ideas of Karl Marx.

410. (D) Britain adopted conscription in World War I, the last country to do so. All other options are incorrect because they happened earlier, starting with France during the French Revolution.

411. (A) The chain of events that led to World War I started when a Serbian man assassinated Archduke Ferdinand of Austria-Hungary. When Serbia refused to abide by the ultimatum quoted in the question, Austria-Hungary declared war on Serbia, and other countries took sides and declared war on countries of enemy alliances. All other options are incorrect because though they took part in the war, they issued no ultimatums, but simply followed alliance obligations.

412. (C) The Treaty of Versailles imposed harsh financial penalties on Germany. These proved quite difficult for Germany to meet and contributed to the economic problems in Germany in the 1920s, and thus, the conditions that allowed the Nazis to come to power in 1933. Option A is incorrect as it did nothing to Brest-Litovsk. Options B and D are incorrect as they had no effect on the breakout of World War II. Option E is incorrect because economic sanctions could occur without the treaty and would have had no effect on World War II, in any case.

413. (B) Lithuania was one of the Baltic countries that were part of the Russian Empire. It became independent following World War I and stayed that way for the interwar period. All other options are incorrect as they were independent countries or the head of empires before the war.

414. (D) The last organized opposition to Communist rule was the Kronstadt Rebellion of 1921. The rebellion was led by soldiers who initially were among the strongest supporters of the Bolshevik Revolution. As a result of the heavy-handed nature of Communist rule immediately after the revolution, the sailors withdrew their support for the Bolsheviks, calling for a government of "Soviets without Communists." Their rebellion was crushed by Red Army Civil War hero Mikhail Tukhachevsky. Options A, B, and C are incorrect because the civil war was still raging during these years and there was still some tolerance of non-Bolshevik groups. Option E is incorrect because 1939 was way past the institution of Communist totalitarianism and the Stalinist purges of the 1930s.

415. (A) "Land, Bread, and Peace" were the main demands of people exhausted by war and frustrated by czarist land ownership policies that favored nobles. The Provisional government could not deliver these demands, so Lenin used this slogan as a pathway to power. Options B and C were never political slogans of any significance. Option D was the slogan of the French Revolution. Option E is the basic philosophy of John Locke, the Enlightenment philosopher.

416. (D) After the March 1917 revolution, Mensheviks supported and worked with the Constitutional Democrats who formed the Provisional government. Bolsheviks condemned such actions and opposed the Provisional government until its overthrow in November. Option A is incorrect as the Bolsheviks would want no such thing, as they were Marxists.

Option B is incorrect as Mensheviks were still Socialists who were more inclined to agree with Bolsheviks on the goal of revolution, if not the means. Option C is incorrect as Mensheviks, if anything, were less ruthless than Bolsheviks. Option E is incorrect as Mensheviks were Marxists.

417. (B) Most of World War I in the western front was fought in northeastern France, where trench warfare had been established after the initial stages of the war. Option A is incorrect as the Germans had entrenched themselves in France at the beginning of the war after going through Belgium. Option C is incorrect as almost no fighting occurred in Portugal, which was in the war on the side of Britain and France. Option D is incorrect as Britain was separated from the main theater of war by water. Option E is incorrect as the Netherlands was never in the war.

418. (C) There were parades, cheering, and a great deal of popular enthusiasm for the war at its beginning in Germany, Austria, Russia, and other countries. Most believed victory would occur in a matter of weeks. The reality was sobering. All other options are opposite to the tone of great support for the war.

419. (D) Czar Alexander II was not a figure in the Russian Revolution because he died almost 40 years before it occurred. Option B is incorrect because even though Rasputin was assassinated the year before the revolution, his influence on the royal family helped create the perception in Russia that the czar and his government were inept and incapable of leading the country. All other options are incorrect because they either fell from power or rose to power because of the revolution.

420. (D) Defensive weapons and tactics such as machine guns and trenches without an improvement in offensive weapons and tactics led to the stalemate of the World War I trenches. It was not until the advent of tanks and accurate aerial bombing that this situation could be changed. Option A is incorrect as airplanes had a mostly minor role in World War I since their bombing was quite inaccurate. Option B is incorrect because snipers were insignificant next to mines, gas, and machine guns. Option C is inaccurate because the fighting took place on plains, which were fine for assembling large armies. Option E is incorrect because there were no night vision goggles at that time.

421. (A) This quote refers to major ethnic groups in Yugoslavia, which was formed after World War I. All other options are incorrect because there were no significant populations of these groups.

422. (B) The Triple Alliance refers to the Central Powers of World War I, which consisted of Germany, Austria-Hungary, and Italy. Option A is incorrect because Russia joined it to oppose the Triple Alliance. Option C refers to an alliance created earlier that included Germany, Austria-Hungary, and Russia. Option D is incorrect because it refers to the winning alliance of World War II, of which Russia was a member. Option E is incorrect because it refers to the alliance of Prussia, Austria-Hungary, and Russia after the Congress of Vienna in 1815.

423. (D) Women in many countries were mobilized for the war effort, freeing men to fight. Even after the war, though most women had to leave their new jobs, newly acquired suffrage and experience in a much larger number of work roles gave women an enhanced status and opened up many areas of employment to them, whereas before they had been limited to such jobs as domestic servants. Option A is incorrect as there were still plenty of male supervisors. Option B is incorrect because women were often used during the war for heavy manual labor. Option C is incorrect because suffrage was usually granted after the war, not before. Option E is incorrect because men did accept such work—before and during the war.

424. (E) It would be absurd to use cavalry to overcome trench warfare. The horses would immediately be mowed down by machine guns, along with their riders. The technology of Option A was used toward the end of the war but was not completely effective as the tanks were primitive and the troops were just beginning to learn how to use them. They will be instrumental in making trench warfare obsolete in World War II. All other options are incorrect because they were actually used and were ineffective.

425. (E) In order to prevent the Ottoman Empire (Turkey) from controlling the Middle East and the Suez Canal link to India, the British helped the Arabs who were fighting the Ottomans. Option A is incorrect as the British did not necessarily want to see these lands become independent and did not come through with promises that the Arabs thought had been made by the British to create a new independent Arab homeland. Options B and D are incorrect as the issue of a Jewish state was not addressed until 1917 and was not a concern for most of the war. Option C is incorrect as there was minimal French and Russian influence at the time.

426. (B) Austria was required to pay reparations to the Allies as a result of the Treaty of St. Germain, signed after the Versailles Treaty on September 19, 1919. According to that treaty, Austria had 30 years to pay off its obligations, beginning in 1921. The treaty did not stipulate the exact amount the Austrians needed to pay, and ultimately, the Austrians paid nothing. Option C is incorrect as Germany had its military forces clearly limited by the treaty. All other options were specifically in the Treaty of Versailles.

427. (E) Wilson's Fourteen Points called for the creation of new nations, an organization for resolving international disputes, and lenient terms toward Germany. The treaty was much more punitive, and included severe reparations and punishment of Germany in particular. Option A is incorrect because, while true, it was not a fundamental difference between them. Option B is incorrect because the Allies did have some governmental restraints on their own diplomacy. Option C is incorrect because the Allies had no such plan to divide up previously occupied countries. Option D is incorrect because if anything, Wilson was more supporting of a League of Nations.

428. (C) The atrocities in Belgium stirred up outrage in Britain at the beginning of the war when Germany invaded France through Belgium. Option D is incorrect as the Germans never occupied Paris during World War I. The other options are incorrect because they are events that occurred later than the start of the war.

429. (D) A mandate was supposed to be a transitional period of administering a nation until it was ready for independence. Option A is, therefore, obviously incorrect. Option B is incorrect as mandates applied to colonies whether or not they were German. Option C is incorrect as a country administering the mandate worked by itself without involving the elites of the society and there was no set time period. Option E is incorrect because indigenous cultures were not considered.

430. (C) Prior to the annexation, 42 percent of Bosnia's population was Orthodox Serbian, 40 percent was Muslim, and 18 percent was Catholic Croat. Naturally, Serbs in Serbia felt that Bosnia should eventually become part of a greater independent Serbian state and, therefore, Austria's annexation caused deep hostility among Serbian nationalists toward Austria. Option A is incorrect as the Ottoman leadership had several separatist movements to deal with and realized that it would be fruitless to challenge Austria over Bosnia. Options B and D are incorrect as Romania and France have no ethnic affinities with the Bosnian population. Option E is incorrect as Bulgarians never had a legitimate territorial claim on Bosnia.

431. (D) Bolshevism became a serious force during the Russian Revolution, but was of little significance before it and had no impact on the causes of World War I. Option A is incorrect because most of the countries were imperialist competitors in the years before World War I. Option B is incorrect as historians believe the alliance system was a clear cause of the chain reaction that started the war. Option C is incorrect because there was a clear armaments competition between the combatants, helped by the greed of arms manufacturers. Option E is incorrect because Balkan nationalism caused the assassination that triggered the war in 1914.

432. (E) Germany and Austria-Hungary were competitors during the German unification process, and Bismarck arranged for Germany to grow at Austria-Hungary's expense. However, common interests led to an alliance during World War I. Option A is incorrect as France and Russia allied with each other in the years preceding World War I. Option B is incorrect as Germany and Italy broke their alliance during the war. Option C is incorrect as Serbia and Russia were natural allies and their alliance before and during the war helped create the war in the first place. Option D is incorrect because Great Britain and Belgium were not allied but became allied when Germany disregarded Belgium's neutral status and attacked.

433. (A) Poland became part of the Russian Empire at the end of the 19th century and stayed that way until it was reborn at the Treaty of Versailles in 1919. Option D is incorrect because Croatia did not come into existence as an independent country until after the Balkan Wars of the 1990s. All other options ate incorrect because they were states that existed prior to World War I.

434. (C) The Schlieffen Plan anticipated Germany being squeezed between France and Russia. Therefore, it called for France to be knocked out of the war early, so that Germany could concentrate on Russia. Option A is incorrect as Germany knew Russia would be in the war and fully planned on how to deal with it. Option B is incorrect as Germany believed the key to success lay on in knocking France out quickly and fully believed this could be done. Options D and E are incorrect as Austria-Hungary, Italy, and the Ottoman Empire were to the south of Germany and would not prevent Germany from fighting a two-front war in any case.

435. (A) Alsace-Lorraine had been disputed between France and Germany for many years. It went to Germany after the Franco-Prussian War. However, it was returned to France after World War I. Option B is incorrect because Burgundy is part of France and has never been disputed. Option C is incorrect because Flanders has always been Belgian and has never been disputed. Options D and E are incorrect because both were always part of Germany and were never disputed, though the Rhineland was demilitarized after the war.

436. (E) The quoted action is the so-called "war-guilt clause" that Germany was forced to sign. It was used to justify the huge reparations that Germany was forced to pay after the war. Option A is incorrect as the League of Nations had no power to impose sanctions of any kind. Option B is incorrect as no disarmament took place other than in Germany. Option C is incorrect as no significant decolonization took place. Option D is incorrect as Germany was excluded from the peace negotiations until the end when it was presented as a fait accompli.

437. (E) England was the last country to enter World War I. It entered the war when Germany refused to withdraw from Belgium, after Germany had invaded that country to get to France. Option D is incorrect because the war started when a Serbian nationalist assassinated the Austrian archduke and Austria-Hungary declared war on Serbia. Option A is incorrect because Russia declared war on Austria-Hungary to support Serbia. Option C is incorrect because the French were allied with Russia. Option D is incorrect because Germany was allied with Austria-Hungary and, therefore, declared war on Russia.

438. (C) France and Germany almost came to war because of the two crises over Morocco. The first took place in 1905, and the second took place in 1911. Germany wanted to have access to the Moroccan ports and the Moroccan market, which France had almost exclusive control of. Option A is incorrect because England and France had just signed an alliance treaty at the beginning of the 20th century. Option B is incorrect because Morocco was a weak independent country that was quickly being colonized by both England and France. Options D and E are incorrect because Italy had almost no interest in Morocco at that time.

439. (B) Italy entered into the war in 1915 on the side of Britain, France, and the Russian Empire. Italy argued that its participation in the Triple Alliance was defensive in nature and it did not have to take part in the war on the side of Germany and Austria-Hungary. Option A is incorrect because Italy had entered on the side of the Entente Powers in 1915 and not on the side of the Central Powers. Option C is incorrect because Italy decided to enter the war in 1915 and not stay neutral. Option D is incorrect because the United States did not enter the war until 1917, two years after Italy entered the war. Option E is incorrect because of no such plebiscite was ever held.

440. (C) None of Wilson's Fourteen Points made any reference to Africa. He was mostly concerned with issues in Europe and the causes of the war in the first place. Option A is incorrect because national self-determination was a cornerstone of the Fourteen Points and was considered to be essential to ending the ethnic question in Europe. Option B is incorrect because Wilson believed the creation of the League of Nations would prevent future wars. Option D is incorrect because Wilson believed that peace without reparations would be a way to declare that the war was not the fault of any one particular nation and would prevent future grudges from being created. Option E is incorrect because Wilson believed that secret treaties were one of the causes of World War I.

441. (C) The greatest naval power in the world at the outset of World War I was Great Britain. With the aid of its navy, the British were able to create a global empire. Since 1898 Germany's naval program had grown, and by 1912 it became a threat to the British. Option E is incorrect because the United States had been growing its navy, but it could not compare to that of Great Britain yet. Options B and D are incorrect because although they were substantial European powers, they did not have navies that could compare with that of Britain's. Therefore the British did not see them as threats.

442. (E) World War I resulted in the destruction of the Ottoman Empire, which had once controlled the entire Middle East. After its dissolution, the Ottoman Empire was replaced by a number of protectorates. The modern-day country of Turkey was created in the area of Asia Minor and the city of Istanbul after World War I. Option D is incorrect because France lost no territory after World War I but actually gained some. Options A, B, and C are incorrect because they all lost territory as a result of World War I, although not nearly as much as the Ottoman Empire.

443. (E) France after World War I sought to remove Germany as a threat. Accordingly, France made sure that the treaty oversight contained provisions that were intended to limit the strength of Germany. This would prevent Germany from attacking France in the future, or so it was hoped. Option A is incorrect because while the French sought revenge against Germany, most French thinking was directed toward future German aggression and preventing it. The French were in no mood to forgive the Germans after World War I and made sure that the Germans paid reparations after the war. Options B, C, and D are incorrect because they described basically the same attitude. The French were clearly not indifferent to Germany and sought reparations and punishment for Germany after the war.

Chapter 15: The Interwar Years and World War II, 1918–1945

444. (D) Hitler was ideologically opposed to Bolshevism. It was the complete opposite of national Socialism. He also believed that the German people were a great race that needed a large territory to settle. This territory would be obtained from the vast expanse of the Soviet Union. Option A is incorrect because the Soviet Union did not control the Balkans or the Near East, and Stalin had already signed a nonaggression pact with Hitler. Option B is incorrect because Japan was allied with Germany and was much too far away from Europe to be any kind of threat to Germany. Option C is incorrect because Hitler had already defeated the French and, if anything, a war with Russia would detract from his efforts against the British. Option E is incorrect because, though Hitler employed a racist ideology, he did not seek to exterminate the Slavic population as he did with the Jews.

445. (B) Radar was a key invention of World War II. It enabled the British to see exactly where the German planes that were going to bomb England were coming from. It significantly reduced the effectiveness of the German bombing and caused great losses of German planes. It is probably the main reason why Hitler was forced to give up on the Battle of Britain. Option A is incorrect because poison gas was commonly used in World War I but not in World War II. Option C is incorrect because V-2 rockets were not used until the end of the war, and they played no significant role in the outcome of the war. Option D is incorrect because the Germans, not the British, used Tiger tanks. Option E is incorrect because, while sonar was widely used during World War II, it had no significant effect on the Battle of Britain.

446. (C) Germany used Belgium to attack France twice. In World War I Germans attacked France through Belgium in order to be able to get to Paris quickly. In World War II the Germans attacked France through Belgium in order to go around the Maginot Line. Option A is incorrect because the military push in the Balkans that occurred during World War II was not until 1941, two years after the war had begun. Option B is incorrect because Germany was not allied with Japan during World War I. Option D is incorrect because the Germans did not respect the rights of American vessels during either war. Option E is incorrect because there was no invasion of North Africa by the Germans during World War I.

447. (A) The main issue during the Potsdam Conference of July 1945 was the future of the Eastern European countries that had just been conquered by the Soviet Union and whether or not they would be free. Elections were one of the main issues being discussed. Option B is incorrect because no discussion of future military forces or their limits were established at the Potsdam Conference. Option C is incorrect because there was no discussion about compensation for the Holocaust, and it would have involved more than Russian Jews. Option D is incorrect because German POWs would have been released in accordance with the Geneva Convention and were not subject to discussions at Potsdam. Option E is incorrect because the Soviet Union was already going to be a founding member of the United Nations.

448. (E) Southern France between 1940 and 1942 was governed by Marshall Henri Petain. The capital was at Vichy, which is why it was called Vichy France. It was a puppet state of the Germans. Option A is incorrect because France never was Communist and there was no such person named Mendez France. Option B is incorrect because no part of France was prosperous during this time. Option C is incorrect because Free French was a resistance movement under Charles de Gaulle headquartered in London, not an area of France. Option D is incorrect because Georges Clemenceau was not a figure in French politics until after the war.

449. (C) The turning point of the eastern campaign during World War II was the Battle of Stalingrad. The Russians stopped the German advance at Stalingrad, and the Germans began a long retreat that lasted until the end of the war. Option A is incorrect because the Germans were not defeated by the Soviets in Poland until the last year of the war. The Germans were already in retreat. Option B is incorrect because there was no major Soviet theater of operations in Iran nor were there any Germans in Iran. Option D is incorrect because there was no German mutiny at Leningrad. Option E is incorrect because Hitler never refused to send supplies to German troops besieging Moscow.

450. (B) The center of Nazi ideology was racism. All races were put on a hierarchy, the lowest being Jews and right above them the Slavs. Accordingly, the Nazi occupation in Eastern Europe and the western Soviet Union was quite harsh. Even people inclined to sympathize with the Nazis were soon alienated after that. Option A is incorrect because there was no difference between Eastern and Western Europe with regard to their inclination to collaborate with the Germans. Option C is incorrect because the Nazis were not known for five-year plans, which were characteristic of Communist planning. Option D is incorrect because while American and British soldiers may have been treated more humanely, that was not a significant difference in the occupation. Option E is incorrect because Jews suffered even more in the East than they did in the West during the Holocaust.

451. (D) Nazi war criminals would classically defend their actions by saying that they were just following the orders of their superiors. Therefore, they could bear no responsibility for war crimes. Option A is incorrect because they were being prosecuted for war crimes and genocide against civilians, not crimes that occurred in the course of war. Option B is incorrect because it is not a justification that would excuse them from punishment. Option C is incorrect because it would not have cleared them of war crimes. Option E is incorrect because they did not claim this, and it would not result in their being excused for war crimes.

452. (C) The Sudetenland, an area of western Czechoslovakia inhabited by German speakers, was cleared for takeover by the Germans at the Munich Conference of 1938. Many considered it to be an appeasement of Hitler. Option A is incorrect because people of the Saarland had voted to reunite with Germany in 1935. Option B is incorrect because the Rhineland has always been part of Germany and had just been illegally remilitarized by the Nazis. Option D is incorrect because Austria had already been annexed by Nazi Germany earlier that year. Option E is incorrect because Poland will be invaded by Nazi Germany only in September 1939, which will begin World War II.

453. (D) The Germans perfected the blitzkrieg, the concept of "lightning war." This was an overwhelming use of force in a methodical and organized fashion to quickly conquer territory and subdue defenders. This led to the quick German conquest of Poland and France. Option A is incorrect because the German technology in World War II, at least at the start of the war, was not significantly superior to British and French technology. Option B is incorrect because there was no clear French insistence on endlessly fighting, and the French command surrendered relatively soon after it became clear that the cause was lost. Option C is incorrect because Britain did not invade Norway until after the initial German victories. Option E is incorrect because the fighting at Tannenberg occurred during World War I.

454. (C) The Vichy government was a conservative Catholic government that passively cooperated with the Nazis. Option A is incorrect because it was a paternalistic, authoritarian regime and would clearly not be described as socialistic or democratic. Option B is clearly incorrect because the Vichy government was a Catholic and conservative government. Option D is incorrect because the Vichy government was not monarchist and there was no monarch around to speak of. Option E is incorrect because Vichy France was not liberal nor did it seek to expand anywhere.

455. (B) At Yalta, the Allies decided to divide Germany into zones of control by the winning powers. The goal was to eventually reunite the different sections of Germany. Option A is incorrect because there was a clear plan coming out of Yalta concerning what to do with Germany after the war. Option C is incorrect because the French were going to be included as one of the occupying powers, which would make three, not two, blocs. Option D is incorrect because the Marshall Plan was not organized until after the war. The Marshall Plan was also a response to the postwar domination of Eastern Europe by the Soviet Union. Option E is incorrect because the French were not making outlandish demands in 1945, nor were they in a position to make outlandish demands at that time.

456. (E) Very little fighting took place between September 1939 and the summer of 1940. This time is referred to as the "Phony War." Option A is incorrect because the French sought to defend their territory from the Germans. Option B is incorrect because the British were actively engaged in the war by the spring of 1940, and the "Phony War" refers to the period of inaction. Option C is incorrect because the Americans were quite angry and ready to mobilize after the attack on Pearl Harbor. Option D is incorrect because Britain and France declared war after the German invasion of Poland.

457. (D) Czechoslovakia was a relatively modern and democratic state in Eastern Europe. Option A is incorrect because Czechoslovakia was not the only member of the League of Nations in the area. Option B is incorrect because Czechoslovakia did not have a monarchy. Option C is incorrect because Czechoslovakia did not enjoy Soviet support at the time. Option E is incorrect because Czechoslovakia was a democracy and did not embrace fascism.

458. (B) Churchill was referring to the efforts of the Royal Air Force to defend Britain against the Nazi bombing during the Battle of Britain. The efforts of the Royal Air Force to protect the country prevented many deaths. All other options refer to events that occurred after Churchill spoke those words. Churchill's words became famous and were used in British propaganda soon after he uttered them.

459. (C) Operation Barbarossa was the code name for the German invasion of the Soviet Union in 1941.

460. (C) Britain was the victor at the Battle of El Alamein, which ended the Africa campaign. The Germans and Italians tried to capture North Africa and the Middle East, thereby threatening English shipping to India and the Middle East. The British victory put an end to this threat and brought to a close the entire African theater of war. Option A is incorrect because the Germans lost the battle. Option B is incorrect because the Soviet Union was not even involved in the battle. Option D is incorrect because even though Americans were present in some parts of the African theater, they did not take part in this battle. Option E is incorrect because Japan had absolutely no part in the Africa campaign.

461. (E) The Soviet Union was not present at the Munich Conference and saw the Munich Conference as a trial. The Soviet Union had a strategic alliance with Czechoslovakia, and the Munich Conference led to the dismemberment of Czechoslovakia and its eventual annexation by Germany. All other options are incorrect because they were parties present at the conference and agreed to the treaty that resulted from it. In that treaty, the Sudetenland, which was German-speaking, went to Germany and the rest of Czechoslovakia soon after that.

462. (B) Neville Chamberlain was the British prime minister at the time, and he famously came back to England after the Munich Conference and proclaimed "peace in our time." This was widely seen as a weak approach to Hitler and a glaring example of the failed policy of appeasement to Hitler. Chamberlain believed he had avoided war with Hitler and Germany, which he did, but only for a year. All of the other options are incorrect. Also, Churchill saw the folly of the appeasement strategy and did not support the Munich Conference at all. Stalin did not even take part in the Munich Conference nor did Roosevelt.

463. (C) The strategy of island-hopping concerns a way to reach Japan with the minimum loss of time and life. Accordingly the Americans attacked smaller, less heavily defended islands as a way to break the Japanese supply lines. This caused larger Japanese bases to be cut off and, therefore, allowed to "wither and die." Option A is incorrect because it is the exact opposite of the strategy proposed by island-hopping. Too much time, money, material, and men would be used if all of the islands were conquered. Option B is similarly not correct because too much time and money would be used to conquer the heavily fortified islands. Option D is incorrect because, while the air force was used extensively, it could not be used to wipe out military bases all by itself. Option E is incorrect because the method that the Americans preferred to conquer Japan was never employed. The Americans simply insisted on surrender after the dropping of the atomic bombs.

464. (C) Berlin lay deep in the Soviet sphere. This was the section of Germany that was controlled by the Soviet Union, in accordance with agreements made by the other Allies. Option E is incorrect because there was no Chinese sphere in Germany after the war. Options A, B, and D are incorrect because those spheres were in the western part of Germany.

465. (D) Clement Atlee was recently elected British prime minister. As the new leader of Great Britain he was one of the three main players at the Potsdam Conference. Option A is incorrect because Churchill had just been defeated in the recent election and was no longer the prime minister. Option B is incorrect because Potsdam was a meeting of the Allied leaders and Hitler was the leader of the Axis. Option C is incorrect because Roosevelt had died by then and had been replaced by Harry Truman. Option E is incorrect because the French were not at Potsdam as it concerned the future of Eastern Europe.

466. (D) The turning point of the eastern front turned out to be the Battle of Stalingrad in 1942 and 1943. After that the Germans were forced to begin a long retreat back to Germany. Likewise, the major naval defeat of the Japanese at the Battle of Midway was a crippling setback for their overall plans for the war and began a slow retreat back to the Japanese home islands. Option A is incorrect because millions of Russians and other Soviet citizens died during World War II, and the Soviet military leadership was quite profligate in its attitude toward human life. Option B is incorrect because the Maginot Line was built between World War I and World War II and yet proved completely ineffective as the Germans simply bypassed it by going through the Netherlands and Belgium. Option C is incorrect because V-E day came before V-J day. Option E is incorrect because military intelligence managed to decode both German and Japanese encrypted messages. This ability proved critical to many World War II battles.

467. (C) Luxembourg is considered a low country along with Belgium and the Netherlands. Together these three are considered the Benelux countries. They are in the low-lying delta of three rivers in northern Europe that empty into the North Sea, which is why they are known as the "low countries." All other options are not low-lying countries.

Chapter 16: The Cold War and Beyond, 1945–Present

468. (B) Tito was the resistance leader in Yugoslavia who later became the leader of Yugoslavia. He had nothing to do with Italy. All other options correctly show the leaders of the countries they are paired with.

469. (E) The collapse of the Fourth Republic was precipitated by the controversy over Algeria. Algeria had been a French colony, but its independence movement created a constitutional crisis. Many white settlers in Algeria favored remaining part of the French union. Charles de Gaulle came out of retirement and forced the creation of a new constitution, with a much stronger executive. This was the beginning of the Fifth Republic. When Parliament voted for its own dissolution, this led to creation of the new constitution. Option A is incorrect because Germany was still partially occupied and was both politically and economically incapable of threatening any other country. Option C is incorrect as there was no breakdown in relations with the United States. Options B and D are incorrect because there was no economic collapse nor was the political crisis triggered by any economic reasons, including social welfare policy.

470. (A) The East German government created the Berlin Wall to prevent the growing tide of refugees that were leaving East Berlin for West Berlin. It was easy for East Germany residents to leave for the West by simply going to West Berlin, which was completely surrounded by East Germany. Option B is incorrect because, while there were plenty of spies in Berlin, they were spying for both sides and the wall did not prevent that. Option C is incorrect because building a wall would not prevent spies from entering East Berlin. Option D is incorrect because the wall was built eight years after the end of the Korean War, and the Korean War had nothing to do with the Berlin Wall. Option E is incorrect because German reunification was never formally disavowed by either the Soviet Union or the Western nations.

471. (C) Yugoslavia, though a Communist state, was officially an independent country and asserted its independence soon after World War II. Marshal Tito, its leader, made a famous break with Moscow and Russian hegemony within Communism. All other options are incorrect because they correspond to Eastern European countries closely allied with the Soviet Union throughout the Cold War.

472. (E) Clement Atlee's postwar Labour government undertook a social democratic legislative program after the war. Accordingly, it strove to build housing for common people and, therefore, undertook a major housing program. His administration had strong support from British trade unions, and part of his program was for the government to take over certain key industries. It also embarked on a large expansion of the British welfare state. Therefore, all options are correct.

473. (C) The overall competition between the Soviet Union and the West concerned the competition over political and economic systems. Option B is a result of Option C. The competition between the East and West was the cause of what to do about the final status of Germany. Option A is incorrect because the Soviet Union was given a very prominent role in the postwar division of Germany, beginning in 1945. Option D is incorrect because Scandinavia played no major role in the Cold War. Option E is incorrect because the border between Poland and Germany was pretty clearly established after the war and has not changed since.

474. (B) Alexander Dubcek, the leader of Czechoslovakia in 1968, sought a liberalization of the Communist regime in Czechoslovakia. This was ended when the Soviet Union invaded Czechoslovakia and reestablished an orthodox Communist regime in 1968. Option A is incorrect because the Prague Spring had nothing to do with any green revolution in Eastern Europe. Likewise, Option C is incorrect as there was no agricultural aspect to the Prague Spring and no drought in 1968. Option D is incorrect because there was no great flowering of Czech literature as Czechoslovakia became a Communist satellite soon after World War II. Option E is incorrect because there was no change in the number of Czech troops to the Warsaw Pact before or after 1968, and this does not have any connection to the Prague Spring.

475. (A) The Sino-Soviet split that occurred in the 1950s created a division between the two most powerful Communist countries in the world. From then on Communism would cease to be a monolithic movement. Option C is incorrect because there were no major Cuban objections to Soviet policy. Options B, D, and E are incorrect because although they occurred, Yugoslavia, Romania, and Albania are relatively small countries and did not present a serious threat to the Communist movement in general.

476. (E) The Marshall Plan was a way to create prosperity and stability in Europe in the face of a possible Communist takeover. By rebuilding Europe, the Marshall Plan would dampen the allure of Communism and also provide a market for American goods. Options A and B are incorrect because there was no requirement placed on countries to participate in the Marshall Plan. Any country in Europe was officially invited to join. Option C would be correct if we were talking about Communist countries. There were no Communist countries in Western Europe, so Western Europeans did not see it as capitalist imperialism. Option D is incorrect because the Marshall Plan was seen as a great success by the time it was over.

477. (A) Gorbachev was not a capitalist, but he saw what was wrong in the Soviet economy and tried to restructure it in a Socialist manner. *Perestroika* was the economic counterpart to *glasnost*, which was a new political openness in Soviet society. Accordingly Option B is incorrect because Gorbachev did not try to create a free-market economy. Option C is incorrect because Gorbachev did not try to create a three-person directorate or create any major change in Soviet political institutions. Option D is incorrect because Gorbachev never sought to abolish the KGB. Option E is incorrect because Gorbachev sought no drastic political restructuring at first; *perestroika* moved along gradually.

478. (A) The Khrushchev era was known as the "thaw." Khrushchev ended severe Stalinist repression and freed large numbers of political prisoners. Option B is incorrect because although Khrushchev created new agricultural programs, these did not create big advances in agricultural production. Option C is incorrect as the Soviet Union never sought to join NATO. Option D is incorrect because Khrushchev tried to increase the amount of consumer goods but did not actually try to create a consumer economy. Option E is incorrect because Khrushchev never sought to hold nationwide elections for the position of general secretary, and an inner circle of Communist party members chose this.

479. (D) The first space satellite launched in history was created by the Soviet Union. The Soviets beat the Americans to this achievement, and it was a particularly impressive achievement seen across the world. Option A is incorrect because although the Soviets created many large and impressive dams, the dam on the Volga River is not the world's largest, nor was it at the time. Option B is incorrect because the construction of the *gulag* network of concentration camps was not a scientific or engineering achievement. Option C is incorrect because, while the Soviet Union created high-quality fighter planes, so did many other countries and the American ones were usually considered to be of better quality. Option E is incorrect because atomic and hydrogen bombs were invented by the Americans.

480. (D) Despite the encouragement of America broadcasts, there was no explicit military assistance to revolutionaries in anti-Communist rebellions in Eastern Europe. As a result, all protests against Communist rule during most of the Cold War were crushed. Option A is incorrect because, though it could be argued that American rhetoric was hollow and failed to support Polish and Hungarian rebels, this option is better explained in Option D. Similarly, Option C is incorrect because all Soviet bloc eastern satellites were expected to remain loyal to the USSR during this time and to closely follow the economy prescribed by Moscow. Option B is incorrect because this is also covered in Option D. Option E is incorrect because there were future protests against Communist rule after the Polish and Hungarian uprisings of 1956.

481. (C) Some gradual liberalization took place in the Soviet Union after the death of Stalin, but this was accompanied by increasing economic decline, particularly after the 1970s. Generally Communism went into a slow decline starting from the 1950s and continuing until its eventual fall. Option A is incorrect because the KGB was not dismantled until after the fall of the Soviet Union. Option B is incorrect as the Soviet Union never solved its agricultural problems. Option D is incorrect as you never announce repression anywhere.

482. (B) Khrushchev strove to create a political thaw by beginning the policy of de-Stalinization, whereby Stalin's policies were refuted and greatly altered. Option A is incorrect because, if anything, Khrushchev condemned many of Stalin's policies. Option C is incorrect because while the Soviet Union supported the Egyptian side of the Suez Crisis, this was not the topic of this congress. Option D is incorrect because Khrushchev certainly could not control Communism in China even if he so wished and did not seek to do that in Eastern Europe either. Option E is incorrect because Khrushchev never ended the competition or animosity between the Soviet Union and America nor would he ever dream of doing such a thing.

483. (A) Charles de Gaulle led France in an independent course between the Soviet Union and the United States at the time. De Gaulle would accept neither American dominance nor Soviet hegemony. He wasn't anti-Communist and sought to make France a power of its own. Option B is incorrect because the goal of de Gaulle was to take France out of military command of NATO in the 1960s, and therefore it could not be the leading member of the alliance. Option C is incorrect because it is exactly the opposite of Option A. Option D is incorrect because de Gaulle distrusted West Germany and Britain and sought to keep Britain out of the common market. Option E is incorrect because de Gaulle was not a Communist and sought no alliance with the Warsaw Pact nations.

484. (B) The European Economic Community had its origins in the European coal and steel community in the 1950s. This was a trade organization concerning steel producers at the time. All other options are incorrect because they have nothing directly to do with coal or steel production.

485. (C) Guerrilla wars became numerous in the 1960s and 1970s because of the continuation of national independence movements and the realization that traditional styles of war might lead eventually to nuclear conflict. Therefore, guerrilla and asymmetrical types of warfare became more numerous during the nuclear age, not less. Option A is incorrect because mutually assured destruction is the theory that nuclear war will eventually lead to the complete destruction of both combatants and, therefore, is not an acceptable form of warfare. Option B is incorrect because nuclear weapons became more numerous in the nuclear age, and eventually proliferated to a number of countries. Option D is incorrect because nuclear weapons are expensive and require delivery systems such as long-range bombers and missiles, which have consequences for national economies. Option E is incorrect because nuclear weapons have direct connections to space programs because the development of missiles to deliver these weapons is also tied to the development of space rockets.

486. (E) After the war Berlin was located in the Soviet occupation zone of Germany. This led to many complications, including walls and separation schemes to keep people from crossing between Berlin and the rest of Germany. Option D is incorrect because there was no United Nations in Germany during the Cold War period. Options A, B, and C are incorrect because they controlled the Western occupation zone of Germany, which was later united to become West Germany. West Germany constituted two-thirds of German territory until German reunification in 1989.

487. (B) The Security Council is composed of the five official victors of World War II—the United States, the Soviet Union, France, United Kingdom, and China. So Germany, the largest Western European state, is not a member of the Security Council.

488. (B) The Greek Civil War and Communist pressures on Turkey led to the Truman Doctrine, a formal declaration of support by the United States for countries being threatened by Communist takeover. The United States pledged its support for anti-Communist forces in small countries. Option A is incorrect because the Truman Doctrine was made in response to events in Greece and Turkey, and there had not yet been any Communist takeover in Vietnam. Option C is incorrect because there have been no Communist takeovers in West Germany or Italy. Option D is incorrect because there has been no Communist threat in Algeria. Option E is incorrect because there have been no Communist events in Japan, which at the time was occupied by the United States.

489. (B) The Iron Curtain got its name from a famous speech by Winston Churchill in 1946. He described areas of Eastern Europe controlled by the Soviet Union as being behind the Iron Curtain. This was an example of early Cold War rhetoric. Option A is incorrect because while Reagan derided the Iron Curtain and demanded the Berlin Wall be torn down, he did not invent the term *Iron Curtain*. The other options are incorrect because they refer to Soviet leaders who would never use this term to describe the Cold War division between Communist and non-Communist. This would imply that their countries were prisons that people could not leave from.

490. (C) Yugoslavia eventually accepted some Marshall Plan money, which was one of the reasons for the break between Yugoslavia and the Soviet Union after the war. Marshal Tito of Yugoslavia took an independent course and was open to accepting money from the West. All other options are incorrect because they were Eastern Bloc countries that had been forbidden by the Soviet Union to accept Marshall Plan money.

491. (C) The Cuban missile crisis was seen as a capitulation of the Soviet Union to the demands of the United States. The United States demanded that the Soviets bring back missiles that had been installed in Cuba, 90 miles away from the American coast. Even though the United States promised to remove missiles from Turkey aimed at the Soviet Union, this was not revealed until many years later, and it seemed as though Khrushchev had backed down, which cost him domestic support. Option A is incorrect because de-Stalinization was a popular policy within the Soviet Union and had created a more open atmosphere. Option B is incorrect because most of the Soviet Union had supported the way the Hungarian Revolution had been suppressed by Soviet troops. Option D is incorrect because the Bay of Pigs was an invasion of Cuba by Cuban exiles, and it probably would have been supported by Soviet people. Option E is incorrect because it is doubtful that most of the people cared about Khrushchev's crude mannerisms.

492. (D) The Brezhnev Doctrine stated that Communist countries or countries within the Soviet sphere of influence could not stop being Communist nor could they leave the Soviet sphere of influence. Option A is incorrect because while the Brezhnev Doctrine might affect Communist countries in Southeast Asia, it affected all countries within the Soviet sphere of influence. Option B is incorrect because the Brezhnev Doctrine did not apply to

NATO countries, which were by definition outside of the Soviet sphere of influence. Option C is incorrect because the Brezhnev Doctrine affected countries outside of the Soviet Union, as it was a forgone conclusion that Soviet republics could never become non-Soviet. Option E is incorrect because the Brezhnev Doctrine affected all countries within the Soviet sphere of influence, not just those in a particular region.

493. (C) Impressionism was a 19th-century artistic movement. All other options are 20th-century artistic movements.

494. (D) Under Communism most ethnic differences were played down or suppressed. Ethnic groups were forced into greater political entities, which they may not have wanted to join. The entire Soviet Union was a nation of 16 different regions all held together by the national Soviet government in Moscow. When Communism fell, the nationalist feelings of various ethnic groups came to the surface, and this has resulted in violence and separatism in the post-Communist era. Option A is incorrect because the free-market economy has nothing to do with ethnic hatred. Option B is incorrect because ethnic and religious groups are not allowed complete freedom under Communism. Option C is incorrect because there has not been a great deal of nationalist violence in Eastern Europe, with the exception of the wars in Yugoslavia.

495. (B) In 1982 Argentina attacked and conquered the Falkland Islands, a small archipelago of islands a few hundred miles east of Argentina that has been administered by Britain for the past 200 years. When Margaret Thatcher, prime minister of Britain at the time, sent a military force to take the islands back, the British people rallied to her support in a wave of nationalism. In the following weeks Britain successfully won the Falkland Islands back from Argentina after a short war.

496. (A) Nationalization of industries would be the exact opposite of Thatcherism. Thatcherism could be described as a policy of clear confidence in the free market, which is the opposite of nationalization of industries. All other options are incorrect because destroying the power of labor unions, reducing taxes, reducing government spending, and close partnership with the United States were all pillars of Margaret Thatcher's policies.

497. (D) The Catholic Church served as a vanguard for the Solidarity movement in Poland. The Solidarity movement in Poland was closely allied with the Catholic Church during the late 1970s and early 1980s. The church strongly supported Solidarity and used its protected place in society, even during Communist times, as a sort of sanctuary for the Solidarity movement and Solidarity figures. Option A is incorrect because the Communist Party controlled the Polish Parliament. Option B is incorrect because while members of the peasantry may have supported Solidarity, it is not an institution and is not what gave the Solidarity movement support and protection. Option C is incorrect because the Polish army did not support Solidarity movements during its heyday. Option E is incorrect because there were no significant numbers of disaffected Communist Party members.

498. (C) In 1991 Slovenia and Croatia declared their independence from the Federal Republic of Yugoslavia. As a result, Serbian armed forces moved in to protect Serbian minorities and carve out areas for them in these former republics. Option A is incorrect because Croatia eventually applied for NATO membership, but this was not the cause of the 1991 war and did not happen for many years afterward. Option B is incorrect because although there was severe fighting between Bosnian Muslims and Serbs in Bosnia this did not happen until after 1991. Option D is incorrect because Slovenia and Croatia did not massacre thousands of Serbs, and there were no great massacres in the Slovenian or Croatian wars of independence. Option E is incorrect because there were no Croatians, Slovenian, and Bosnian attacks on Serbia.

499. (B) Czechoslovakia peacefully broke into two different ethnic enclaves in 1993, the Czech Republic and the Slovak Republic. This was done via a simple vote of the Czechoslovak Parliament. Option A is incorrect because Czechoslovakia will eventually join the European Community and NATO, but not for a number of years. Option C is incorrect because Czechoslovakia never suffered a violent civil war. Option D is incorrect because while Czechoslovakia allowed more local autonomy for ethnic minorities, the nation divided into two main ethnic groups, Czechs and Slovaks.

500. (A) Women in Western Europe in the second half of the 20th century have achieved much greater equality with men in the workforce than ever before. Women participate in equal numbers with men in many occupations. Option B is incorrect because although women have made great strides in the workforce, they still do not have wage equality with men. Option C is incorrect because women in Western Europe live longer than men; this is true of almost all Western European countries. Option D is incorrect because family size in Europe has gotten much smaller over the past 40 years, and some European countries do not even have enough children to replace their populations. Option E is incorrect because women attend more institutions of higher education than ever before, and almost no institutions of higher education are closed to them in Europe today.

BIBLIOGRAPHY

Barzun, Jacques. *From Dawn to Decadence 1500 to the Present: 500 Years of Western Cultural Life*. New York: Harper Collins, 2000.

Chambers, Mortimer, Barbara Hanawalt, Theodore K. Rabb, et al. *The Western Experience*. 8th ed. New York: McGraw-Hill, 2003.

Curtis, Glenn E., ed. *Russia: A Country Study*. Washington: GPO for the Library of Congress, 1996.

Duiker, William J., and Jackson J. Spielvogel. *World History*. 3rd ed. Australia: Wadsworth, 2001.

Hunt, Lynn, Thomas Martin, Barbara H. Rosenwein, et al. *The Making of the West: Peoples and Cultures*. 2nd ed. Boston: Bedford/St. Martin's, 2005.

Kishlansky, Mark, Patrick Geary, and Patricia O'Brien. *Civilization in the West Since 1300: Advanced Placement Edition*. 6th ed. New York: Pearson, 2006.

McKay, John, Bennett Hill, and John Buckler. *A History of Western Society Since 1300: Advanced Placement Edition*. 8th ed. Boston: Houghton Mifflin Company, 2006.

Palmer, R.R., and Joel Colton. *A History of the Modern World*. 8th ed. New York: McGraw-Hill, 1994.

Spielvogel, Jackson J. *Western Civilization: A Brief History*. 6th ed. Australia: Thomson Wadsworth, 2006.

Stavrianos, L.S. *The Balkans Since 1453*. New York: New York University Press, 2000.

Viorst, Milton. *The Great Documents of Western Civilization*. New York: Barnes & Noble Books, 1965.

http://www.diplomatie.gouv.fr/en/france_159/institutions-and-politics_6814/the-symbols-of-the-republic_2002/liberty-equality-fraternity_1503.html

BEAUTIFUL
MUTANTS

by the same author

Ophelia and the Great Idea

DEBORAH LEVY

BEAUTIFUL MUTANTS

VIKING

VIKING
Published by the Penguin Group
Viking Penguin, a division of Penguin Books USA Inc.,
40 West 23rd Street, New York, New York 10010, U.S.A.
Penguin Books Ltd, 27 Wrights Lane,
London W8 5TZ, England
Penguin Books Australia Ltd, Ringwood,
Victoria, Australia
Penguin Books Canada Ltd, 2801 John Street,
Markham, Ontario, Canada L3R 1B4
Penguin Books (N.Z.) Ltd, 182–190 Wairau Road,
Auckland 10, New Zealand

Penguin Books Ltd, Registered Offices:
Harmondsworth, Middlesex, England

First American Edition
Published in 1989 by Viking Penguin,
a division of Penguin Books USA Inc.
10 9 8 7 6 5 4 3 2 1
Copyright © Deborah Levy, 1989
All rights reserved

Grateful acknowledgment is made for permission
to reprint excerpts from "Falling in Love Again" by
Frederick Hollander. Copyright © 1930 by
Famous Music Corporation. Copyright
renewed 1957 and 1958 by Famous Music Corporation.

LIBRARY OF CONGRESS CATALOGING IN PUBLICATION DATA
Levy, Deborah.
Beautiful mutants / Deborah Levy.
p.   cm.
ISBN 0-670-82892-0
I. Title.
PR6062.E9255B4   1989
823'.914—dc20   88-40644

Printed in the United States of America
Set in Melior

To my mother Philippa Murrell,
my father Norman Levy
and Hoôvés from, amongst other places, Lebanon

My mother was the ice-skating champion of Moscow. She danced, glided, whirled on blades of steel, pregnant with me, warm in her womb even though I was on ice. She said I was conceived on the marble slab of a war memorial, both she and my father in their Sunday best; I came into being on a pile of corpses in the bitter snows of mid-winter. Afterwards they bought themselves a cone full of *ponchiki*, doughnuts dripping with fat and sprinkled with powdered sugar, and ate them outside the Kursk railway station, suddenly shy of the passion that had made them search for each other so urgently under all those clothes. On my fifth birthday, my father stole a goose. He stuffed it into the pocket of his heavy overcoat and whizzed off on his motorbike, trying to stop it from flying away with his knees. We ate it that evening, and as I put the first forkful into my mouth he tickled me under the chin and said, 'This does not exist, understand?' I did not understand at the time, especially as my mother stuffed a pillow full of the feathers for me, and soaked the few left over in red vegetable dye to sew on to the skirt of her skating costume.

When my parents died, I was sent to the West at the age of twelve by my grandmother, survivor of many a pogrom and collector of coffee lace handkerchiefs. She said it was for the best, but I think she just wanted to enjoy her old age without the burden of yet another child to look after. I was to stay with a distant uncle in

London. When I asked my grandmother why he had left Russia she whispered, 'Because he is faithless,' and busied herself wrapping little parcels of spiced meat from Georgia for me to take on the ship. Her letters were written on torn sheets of brown paper, three lines long and usually the same three lines in a different order; short of breath as always.

In London, where women were rumoured to swim in fountains dressed in leopardskin bikinis, I unpacked my few clothes, books, photographs, parcels of meat, and wept into the handkerchief my grandmother had pressed into my hand, embroidered in one scarlet thread with my name ... L.A.P.I.N.S.K.I.

The Poet smells of cashew nuts and cologne. She drinks tea from a transparent cup of cheap rose-coloured glass and says, 'This is the age of the migrant and the missile, Lapinski. In some ways you could say our time has come.' She laughs and her gold teeth rattle. Her hands are raw from making frozen hamburgers which is her job. Every morning a coach takes The Poet and other workers to an industrial estate on the outskirts of the city, clutching bags full of shoes to change into, hand-creams and hairnets. 'Exile is a state of mind.' She taps her wide forehead.

Tonight I will cook for the Poet a stew my grandmother taught me called *Bigos*. She watches me put cabbage, rabbit, fungi, lilac, mushrooms, prunes, honey, red wine, salt and peppercorns into a pot.

'We on the meatbelt, Lapinski, blood under our fingernails, are not in a factory on the edge of the motorway, we are somewhere quite different. We are decorating our bedrooms, cleaning the house, making up conversations that will probably never be spoken, on a mountain, writing a book, trying out a new mascara, making plans for children, or for the future which is one day, at most one week, ahead. I myself am alone on the shores of the Black Sea coast or sitting under a fig tree in the paradise of Adam and Eve. If you were to count the thousands of miles between us as machines hum and our fingers linger on control buttons, you could cover the universe. We take ourselves through borders of every kind and carry no passport.

'I know women who work in their sleep and wake when the bell goes, women who sing lullabies, laments and pop songs in time with the machine, women who unknown to themselves make sculptures from meat, the burgers take on the shape of their thoughts; I have seen great pyramids of thought sail across stainless steel into another life. My good friend emigrated from the gasworks of her home town, via detours of all kinds, to the meatbelt. She threads shells through her long black hair – in the tea-break she says she can hear the sea and swallows two spoonfuls of a thick expectorant for her imaginary cough. Sometimes she can see a flock of birds fall into the meatmound and who am I, Lapinski, to disagree. Her fingernails are the colour of Portuguese oranges, defying the cardboard pallor of meatbelt life; when she was a child she waded through a kitchen swamped with spilt milk, now she paints her nails and dips them in the spilt stuff of her life. We have displaced our selves, banished ourselves. We are in exile.'

The sulphurous light of the city glows on The Poet's fingertips. She has carried sacks of tea on her head through plantations of hazelnut and tobacco in the burning late morning sun. At five she sold gum and matches in Eastern villages. At seventeen she cut off her beautiful hair and unlike Samson found strength in the birth of her strong neck. In the slum cities of Northern Europe she lost her health. Coffee cups in greasy cafés offered her dark and difficult visions. And then she lost her mind. She lost her self in the architectural, rational, cultural, political, anatomical structures of Northern European cities and began to vibrate with confusion and pain. She turned inwards and lay in the damp crease of her pillow for twenty-eight days and nights.

4

The sound of police sirens replaced the song of lottery callers, chestnut sellers, canaries and laughter. In her dreams she became a stone, eroded and reshaped by the tides, on the telephone she tried to talk to her mother but found she no longer had a language they both understood.

She held on to the bloody threads of each day, invisible with hundreds of other foreign workers, the brown underbelly of the city, some broken, some brave, but always dreaming, writing letters home, thinking of loved ones, hoping for better times. She survived on odd jobs, cleaning, sewing in sweat shops, looking after other women's children. It was at this time that The Poet mistressed the skill of metamorphosis. She learnt she had to become many selves in order to survive. Through observation, study and meditation she taught herself to change from one self to another, from one state to another. If she had no identity she would have many identities; she learnt she was engaged in a war and saw how those who are confused and in pain or have some secret sorrow of their own, bring out an instinct in others who refuse to acknowledge the possibility of this pain in themselves, to crush, humiliate and hurt. The Poet refused to be crushed.

She waited for the storm inside her to be over. And when it was, in the parts that were torn, she planted sunflowers. She finished her cleaning, bought bread and dates, sat on benches in city parks looking at children scuff their knees in cement.

Chewing the white unbleached flour of the bread she liked best, she decided that the word justice did not mean law and order, and the word opportunity did not mean organised human misery. And as she swallowed the bread she also swallowed the humility of being a confused human being; devoted herself obsessively to understanding her condition and thus the condition of

5

others. 'Lapinski,' she croaks, eating an iced bun, for she is no exotic, 'I have been a foolish casualty, a bitten fruit.'

Tears trickle down the veins of her brown arm.
In her eyes, whole continents seem to flicker.

It is true she turns her male lovers into swine.
It is true she rides over corn and heads of grasses.
These are merely images.
She is a poet.

'Please forgive me ... please don't hit me ... please forgive me ... please ... please... please ... please ... please ... please ... please.' It is a woman's voice, breathless and monotonous, and cutting through her, the smoky drawl of a cowboy on television saying 'Y'know ... it could be'. I run upstairs and bang on the door with both fists, cigar in my mouth, 'Please ... please ... please' getting louder as I bang again and ash falls down the front of my summer dress. The man who lives there opens the door, first a little and then wider; tears stream from his eyes into a little pot of pink yoghurt clasped to his chest. 'Hello Lapinski,' he says. We stare at each other and all the time, she, the woman is saying 'Please don't hit me ... please don't'. He smiles, 'She comes in three sizes,' and points to a doll, five-foot-long, lying in front of the flickering television, yellow plastic skin, black hair and slanting eyes. 'Just taming the savage,' he says.

As I turn to go he shouts, 'Lapinski you're a cunt. Don't go away ... I'm only relaxing. Do you know my dolly can eat chips and talk at the same time?' All I can see are the black holes of his nostrils and mouth. 'Come in Lapinski, have a beer, got some paté from the deli ... why does it bloody rain in June? ... I've got an eye infection dammit ... let's go stomp at The Savoy ... I'll pay. C'mon Lapinski put your gladrags on it's party time ... tills are ringing ... corks are popping ... mortgage gone up another sixty quid a month ... you help make an Eden and then you can't afford to live in it ... got a fucking skin disease on my elbow ... do you know my compact discs are self-destructing themselves?'

The sound of a piano playing in some hidden part of the city drifts ghost-like through the walls. A strange, ecstatic sound; fragile and triumphant and full of bones. The Poet wipes her eyes on a corner of my tablecloth. 'Perhaps the modern tragedy, Lapinski, is that we weep and do not know what we are weeping for. This is quite different from catharsis.' She suddenly throws back her head and roars with laughter; her gold teeth rattle and my cat stares into her mouth with wonder. 'Today I saw a band of clowns in the street, banging drums, dancing, red noses and baggy trousers. They were shouting "Join the community church ... join today ... Jesus enjoyed a good joke ... Jesus liked to laugh too" and they gave out free balloons to passers-by, who were desperate to laugh and so they did. They didn't know what they were laughing at, except they wanted to be happy. A man said to me, "I've got a red nose, too much Guinness ... and I always wear baggy trousers but everyone thinks I'm a very serious person."'

We have finished our stew and I am polishing The Poet's boots. She has only one pair and they have to last. My cat loves The Poet. They watch fat moths circle the lamp and when I hear bird noises I don't know which of the two is making them. They have long conversations I don't understand. I pass her the gleaming boots – my father taught me to polish my school shoes every morning in the special way an icon maker from Yalta taught him – and tell her about the ice-cream man at the corner of the market. He shouts 'Get yer Cornettos here Ladies and Gents and dwarfs and sycophants and piss-stained nihilists and ruddy-cheeked ruralists and podgy little alchemists, get yer Cornettos here, like the Italians don't do it, we're all Europeans now.'

The Poet grudgingly admires her boots (the icon maker was a vain man and made sure the tricks he passed on would be admired),wraps a shawl around her shoulders, pins it with a glistening brooch. 'I'll be off, Lapinski, I can see from that glint in your bleary eyes you want to light your second cigar of the evening and summon a few demons. Oh don't deny it ... don't deny it ... like all people who feel uncomfortable in an uncomfortable world you want to make a map. Well let me tell you it is difficult to make a map in splintered times when whole worlds and histories collide.' She kisses me on the cheek and says goodbye to my cat with her eyes, which are turquoise tonight. 'When I first met you, Lapinski, you were attempting to brew vodka from peach stones ...' Small and bright and certain against the night sky, she walks in the direction of the zoo. As she turns the corner, she looks like a beast of burden. A llama. An animal that survives in harsh climates. Hunted for meat, milk, wool, dung.

Rain falls from a luminous sky on the broken wing of a Chinese umbrella, and under it a woman walks through the heart of London, with fast little steps in the dir-ection of the hospital. She thinks she can hear voices, maybe from the cocktail bar where a young entrepreneur in sunglasses talks feverishly, breath quickening like an eroticised mercenary planning a raid, pointing to his 'joybox', a Ferrari parked out-side. She says to the boy leaning against the wall, a little ivory skull glued to the toe of his shoe, 'It's happy

8

hour and my friend is dying. I have to find the hospital.'
He gives her a cigarette which she lights, balancing
her broken umbrella

On your old breast, dear
My permed head I'll rest, dear

wipes the rain out of her eyes and stares into his with an
expression he cannot meet. 'Don't worry about me. I'm
raging with grief. We must treat the dying like kings you
know.' She looks into the window of the bar where two
waiters, blond hair gelled and parted immaculately in
the middle, serve pink champagne and langoustines;
skin incandescent, they glide from table to table carrying pecan pie and crème caramel on the dip of their
wrists, the backs of their long necks shaved in symme-
trical sculptures. The blondest waiter of all gives a
customer a small pair of metal pliers to crack the claws
of his lobster. The woman looks at the boy again, smiles
a ravishing smile, adjusts the lemon silk of her best suit
and says, 'It's all a wilderness, lobster or no lobster.' She
crosses the road and, blinded by the rain, walks straight
into the headlights of the growling Ferrari.

Lapinski is a shameless cunt. I don't know what accent she's wearing today because it changes like the English weather, but I do know she swings her lies, attitudes, hips, cheap cotton and broken reading glasses like pendulums to con and confuse normal people like myself. She makes me feel weird under my suntan. Her eyes have this faraway look in them but that's only a trick; they gore into your ribs and crack them just when you think you've impressed her. She's a cunt.

When she comes to see me upstairs, something I try hard to avoid, I have to spray my flat with a lavender aerosol because she stinks. I think it's the stench of ... otherness. Or it could be because she seals the soles of her flat brown shoes with donkey dung – or so she says. I put newspaper down when she walks in just in case there's some truth in it. It's as if she's been places I never want to be – I am frightened by what she asks of me, not in words, but by insinuation. I do my best not to take a swipe at the cunt's neck because she sometimes brings me frozen hamburgers some mate gives to her; I think she rubs garlic under her fingernails – I have to rush to the fridge, grab a beer and gargle with it to get a hold on things. Don't ever expect a simple answer to a simple question from Lapinski. She doesn't know how to talk straight. If you ask her if she likes dogs (I have a terrier) she says 'only curried' and guffaws behind her hand. She's not very well off, got a job cooking in a café for foreign people. I tell her to write everything she spends

10

in a little book so she'll know where she is. But no, she looked at me as if I had suggested she slit her wrists.

I want to be master of my own fuck-ups. My dad was the last blacksmith in our town; he worked eleven hours a day, as a welder. When I was young my mother still had to ask the butcher for bones for the dog and then make us broth with them. He wrote songs about things that happened to him in his life, the everyday struggles of people he knew, thoughts and feelings that went through his head while in the dark with fire and metal. He sang them in the pub dressed in a suit the colour of granite. Well I don't want to be a stone — there's too much blood in it, too many late night tearful conversations about how to get by in it — too many fucking dog bones in it. Thoughts and feelings won't buy me a Jacuzzi. I prefer the wine bar. In the city, as long as you're generating revenue, bringing in the money, you can be an Extra Terrestrial and no one will blink — it's what you're worth that matters. When I go back to see my mum I sometimes catch her looking at me as if I am a complete stranger; her eyes settle on my white suit like a half-starved fly — I feel stripped in front of her large stupid body, shuffle about the house trying to find words that will make her like me. She gave me some runner-beans from the garden and I threw them out of the window on the motorway.

I have bought myself a new toy. It's called The Revenger — a compact disc that I slip into the dashboard of my Nissan whenever I feel like relaxing. When you press the button you hear the sound of machine-gunfire as you crawl from red light to red light in the rush hour. Yesterday I had the gun belting out and saw a tart waiting on the kerb. Red fishnet tights and blonde ponytail; she made me tremble so I wound down the window. She looked beautifully shocked, it wiped the snarl off her Max Factor lips. I wanted her lips. She ran

11

away – did she really think I'd fill her lovely soft belly with bullets? I followed her for half a mile down the road and when I caught up with her fishy legs said, 'What's your name?'

'Tremor.'

'Well Tremor, you make me tremble, how about a massage?'

The thought of a massage during a massacre, rattttttttta-tatatata ... oooh ... ratatataratataratatatata ... oh ... appealed. Like perfume in the trenches, or pristine peach satin under the rags of a whore in Tokyo where I sometimes do business. We had good sex on the back seat, with the engine running so I could keep the machine-gun firing. Her red tights lay like a puddle of blood on the floor.

I take orders to help shape the world's economy, so she can take orders from me. She said I hurt her, I said I pay to hurt her. I don't like them with stretch marks on their stomachs – it's a turn off to think of tarts as mothers. When she put the money in her handbag I saw she had a little plastic duck in it, the sort babies float in their bath. The next morning her hair was all over the seat cover.

Lapinski's cat is almost as vile as she is. She calls it, how do you say it, K.R.U.P.S.K.A.Y.A. No wonder he's nearly as far gone as his mistress. I think Bill is a reasonable name for a tom. The other day that cunt of a cat bit my terrier. On the ear. I kicked it down the stairs and bathed Duke's ear with Dettol. She talks rubbish all night with her friends and smokes disgusting little cigars from Cuba – they arrive for her every month in the post in a little wooden box – I can smell them upstairs and have complained twice. She swore at me in Russian through the black stumps of her teeth – her breath makes me cry.

I was buying an electric blanket in a department store

and there was Lapinski turning out her purse to buy a lipstick. A fucking expensive lipstick in a gold case – yet her cardigan's got holes in the elbow and she had to walk home because she didn't have the bus-fare. She cupped it in her hands like a little frog, skipping over the lines of the pavement. It's probably blue.

Maybe it's the Muzac coming in through the window, someone playing the piano, tonight I feel a bit down – have been feeling like this for some time now. Perhaps I should dismember the telephone or something. It's fucking unfair – I don't think patriots should get depressed. The doctor has given me some pale pink pills, which was thoughtful of him because they match my tie.

I'll tell you something about Lapinski. When she gets a gas bill, she writes all over it with a thick black felt tip, THIS DOES NOT EXIST, and sends it to the gas board. Her eyebrows meet in the middle.

Dear Lapinski,

In the mellow autumnal breeze I had a farcical chase after your lipstuck Rizla which got blown about and nearly lost. But I'm going to save it until we are next alone when I shall offer it to you wrapped around something appropriately aphrodisiacal.

Freddie

I have summoned my first love demon and he has answered my call. This is no act of the supernatural, more to do with the art of suggestion. I kissed the transparent skin of a Rizla, thinking of the cold wars we raged on each other's skin, tucked it behind Krupskaya's ear and watched her disappear into the night. She is the Messenger Of Broken Dreams. These errands keep her fit and sleek. I journeyed from the iron curtain to the black Venetian blinds of a Western man's bedroom, and learnt love alone will not smash the atom.

We are walking on damp cement. Hand in hand. I wear a dazzling emerald dress. He tells me every time he makes an inspired brushstroke on canvas he hears the voice of Salvador Dali whisper *Ole!* and last night, which he spent without me, he found three snails on his hot-water bottle. At his studio we eat rice with red hot pepper. 'I am tinged with genius . . . and that paint-

14

ing there . . . ' he points to a large canvas propped up against the wall, 'glistens with obscure clarity.' His long lidded eyes settle on my body like the Inquisition. Light shines on his short corn-stubble hair, his large hooked nose, his apricot body and thick lips. 'Charisma depends almost violently on beauty,' he says, stroking the thin emerald cloth on my breast. I am pretending to look at a small painting of a mermaid holding a hammer and sickle in her hand. His fingers make little ripples under my dress and all the time the sun is shining on him. I begin to sting and smart. The red hot pepper on his fingers and the possibility of love, yearned and dreamt for, the possibility of great love for ever and ever two inches away from my singing heart.

In a caravan surrounded by geese and nettles, we eat a selection of cheeses. Goat, cow, sheep. We drink red wine. I am thinking this is the Last Supper because Freddie has been sleeping with a woman who plays the violin and I am upset. He bought her a bottle of lime pickle which seems to me a very intimate thing to do; it suggests he knows what she likes to taste. Just as my mother and father slipped away from me in a tram crash on a bridge where, months after their death, I'd stand looking down at the water below and imagine I could see them floating – a shoe, my mother's green skirt, my father's heavy overcoat – floating down and away from me; so I feel his love slipping away from me, and into her. I want him to declare his love so I can give him mine; instead he looks out hungrily, loots other sexual scenarios, comes to me changed, and fumbling and shy we have to find where we last left off, who we were before. Now he strokes my neck while geese run about the field and wind rocks the caravan. It is late autumn and loss is in the air, I am too familiar with its sensation; it haunts me in dreams and at unexpected moments, brushing my hair or waiting for a bus. He says, 'Where'd

15

ya lose your heart?' I look down and see the gold heart I wear on a chain round my neck has fallen off. I search the floor of the caravan, hand clutching the place my heart once was, my very very precious heart, given to me by my grandmother that day she pressed the hand-kerchief into my hand. He comments on the blue black colours in my hair, yawns, smiles, stretches, says, 'You know, a lot of fashionable and influential image-makers would say that gold heart is naff. You have nothing to lose but your chain.'

On the beach we look at each other through a hole in a stone. He sucks all the green from my eye. He is a reader of colour, texture, signs, of the space between things, of light and dark and gesture. He stands outside himself and observes. He is interested in sensation. He is sensual. He admires me. I say, 'When I was twelve I ate spiced meat from Georgia and sipped Pepsi-Cola.' He likes bizarre juxtapositions and contrives them in his paintings, his love play, his clothes, his conversation. I love him with as much protest as I can muster. I make him cry. His tears intrigue him. He stands outside his tears and sculpts meanings with them. He makes me cry. He is bewildered. He stands outside my tears, and watches them in relation to the window frame and straw chair.

On the beach we stare at each other through a hole in a stone. We suck all the fear from each other's eye and then we look away. He sings

In a fishing boat
when the light turned blue
you burgled me
and I burgled you

We are East and West looting each other.
We hang a washing-line across the room. It is draped

16

with feathers and rags and flowers and bones found on walks, the insides of clocks and cars and TV sets. It is the Berlin Wall. We declare an uneasy peace. War is more sexy. We are afraid to make peace. We sharpen our weapons. We pride ourselves on our weapons. If we were to make a peace treaty, to disarm, we would have to come to the conference table naked and we are afraid of our nakedness. He falls in love with someone else to punish me.

I am thinking of his mother. How she once told me she was merely alone and not abandoned. He says, 'Your dizzy eyes.' I am thinking of his father. How in the war he brought his girlfriend home to live in his wife's house and how she, who is merely alone and not abandoned, washed her husband's girlfriend's clothes in the bath. Peering at the labels. Good clothes. And how his father (after he had abandoned his wife) got a disease that made him shake so severely he could no longer play cricket in his immaculate whites on England's green killing fields. He says, 'I have the body of Jesus Christ and the soul of Lenin. Are you going to crucify me then with the curl of your lips?' No I am not. I am going to abandon you. He cleans his paintbrush with a rag, feeling abandoned and exhilarated.

'In fact, Lapinski,' says Freddie, in his mellow autumnal backyard, waving the lipstuck Rizla, 'dressed as you are in creams and blues you look like a gentle bruise.

'Forgive me I am shaking. There are roots poking through the walls of my flat, through the floor and through the ceiling, and I thought of you because you always said you had no roots. Perhaps you dropped a few seeds all those years ago. Yesterday, Lapinski, I stole a statue of Freud from a London park and carried him home. And I danced for him, swinging my hips, until I became paralysed, First my neck, but that was okay, it was interesting, I could still move the rest of my body. Then my arms froze in a great O shape above my head, wrists turned in on themselves, but my legs still danced on. I explored the family trees in my joints, muscles, bones, and then I became totally paralysed ... statue-like in front of the statue Freud. He watched me and then he spoke, asked for cocaine, books, a cigar, a florentine from a Viennese pâtisserie. I asked him whether my paralysis was real or a state of mind, but he was silent and staring. Staring at my penis, so I got an erection, and that became frozen too, which is to say, Lapinski, what am I to do with this lipstuck Rizla? Am I to attempt trans-meditational coitus with you – Lapinski who dropped her seed somewhere in me, like the male fish who carries eggs in his mouth?

'Lapinski, I have desires I don't understand. I dreamt I was a torturer. I made women do things they didn't want to do, made them squeal with pain and ecstasy, tied them up and beat them and fucked them in their most secret places. I woke up sweating, it was terrible and wonderful, and as women walked the streets on the way to buy milk or cigarettes I thought ... it could be her, she's the one. I will take her back to my chamber of ferocious fumbling, my chamber of a hundred hidden orifices and she will enjoy it. I will make her queen and I will be king. Lapinski, I want to repent for the times I kicked you in your soft stomach, metaphorically you understand, I am not a brute in that sort of way ... I do not have steel tips on my boots ... I want you to be strong and brave and beautiful but I also want to crush you ... want you to be wild and spontaneous but I also want to tame and domesticate you. I want you to want me but I don't want you. Lapinski, I have had many lovers but they do not satisfy. Remember when I

18

deserted you and went off with the woman of the lilies, and the woman with the straw hat, and the woman with the boils, and the woman with the kid gloves, and the woman with the ideas, and the woman whose bones I sucked till the sun disappeared for ever, and the woman who kept Valium in her sugar tin, and the woman in the apple orchard, and the woman of the swamps, and the woman who bit her fingernails until they bled, and the whore in rue Chartreuse, and the woman who ate and ate and then sicked up in gutters and washing-up bowls, and the woman who made necklaces from pistachio nuts, and the woman who wore tattoos instead of clothes, and the woman who smelt of cheese, and the woman who wore knickerbockers to polish her floors, and the woman who cooked curries that made me hallucinate. Well, Lapinski, they were ponds, ponds to drown my feelings of loss and pain, to drown my feeling of disconnectedness. I am trying to confess, Lapinski, I want to paint you who abandoned me, in a room full of light. My woman from Moscow. Oh kiss me here . . . here . . . here . . . Make me better. I want to fill myself up with moments that shimmer, with moments that give me reason to continue . . . but I don't know where to find them.'

He is shaking. Shaking. Freddie is breaking down. He weeps and laughs at the same time. He carries the scent of a thousand women in his armpits, his tears are the jewels they took off, or put on, for him, he is shaking just like his father shook before him, shaking into the moon, lipstuck Rizla spiked on his forefinger. Who will put him together again? Nurses, books, Beethoven, shock machines?

'Lapinski.'

'Yes?'

'I am going to break into the zoo.'

He disappears in the direction of the zoo, where once

19

in a while wolves can be heard howling just as men have been rumoured to howl in forests and phone boxes, in snow storms and bars. Howling into the culture like maggots in an apple.

It is the age of the Great Howl.

No woman has ever fallen in love with me.

I once fell in love with a police woman but in the end she married a PC from her station. I liked the glint in her eye, and the streaks in her hair. And she was bloody brave. Last time I saw her, before she got engaged, she said they were training her up to drive a tank. I said, 'Is there going to be a coup then?' She gave me a mean look that made my penis stir, but I think it put her off me. You make do with what you've got, unlike that cunt Lapinski who reckons the world owes her a living just for thinking. Last Sunday I went to a pub on the borders of West Sussex with Peter and Fiona from the office. We had Chicken Kiev. And then I had this dream that Lapinski and all her mates walked into the pub and as they went to the bar to order I took out a machine-gun and shot them all down, one by one. They fell in slow motion on top of each other, scattering books and feathers, junk jewellery, notebooks, turquoise stockings, bicycle pumps, children's toys and dried flowers which smelt of something that made my hand on the trigger shake. The owner of the pub came up to me and said, 'Glad you did that, this is an *Olde Worlde Pub* and we want to squeeze out people like that. They've got no respect for bricks and mortar, they want to storm our paradise, they are the buffalo. Pick 'em out and shoot 'em. They are the slow-footed among us, if we were to slow down what would we think about in the time it took to put one foot in front of the other − if we were to think like them what would the shape of our settees and garden furniture be? Could we still squirt sperm into geisha's bums or would we have to browse in libraries? They are spirits from a dying world knotting our hair in sleep we worked hard to buy.'

For the last three nights I've heard Lapinski crying through the early hours. I don't know what's happened and I don't like to ask because my dream of shooting her is still fresh in my mind. When I see her walking to work I see another picture of her, face down on the pub floor, blood pouring out of the holes in her back — like one of those abstract sculptures I bet the cunt loves. Her cat *Krupskaya* made a jump for Duke yesterday. Duke gets annoyed and tries to bite her head off. So what does *Krup* do? Run away? Not on your life. She jumps on top of his back and sticks there like a pot of glue. Duke begins to run about in circles and whine so I have to call Lapinski up. She stomps in leaving mud, or donkey dung, all over my carpet so I have a go despite the fact her eyes are red and swollen. She says, 'I might have mud on the soles of my shoes but at least I don't have it between my ears,' and starts to unstick her cat by promising all sorts of treats, like milk and tuna, and things like that. Duke licked his wounds and growled at her shoes — not that he's ever seen a donkey before. So Lapinski gets the huff, draws on her cigar in a temper, tells me I should have my dog put down and slams the door. I've got a horrible feeling she said I should be put down too. Cunt.

I'm going to give my mum a razor and shaving-cream for her birthday. The poor old dear is growing a beard. I wake up in the mornings in pain. And there's no one to tell.

It is by the mirror, where I practise narcissism, that I summon my second demon. For it is she who wrote me letters of love, written backwards so I had to read them through the looking glass. 'Backwards letters are my escape,' she said.

She is fifteen years old, voluptuous, ribbons and flowers and bits of old lace tangled in her mane of blonde hair; she wears Mexican smocks embroidered with silken greens on crisp white cotton, lips shining, a pot of gloss always at hand so that crumbs stick to her lips. She is full of fury and smells of roses.

'This, Lapinski, is my family.' She points to each of them, '... this is my father who has forgotten how to love; this is my mother who has forgotten how to think; these are my sisters who will all go into the wine trade ... and this ...' she bursts into tears, 'is my life.' The aroma of freshly ground coffee lingers about the house.

She is on holiday with her business tycoon daddy and her sisters. An oily pensive anchovy on the beach, ashamed of her large breasts and little broken finger-nails, surrounded by her father's girlfriends, film cronies, American and English exiles, models, villa owners, local boutique owners and hangers-on, she feels flawed. They swim, eat, arrange barbecues, play backgammon, strip poker, have massages, manicures, sunbathe, swap gossip. She watches them, her mouth tingling with ulcers.

Her fists beat the burning sand.
'I will escape,' she writes.

A glamorous model drapes her long tanned legs over the business tycoon's lap. Gemma stares sulkily at her daddy, who playfully slaps the bottom of the model. The model turns to Gemma. 'We're being nice to each other because I'm filming in the Caribbean soon and we won't see other for too long.' She kisses the tycoon's ears. 'I am a very busy woman, Gemma,' she smiles. Gemma snaps her book shut, and stands up, scattering sand and suntan lotions. *'Your very busy life and very empty mind are what I want to escape from.'* The truth is she doesn't really know what it is she wants to escape from.

Gemma, who will later become The Banker, is seventeen years old; she gives me her cast-offs and I go home to my uncle's with carrier bags stuffed full of shoes and dresses, and Charles Of The Ritz lipsticks. Years later, Freddie, who has a liking for silks and cashmeres, will run his hands slowly down my body, in Gemma's clothes, exploring buttonholes and pleats and the cut of a sleeve. And years later I will look into the mirror and see his tongue inside Gemma's mouth as they writhe about in a bed of flames.

Gemma stamps the floor with her high heels. We fight about money and class and privilege. She cries prettily, passionately, stops, reads me my horoscope, squeals and squeaks 'eeeeeeeeeek', calls me a 'meanie', flicks through magazines, works for hours in the school library. She is brilliant and sharp, asks teachers a

24

hundred questions they cannot answer, shouts in exasperation. She loves me, she says, and asks me to trim her hair with a little pair of blunt scissors. She doesn't like pubs because they are full of 'sad people.' She is afraid of poor people.

After school she buys me a hot chocolate at the bus station. I sip it very slowly and then she finishes it off for me, a chocolate moustache on her immaculate face, waving goodbye and blowing kisses.

The morning after she has finished her Oxbridge entry exams, we sit on a bench eating monkey nuts, feeding pigeons with the shells. Her fingers are covered in ink and all the flowers have fallen out of her hair. She tells me she no longer wants to escape.

At Oxford, military types in swords and spurs swarm around the gardens. Gemma fluffs her hair, glosses her lips and tells a swarthy Italian economist at a cheese and wine party she despises her hall full of simpering ninnies running baths of Avon bubbles and cooking little pans of sensible soup. 'They're so prim.' He smiles, offering her a sausage on a stick. She eats it fast, and guiltily. 'Even a sedate patch of *blue* on the eyelids is considered fast.' He doesn't know what she's talking about, but her cleavage is exciting and she displays it with pride. His suit is dull but well cut, his white shirt starched. She says, closing her eyes and giggling inside, 'I like men in suits.'

Gemma invites him back to her room for water. She drinks pints and pints of it a day because she read in one of her glossy magazines it will make her thin. She shows him a picture of me, in a polka-dot dress. 'This is my friend Lapinski. The dress she is wearing is the same dress her grandmother wore to slaughter chickens to sell in her grocery store in Russia.' The economist nods,

25

fiddling with his cufflinks. 'When Lapinski was five, she collected chicken heads from the yard for her grannie. When I was five, I rode an antique wooden horse in my Hampstead playroom, and wanted to escape. When I was fifteen I escaped into Lapinski's arms. I love her passionately.' The Italian economist leaves immediately. Tomorrow she will dine with a Panamanian economist she met in a Marx lecture. Apparently he is very rich and owns a plantation.

The Panamanian economist and Gemma fondle each other in her single bed. He cups her face in his hands, stares into her eyes, asks her to put some ice on his penis.

'Ice?'

'Yes pleeeeeeeeeeease.'

But the future Banker is intrepid and creeps to the communal kitchens where she finds one of the simpering ninnies brewing cocoa in her nightdress.

'Hello Gemma,' she blinks dozily.

'I'm looking for ice.'

'Ice?'

'I'm very hot.'

They yank out a large jagged slab of ice from the freezer and Gemma trots back to her economist trailing her kimono on the corridor floor.

'Tra la la tra la la la la.'

She throws it on to his penis and, still singing, climbs on top of him.

'Aaaaaaaaaaah.' He comes immediately. The smell of fish fills the room. Wafts between them. It reminds the Panamanian economist of the fish markets in his home town, flies swarming around piles of roe and guts, and the jokes told by men about the whores they'd had the night before. Both attribute the smell to themselves and feel humiliated. Gemma sings 'tra la la tra la la' and sighs. The truth is one of the simpering ninnies put her

26

little slice of cod on to the slab of ice that afternoon, and its juices became one with the ice, and now with the Panamanian economist's juices too. Gemma, wet, fishy, blushing and unsatisfied, sprays the room with Chanel No. 5.

She wears her Cardin suit for her first terrifying tutorial with three boys from Balliol College. The tutor, little black hairs on his knuckles, clenches his knees and taps a fountain pen on the mahogany desk. One of the boys presents a paper called NOTES TOWARDS THE DEVELOPMENT OF A THEORY ON THE RELATIONSHIP BETWEEN MARXISM AND FEMINISM. The tutor and the boys scribble fast little notes on the back of their folders, sometimes nodding, other times frowning, eyebrows raised. Gemma understands nothing, and when the tutor asks her to comment on the paper, bursts into tears. The men do not know what to do with this elegant glossed woman who has a reputation for scorn, strength, savoir-faire, intellect, and is now squealing and squeaking like a plucked chicken behind her jasmine-yellow note pad. 'Seems like *Capital* has been your bedtime reading these last ten years,' she weeps into her cuff. The boy who gave the talk passes her his handkerchief, shuffling his feet in irritation. He has spent long nights working on his paper and wants to discuss it; now this fat, stupid female is blubbering away all his tutorial time. Gemma cries some more and runs out of the room on her pointy heels, clattering down the corridor while the boys discuss alienation.

In the corridor she bumps into Eduardo the Italian economist, who cheers her up by taking her up to his room where he whips up a steamy dish of pasta with clam sauce. While he cooks he tells her he hopes Oxford won't be swamped by 'aliens' like the redbrick

27

universities. They snuggle up together and Gemma falls asleep, waking up with pain that surprises her. She stares at Eduardo and wills him to take it away.

Dear Gemma,

   Thank you for the invitation to the ball. I have a lovely dress with scarlet netting at the bottom like a mermaid's tail. If my grandmother could see me in it she would demand I dive for beluga caviare. The only trouble is my arms and legs are covered in flea bites. Yesterday, I shampooed Krupskaya, my cat, and hope that has put an end to the central committee that debate in her fur. Is it possible for you to meet me at the station? Perhaps we can go for a drink first, I will buy you a pint of water and we can talk. I have been thinking of my mother and sometimes when I cook at the café, big stupid tears fall into the meat and tomatoes. I can't help feeling bad for the poor people who have to eat it – they have sorrows of their own without paying for a stew flavoured with mine.

   Love Lapinski.

Dearest Lapinski,

It is not a good idea to come up for the ball after all. I have promised Eduardo (my Italian economist) that I'll spend the weekend with him, and the thought of you two meeting is not calculated to send warm feelings down my spine. Perhaps you could delay the trip until I find an ideologically correct young man. Eduardo's consciousness is somewhat intractable and I have no hope of bringing him into the bright light of socialist truth. Oh Well. So long as we keeeeeeep kisssssing we don't have to talk much.

Love love love to you sugar plum

Gemma xxxxxxxx

(from a putative member of the ruling class)

In the library which she loves and where she consumes packets of rice crackers, she follows up footnote clues and obscure details on the sociology of political parties.

She thinks about Eduardo.

He is cold, cold, and *dead* inside.

This thought, to her surprise, is very sexy.

'EEEEEEEeeeeeeeeeeeeeeee   eeeeeeeee   ee   e   eee eeeeeeeeeeeee!' Gemma's orgasms are the loudest in hall. The simpering ninnies next door have to put pillows over their heads or run to the bathroom or into each other's rooms. They do not always know whether she is screaming with pleasure or pain. She sounds like a squealing pig and this turns Eduardo on. While he fucks her he tells stories about killing deer on his uncle's farm, other women he has fucked, the professor he thinks is a communist; he bites her nipples and thighs, leaves blue crescent moons all over her white body. Their bed is littered with blood, condoms, chocolate, hair, peanuts, stockings, his leather belt, knickers, cartons of milk, pitta bread, taramasalata, come stains. Gemma discovers she is brilliant at economics, better than Eduardo (he finds all sorts of ways to punish her for this), and has no problem demonstrating the difference between Returns to Scale and 'EEEEEEEEEEEE-EEEEEEEEEEEEEEEEEEEEEEEEEEEEEEEE EEEEEEEE-EEEeeeee' Diminishing Returns to One Factor.

While my children beg on trains, I am paid by disturbed men to let them put a part of their body into a part of my body. What they don't know is they are fucking a ghost. They are fucking a ghost because my spirit and soul are somewhere else. You could say I have lost my self, which poses an interesting philosophical question. If I have lost my self how can I sell my self? The answer is I sell my body in parts, some more expensive than others. I am my own butcher. Most of my customers are businessmen with wives in the counties and shires; they spill a day's worth of wheeling and dealing into me and I receive it like sewage dumped at the bottom of the sea. Some want to beat me, some want me to pretend to love them, others to be violent with me in a way that would be unacceptable anywhere else. Most want me to pretend to be someone I am not. But that's OK, most people spend the whole of their lives pretending to be someone they are not. My names are Tremor, Gina, Ninette, Sam, Tina, Cleopatra, Iris, Suzie, Malibu, Alex, Blondie, Maggie and Stardust.

One customer wanted me to pretend to be his wife in real life – he was part of something called a REGENER-ATION CONSORTIUM and his firm had an open day 'party' where the local people could meet the developers in the flesh, as I have met them, membrane to membrane, many a time before. He bought me a chiffon dress with a daisy print on it and white gloves – and I took the kids, which made him bite his lip with that sharp tooth of his. The whole event smelt of melted cheese. Clowns they'd hired for the day went around banging people on the head with foam rubber hammers and, when the kids threw stones at them, they gave out funny hats with red, white and blue stripes on them — they looked like whip marks on pale English skin. Then the magicians started to take rabbits out of hats, and the rabbits squealed so loudly they drowned the jazz band in the corner. A woman with a broken Chinese umbrella was the only one dancing anyway, twisting her wrists to some music inside herself, while the waiters went around with sausage rolls on silver trays and this bloke whose wife I was shook people by the hand, saying, 'Enjoy yourself — you're in an enterprise zone now,' to which the woman dancing replied, 'The philosopher has got his spoon stuck in the fromage frais.'

The highlight of the event was the free bus-tour around the area they were developing. We all trooped on to the coach and our compère was a woman in pink shorts called Belinda. She talked through a microphone in a squeaky voice, telling us what we were passing, 'This is a waterfront conversion', and the history of the place. The driver kept ignoring her directions (I think he'd got stoned to survive the day), so she would say, 'In the 1920s produce used to be freighted here all the way from Yorkshire,' and where she said you were, you were not — she'd point at the waterfront and it would be the railway station. Or she would say, 'On the left you will see two new wine bars and a boutique,' and it would be a 1950s office block. The driver would be cruising down some high street where the police were patrolling estate agents' shop fronts because of acid being thrown at the windows, and she would tell you it was a car park. Everyone lost all sense of time and place and the old lady sitting behind me said she'd need a guide book to find her way home, all the while Belinda squeaking, 'Instead of Purism we now have Populism,' and my husband muttering to someone who held an oxygen mask in one hand and a cigarette in the other, 'We're restoring the city and packaging is a pretty important consideration in marketing nowadays.' At the end of the day he kissed me on the cheek and said loudly, 'Hope you had a pleasant day out dear – thought it would do you good to see for yourself why I am away from home so much,' and told me he was just off for a jog on the new track they had built where the share index flashes up on a screen as you run. 'We all have so much to look forward to,' he said to the two people left, a boy in a fez wearing a skirt and football boots with I AM THE BEAST THEY CANNOT HANDLE written on his T-shirt, and the woman with the Chinese umbrella finishing off the sausage rolls and singing

sa ra bo ra
ra bo ra sa
sa bo bo sasa

My most recent customer brought his terrier dog with him – it whimpered under the bed for the ten minutes it took. He has a tattoo on his upper arm, an anchor with roses, and underneath the word MOTHER. A lot of men have tattoos with MOTHER written on parts of their body. After he had finished he said, 'Are you alright then Duke?' I don't know why he doesn't fuck his dog for free. Sometimes he pays me extra to fuck in his car to the sound of rattling guns – but I survive all the wars they rage on me. And I have never gone gently into those long nights of mothers, flowers, aftershave, tears, spunk, sweat, beer and skin.

My son has discovered he is good at making things grow. He's got green eyes and green fingers, and he's hit on the idea of growing roses in the window-box to sell on trains. Despite the lead from the traffic they are blooming blooming blooming. We bought everything together, the soil and seeds, read how to plant them, the light and position and how much water; I watch his seven-year-old body bent over them every morning and feel full of hope for him.

Yesterday, when we were having supper together, my youngest daughter started to sing

Lavender's blue, dilly dilly
Lavender's green
When I be king
You shall be queen

and we all joined in because we know the song has a special meaning for her. She had two budgies, one called Lavender Blue and the other Lavender Green and they died seven months ago. She told me she'd buried them in the park. But yesterday she said, 'Mum, you know how I buried Lavender Blue and Lavender Green that day ... ' and I said, 'Yeah,' and she said, 'Well I didn't.' My mouth was full of baked beans; I spat them out and stared at her. 'What do you mean?' She stood up, perfectly natural and serious, took her pencil box off the sideboard – one of those wooden ones with a sliding top – and, in front of us all, opened it up. There was Lavender Blue. Just lying there like he's having a blissful night's sleep, except his eyes have rotted. She said, 'I put scent on him.' By this time we had all spat out our baked beans and I said to her, 'Where's Lavender Green then?' She shook her head and said she couldn't remember where she had put him. Her brother and sister began to sing

35

Call up your men, dilly dilly
Set them to work
Some shall make velvet
And some shall make shirts

giggling and nudging her until she gave up and told us
to be quiet while she led the way to my bedroom,
smiling at me to see if I was cross. She crawled under
my bed, her little feet sticking out, and reached for an
old shoe. Nestled in there, wrapped in tissue, was
Lavender Green. She said, 'I put scent on him.'

So this little corpse has been lying on its back,
scented, under my customers for seven months now.
Just like me. I would hate my daughters to have my life.
To see the dark side of the moon of a man like I do. I
would rather they grieved in their own way for the
things they have loved and lost, than like me, become a
kind of refugee searching for an identity to describe my
self to my self. I do not know where I have buried all I
have loved and lost.

Tonight, Jupiter, the God of animal metamorphoses, rules the stinking animal pits in the zoo. Urine and shit trickle into a ring of rage, a ring of starless moonless night.

The rage of animals imprisoned by a clumsy culture.

The smell of garlic oozes into the air, wafts over from the gorilla cages; the sweat of images behind the eyes, under the skin and in the cracks of lips. In the reptile house a python feeds on twelve dead rats. A mongoose eats a scorpion without removing its sting. The elephants lift up their trunks and bellow out, over London, and the refuse trucks collecting the shedded skin of the day gone by to take to incinerators and burn.

Freddie lies on his belly outside the llama cage. He is covered in mud and worms, and the llama, all soft curves and very golden, bids him to speak. 'Where are your words?'

'I am unemployed,' says Freddie. 'That is to say I have no place in the scheme of things. No role to put on in the mornings and take off in the evenings. I am of the hungry species and I am alone. A stranger in a familiar land. I have no place to put my head, no thighs even in which to bury my head, no shoulder or lap or concept or cup of happiness or red rose in which to bury my head. No employment of any kind.'

'Unemployed?' says llama. 'Oh come on. There are zillions of jobs for a slut. Why not acccccelerate, put your foot down on that steely pedal, how about a career

37

in the citeeee? Penetrate the city like a hungry blue worm, find the worm in your self and become it. Innovation breeds success and success breeds delicious hungers of all kinds. How you do enjoy your pain, Freddie!

'Go into international finance, become a dynamic sales manufacturer in a high-growth computer company, become a senior sales consultant, a marketing manager, a business analyst for a billion-dollar corporation, become a technical support analyst with BUPA membership and relocation expenses, relocate your ambitions, relocate your self from here to there and beyond. Relocate your head and you will find a zillion homes for it.'

'But ... ' and Freddie weeps, 'I don't know HOW to become those things. I don't know what will become of me at all. I am lost llama lost and lost and lost. How do I begin to become a corpuscle in a corporation?'

'OH SLUTTY SON be result motivated! Think of those mortgage subsidies and executive benefits. Be a self-starter, be profit-motivated. Learn to Be. You need enthusiasm, no one invests in depression. Try harder and you will get the right package because you are the right person. But first you must emigrate. Pack up your head and heart and will and move to a different landscape. It is called, let these words shimmer above your poor ruined head ... The Real World.' The llama giggles.

'Oh ... llama ... I defend The Naked Truth Of Dreams.'

'The Naked Truth Of Dreams? Oh Freddie. You are indeed a funny little thing. A funny little flower.'

Freddie buries his toes in the mud and watches two apes groom each other. The giant panda stares out into nothing, melancholy as she chews a strip of sugar cane; mosquitoes wail above her head.

'What dreams are you talking about, poor Freddie?'
Llama's eyes widen.
'I used to have dreams, llama. But I've lost them. I search in gardens for them. It would seem it is a family I want. Do you know male seahorses give birth? They have labour pains, curl their tails around a plant stem, bend backwards and forwards with the pain, with severe cramps, until they empty their pouches. I have severe cramps and no baby. I want a baby.'

'You digress,' says llama, digging the earth with her hooves. Digging the British soil up. 'We are talking of Enterprise. Why not have a baby syndicate? If you want a family there are

hardware families
and
software families.'

'What is there left for me to become if not a father? I will take my children to swing in parks, to swimming pools, rock them to sleep, mash them bananas ... '

'Freddie, I fear you are talking about a Family in the bigger sense of the word. You are perhaps talking of sisterhood? brotherhood?' Llama sticks out her tongue to catch an invisible fly.

Freddie's tears fall like pebbles on to the mud. 'I don't know what I want, llama. I would like to be happy.'

'Poor Freddie. You have lost your way. Lost your silky slutty senses. I confess I am rather fond of people who have lost their way.'

'Aw, fuck off, llama ,' weeps Freddie, 'I just want to be loved.'

Llama scratches her ear.

'You want to be loved? Ah. Aaaaaaaaaah. But can you love, Freddie? Remember the woman with the lilies, how she sang for you, how you became a flower in her bouquet, and how you ruined her? Not because she was stupid but because she was brave. I see her now with your daughter, her little love child. It is she who fries her potatoes, pushes her on swings, buys her crayons and paper and plasticine. Your daughter makes green and blue daddies in front of the television. And the woman with the violin who mothered your son, bought him plimsolls, introduced him to The Story, took him to libraries and cinemas, played tunes for him on her fiddle to send him to sleep. And where were you Freddie? Here with me searching for your head? Wanting children you already have? You were drinking brandy in an art gallery when her waters were breaking and she was trying not to drown. And you went home with Mary Magdalene to wrap your soul in her hair, and while you screamed on top of her your child screamed coming out of another. Excuse me, Freddie, I have a stone in my paw.

'If you cannot love, Freddie, do something radical with your condition, service systems that manufacture sorrow instead. In this way you will hate well rather than love badly.'

A baby chimpanzee pulls at the long black nipples of its mother who has her arm crooked to hold its head; her mouth opens and closes in time with the suckling.

'Llama,' whispers Freddie, 'I have tried to change. I know indeed that human nature is an invented thing. I have tried to reinvent myself but confess I am reluctant to give up the little power I have on this earth. Yes, I am weeping again, I don't know when I'll ever stop or why. It seems there is no longer any grass to dream on. I hurt, llama, and I want someone to make me better. Have I really missed out on my children? I try to dream about women who have loved me but they refuse to appear. I want peace of mind. I want some peace but I don't know what it is. Anything to get rid of this . . . stuff . . . inside me, this fear, these tears, this shaking. I would shoot guns and thrust bayonets through flesh to distract me from myself; I would whip, torture, wrestle, drive racing-cars over cliffs to distract me from myself; jump from helicopters, throw hand grenades to distract me from myself; I would march right left right screaming orders in my throat, obeying orders in my throat, to distract me from myself. I would build muscles I never knew I had, to distract me from myself.'

Llama shuts her honey eyes. Her belly rises and falls. It is as if her breath is a gentle wind; it makes the salt on Freddie's cheeks smart and sting. He notices three cards pinned to her cage. The blue card says History, the white card says Behaviour and the pink card says Medical Record.

10.15	Specimen sounds as if she is coughing slightly.
10.40	Specimen vomited a little fluid.
1.10	Specimen restless.
1.40	Specimen has stomach contractions.
2.00	Specimen lying on back with periodic grunts.
2.30	No change in position.
4.10	Specimen throwing her weight against cage bars.
	Seems agitated.
5.10	Specimen shows evidence of some nasal discharge.
5.30	Specimen shows no reaction to noise.
5.45	Specimen refusing food. Eyes shut.
6.00	Specimen runs and falls over on occasions.
7.00	Specimen co-ordination much improved. Saliva around mouth.
	If no change tomorrow take swab.

'Are you ill, llama?' whispers Freddie.

'Are you ill, Freddie?' whispers llama.

'I think I might be very sick, yes, llama. And I cannot afford health.'

Llama smiles, or she could be in pain. 'The only freedom you have, Freddie, is the freedom to be sick. I am no barbarian. I do not come from your country. By a strange set of circumstances I find myself locked up here. How strange it is I find myself teaching you the hieroglyphics of your culture.'

'Oh God,' Freddie howls. 'Oh God.' He scoops up mud and begins to eat it. 'Llama ... perhaps ... you could ... could just bite my artery here. Put me out of my misery.'

'My teeth are blunt,' says llama. 'The zoo keeper filed them down.'

Freddie lies on his back and listens to the owls hoot into the night.

The lion shuts his eyes. He dreams he is lying in the shade of the acacia trees. The sound of that strange piano from an invisible part of the city dips in and out of the pictures behind his eyes. To the lion it is the wind. In his dream he prowls over to a nearby water hole only to find it on fire. Fire over water. The smell of burning flesh wafts over the long bleached grasses. He opens his eyes. The grass has turned to cement.

Outside the zoo, a young boy and girl in their early twenties sit against a wall. A tattoo on their upper arms says THE INNOCENTS. Their eyes are closed as they sing in harmony

And then the knave begins to snarl
And the hypocrite to howl;
And all his good friends show their private ends
And the eagle is known from the owl

They both think about hitching to a forest where they spent two summers and remember one particular tree.

A pine tree. But the forests have been blown down in a small hurricane, the night the Stock Exchange crashed, and no one is planting things any more. They remember the evergreen of this tree and how it collected water on the tips of its needles; they would take it in turns to rip off their clothes and one of them stand under the tree while the other shook it by the trunk as it bowed this way and that way and little drops of water sprinkled the head of who ever stood under it.

The Innocents open their eyes. They feel the wall behind their backs and take deep breaths of the city's air.

Dear Lapinski,

It is so HOT here in New York. I'm sitting naked at the table writing this. Sweat keeps dripping on to the page. Eduardo and I are now married. He works in Rome and flies over to see me at weekends. Instead of diamonds he brings me sachets of sugar and salad cream from the aeroplane – I have a whole closet full of them.

As words have never been our strong point we sit in front of the television flicking the remote control and eating our way through cartons of popcorn. The wedding was wonderful. When I cut the cake I cut my finger too and blood dripped all over the icing the Italian baker had taken three months to make into the columns of the opera-house. It was OK. Eduardo has always found blood sexy and sucked my finger for the photographer. My lips are covered in blisters. It always happens before I have an appraisal of my performance by the company. This is difficult to write. I feel very far away from you, both in experience and distance. Last time we met you looked at me as if all the worst predictions you made for me at fifteen had come true. More sweat. Blanche would have worn a floral wrapper but otherwise it's very Tennessee Williams.

Love Gemma

Gemma has become The Banker; a super-rich money marketeer whose qualities of commercial acumen, aggression, energy, contact ability (most of her colleagues at Oxford), motivation, ego drive and adaptability earn her a salary she will not disclose. She has closed up like a seaflower, her voice on the phone is expressionless and brief; at the hairdresser, under the bright lights, she catches up on sleep. Nights alone are very still and black, she prefers to sleep with people around her. She pays a special consultant to buy and choose furniture for her New York apartment, a mixture of old and new; a telephone from a 1930s Hollywood movie, two chaise-longues from an auction, a Perspex table, a bunch of glass poppies that light up at night, two Magrittes for the white walls, theatre posters from sell-out Broadway musicals, a sculpture made from nails. Her wardrobe is full of navy suits and leather pumps to match, she is a feminine master and long ago threw out the wild Mexican smocks, orchids, glittering shoes of her school days, and camouflaged herself in the discreet colour and cloth of money. Her towelling robe is yellow and so is the bathroom soap; such attention to detail is what the consultant is paid for.

She jokes that she is not complimented on her bone structure any more, but on her bonus structure. Yesterday the blisters on her lips popped. On summer evenings, The Banker sits on her tiny balcony eating artichoke hearts, vitamins, Swiss chocolate and aspirins, watching the Empire State Building twinkle in the distance.

From dawn to dusk she is surrounded by computer screens and telephones. The day starts with a pep talk from the company analyst on the microphone and then she begins selling. In her lunch hour she either has a pregnancy test (she does not want to be pregnant) or eats stuffed bagels on the edge of the desk watching the screens. She is capitalism's astrologer; instant reactions to information means time is of the essence. The slightest flicker and her jaws stop chewing on turkey mayonnaise. Her ruby nails dig into the black silk of her stockinged thighs, every rip equals a decision, and she has to buy them in bulk each week. Torn, laddered, full of tiny holes, they are her calendar to judge the stress of each day.

On Saturday mornings she works out in the bank's gymnasium and then meets a colleague for a Mexican meal. She has got short of breath but her lips still shine. Sometimes when Eduardo is asleep by her side she sobs like a wolf cub. The strange thing is there are no tears, she is dry-eyed even after hours of sobbing. Once when Eduardo woke up to find her body shaking and heaving he put his arms around her and asked what was wrong. She just buried her head under the pillow, lying on her stomach, and continued to sob, sometimes surfacing to look at the clock.

Eduardo thinks about the week ahead and the small sleek whores in Bangkok, always smiling and ready to please because they know grief is not good for business.

In the morning he takes her shopping. He buys her spiky shoes, suspenders, petticoats, wigs she will never wear, a briefcase with a combination lock crusted with emeralds and a small revolver. She buys him the best cigarettes, starched white shirts, a cap with checks the shop assistant said was his tartan and twelve pairs of socks. Afterwards they eat ice-cream in parlours all over the city and then she takes him to the Waldorf where there is a little red bus in the window with HOVIS AND BUTTER FOR TEA written across its side. 'Makes me think of home,' she tells him as the Barts Bells chime twelve. Her sobbing fits stop and she knows they will never, never happen again.

*   *   *

She is shaking hands with a fat man in grey flannels and a bow tie who thanks her for her help and promotes her to their branch in London. He says, 'You are a real star, here's wishing all sorts of glamorous things for you, kid.' She says, 'I guess I'll miss the pace, Joe,' and jumps into the scarlet company car. As she looks in the mirror we catch each other's eye. We are startled voyeurs. The last time we were this close was when she took the glass of hot chocolate from my hand and put it to her lips.

Her eye is as blue as meat,
We stare into each other and then she cuts me out.
She shuts her eye.

The Banker taps her manicured fingernail on the window of her Cadillac. It is as if she wants to tap the irritation out of her self. She turns up the air conditioning, stops at the traffic lights, brushes her hair, glosses her lips, swallows vitamins, eats chocolate, checks her watch. The back seat is piled high with Gucci bags. As she boards the aeroplane to Heathrow, gold wedding ring glistening in the sun, she turns to me and says in transatlantic English, 'Don't pride your self on being a small bird perched on my shoulder, Lapinski. I am just about to enter a huge bird, to be carried through the clouds and home again. You are a still-born bird somewhere at the back of my head, a cold-war baby who wants to make peace when there is no peace to be had. Life *is* a nightmare, it's more interesting like that. You are no great shakes. It's my job to invent reality, not fiction. I invent the world. You just figure out ways of surviving in it. You are the dispossessed cringing somewhere on the corner of this earth. I am in its centre, a bright burning light, and you in the corner will be dazzled.'
The air hostess offers her mineral water and prawn

mousse. Down below, people get smaller and smaller as the engines roar and The Banker melts little dabs of orange shellfish on her tongue.

While the hares at John F. Kennedy airport race the plane on the runway, an old man in Piccadilly, London, screams in the middle of the road, hands stretched above his silver hair. A line of cars comes to a standstill; the people in them are secretly afraid to get out and move him on. They laugh nervously behind the wheel; his screams pulse through their hearts. The Innocents watch him. They know his name is Mac and that he is homeless too. When he has finished screaming they saunter into the road and help him to the pavement. Mac says, 'Okay you bandits give the old shaman a smoke. See this white skin over my left eye? I'm screaming so as to break it ... to get to the green underneath.'

On the edge of the motorway, a woman in a headscarf that hides her long black hair plaited with seashells sits on a high stool by the stainless steel meatbelt. She remembers a dream in which great clumps of small eggs, like spawn, leak from her and are put on a slide in a laboratory. Her mother, sister and a nurse are present. The nurse tells her that the red eggs are normal, but there is a chance that the white eggs contain 'abnormalities'.

An aeroplane has just flown over. It even drowned the sound of the machines on the meatbelt, which is quite something because they hum within as well as outside me; we have become one body. I am doing the night shift and miss my friend The Poet. She has not been to work for three days now. I don't know where she is but I suspect she is trying to do something impossible. The lights from the factory guide planes that fly over us. The Alsatians outside bark at them. Sometimes I wish they'd just crash into us and we'd all die very quickly in a pool of duty-free gin. When for that one moment I could no longer hear the sound of the machines I thought I had died. That my heart had stopped and I had become meat too, splattered over the walls and floor.

I ached to be different from the women in my home town. But it's hard to be enchanting and carefree and spiritual when you're dead broke. I wanted to either participate in the world, to taste it, to dare search out joy and claim it, or not be here at all. I wanted there to be more to life than just surviving it. I wanted and I wanted. When I went to university, someone said, 'Are you going to piss in the outside loo in silk knickers then?'

I laughed and laughed and laughed when I first fell in love – as if I was making up for a lifetime of stern set lips; it was at that time I realised to be in love is to dream inside the other person – which was thrilling because he was a big bad boy from Barcelona and wore blood-red espadrilles even in the rain. Some afternoons we would skip lectures and climb up on to the roofgarden a friend had lent us with a bottle of wine, and fuck for hours; we talked about books and revolution, our lips wet with Rioja and each other. He said, 'In Spain every man is the toreador/Christ: we like to conquer death and pierce our flesh.' If I was brought up on chips and the Easter fair, he was brought up on rice, cheap meat and mass. Agreeing that cynicism was a modern condition worth keeping, we made no plans for the future – we assumed our lives would be rich in ideas and events, that we would always be curious, searching, full of questions and sensations. We assumed this because we made each other feel beautiful and interesting; I never thought it possible, then, that ideas could be bashed into stupid blue meat, and people encouraged to eat them like fast-food burgers. I often wonder where he is now, what he is doing, and whether he still feels able to conquer death.

When I visit my home town it's like going back to the scene of some silent, unrecorded massacre. Newspapers full of obsolete tragedies flap around the gasworks like dying birds. Condoms cringe in gutters. Pregnant prostitutes stand on street corners. Some men like it like that. There are regular floods of cancers for the undertaker to get rich on; cancer is gold to him. Young unemployed men and women suicide themselves all the time; leave little notes hidden in secret places for someone who might have cared for them to find, testimonies to their punctured spirit, their wasted contribution to life in this ruined pit of sorrow. If all their testimonies were put together they would make a new Bible, its prophets dead in battered cars, garages, and the bottoms of cliffs.

There is a war on. Everyone is separated and afraid. No one tells stories any more. It is as if we have been robbed of a language to describe the bewildered brokenness we inhabit; there is nothing to measure ourselves against. Our history is being wiped out like a stain. Relandscaped. So I buried a photo album that spans three generations of my extended family in rubble nearby, and hope it will be found one day, just as the bones of prehistoric animals were found and put together – if only that the gift of accumulated experience be used to make someone's life happier.

And here I am on the meatbelt. Tonight I am a blues singer. Yesterday I was a great woman orator, rallying our people to get up and change things. To put their shoulder to change and push. It seems we all wait for someone else to change things for us. To sacrifice their life for us. To somehow voice our most secret desires, our hopes and yearnings for us. We wait to be made brave by someone else's courage. We wait and wait.

Last year I took my first holiday in Europe. I did not find myself in some golden paradise – but on an industrial beach, blue and pink corrugated iron shacks on the shore. Little fires and local people frying sardines. Dogs asleep on the sand. Football posts. Gulls with filthy wings swooping down for sewage and bread. High-rise flats. Patches of grass. A goat. I felt perfectly at home. I bought some candles from a holy shop with handmade roses climbing down their sides. A man was standing in the rain holding out his shoe to collect coins. A woman was begging as if her hand was made that way. On the last day, I took a bus to the nearest big city. Ate pork and cockles in cafés smelling of aftershave and pastries. Drank lots of little cups of coffee with almond cake, smoked strange cigarettes in red packets. Next to the big international shops, traders had set up barrows heaped with nuts, cheap glass, earrings made from shells and tinted crystals (I bought some for The Poet), and flowers, so many flowers, sold by gypsies from the country. Organ grinders, church bells, chestnut sellers, students drinking beer at cafés, flute players busking on pavements, an ancient blind woman banging a triangle and singing about orange trees and lost love, chocolates filled with liqueurs distilled in Gothic monasteries, taxis, trams, piazzas, boulevards, tables and chairs out on the pavements in the sun and tourists with shopping bags by their feet staring numbly at everything. Men kissing each other, twice on the cheek, holding each other as they talked, seagulls shrieking above them. Mothers and daughters with blossom in their button-holes. They reminded me of a woman at home, with blue lips because she had a bad heart, who pinned a flower from her garden on to my heart. Once I went to a café with a huge clock on the wall; its hands kept swinging out of time with real time, so the waiters had to climb up the ladder to put it right. I went to art galleries full of the work of modernists and I went to bookshops to look for native poets in translation. I even lingered in the foyers of glittering fragrant hotels and when I got tired slipped into churches to see the frescos, listen to the service, watch people cross themselves. It struck me that the hands of the clock and the hands of the holy are almost the same gesture. Among the elabor-ate gold leaf on the walls, one painting shocked − a priest standing against a cold snow sky and, stretched across the sky, a thin icy spiked line of barbed wire, the expression in his eyes chilled, as if at the moment the artist caught him he had lost his faith and was filled with some unspeakable fear too terrible to contain. And then I bought a chocolate priest, and wondered if the priest in the painting, like me, had eaten God and was disappointed by the taste. I looked at statues, touched them, sat under them reading maps, fingers sticky with watermelon, legs tanned; I met a woman scientist and she took me home to her family. I played with her children, drank wine, talked for hours, wrote diaries on the balcony of my *pensione*, loved the twittering of canaries in the light, the way my hair started to curl when it had always been straight. I came back full up. And realised how empty I had been.

That aeroplane has frayed my nerves. And they are not too good at the moment. I wake up thinking I can smell something burning, and in the moment of waking know my fears have taken on a smell. These days the most innocent of things can have a myriad of fearful associations for me. I feel psychically assaulted and I feel scared. I feel there is something leaking from me, that I am spilling myself, that I need to save myself but I don't know how to. If I didn't think things were going to change, I would simply give up, walk into the water, like a hundred cowards before me, and give it my last breath. Just as life began in water, so I would end mine there too.

The lights are beginning to dim which means the night shift is nearly over. It is as if we women are returning to each other after a long separation and are startled by the distance we have travelled even though we are standing shoulder to shoulder in the same room. Once, when I was watching The Poet work opposite me, for one mad moment I thought she looked like a Messiah with no cross to hang on. The job of The Poet is essentially to prepare the imagination of the people to receive metaphors of all kinds. I have a feeling that right now she is trying to turn herself into a fish. She loves a good joke.

7.15   Swab taken from specimen.
7.30   Specimen runs and falls over on occasions.
8.30   Specimen stands and falls over on occasions.
8.40   Specimen shows evidence of distress.

The llama's breath rises and falls. Like the dollar thinks Freddie. He wants to hold her. Bury his face in her fur. He sticks his hand through the cage bars but he cannot reach her. She seems to be sleeping and shivering at the same time. An aeroplane flies over the zoo and the animals become restless. The sky is scarred with a thick white line. The chief gorilla smooths the scar on his own chest with hands that are not so different from the hands of the old zoo keeper who rolls oranges into his cage every evening. The animals call to each other, ears alert, they murmur, scratch themselves, bellow out into the thick night of the city. It is as if the passing of this winged beast is an omen for some terrible happening in the future. The bird cages are full of fallen feathers; in a corner the Marabou stork hides her head under her wing. The white-tailed mongoose eats without tasting what it is he's eating. Toads croak. The cats lick invisible wounds with long sideways sweeping movements of their tongues. The elephants plaster mud on their skin, roll about in the dust and rub themselves against the wall of their compound. Their ears flap and spread, grey circles of time imprinted on their mud-soaked flesh, just as the hearts of trees have circles of time marked within themselves. The elephants dimly remember moonlit nights drifting through the bush stripping bark; tonight time seems to have stopped and the wind is hot.

In the city, three cabinet ministers in navy serge suits, cufflinks and well-polished brogues, dump their briefcases on a hotel bed and pour themselves large gin and tonics. They raise their glasses and sing

England here
England there
England every fucking where.

Outside, on the high street, people put bits of plastic into a brick wall and in return get money. They carry their personal number around with thèm, in their sleep, during meals, love play, in swimming baths and offices. The computer in the wall is hot, like the forehead of a person with a fever, burning into the bricks and mortar of Europe.

09.00   Specimen shows evidence of discharge from eyes.
09.30   Specimen refuses to stand up.
10.30   Specimen still shows evidence of distress.

The llama's eyes have turned into a lake. She rolls on to her belly. For one mad moment Freddie thinks he can see her tail flicker, as if she is diving into her self. He touches his forehead for no reason at all. She looks like a fish with fur. Her belly is silvery grey. Freddie realises he has been looking up into the sky which seems to be a great fathomless pool of inky water, and on the rippleless surface he can see the reflection of the llama's thoughts. At this moment she is a salmon, still and silent as the beginning of the world.

A woman with green wispy hair bends and bows over the black keys of her piano like a small tender willow. It is she who plays only those notes forbidden by the Catholic church in the days of the Inquisition, who scents herself with Chinese cedar and twenty-five oils that are not for the timid, whose ribs stick out like needles, whose music spreads itself over all bedsit London, music that is full of questions, discord and joyful contradictions. The Anorexic Anarchist.

She says, 'No No No, Lapinski . . . I will not let you be an autocrat. I will break the pattern of your summoning which I hear through my little diseased cherry tree that refuses to blossom in this time of the accountant, prison warder, soldier, in this time when cathedrals of Armageddon are built to house nuclear icons, and battery chickens become things called golden nuggets in boxes that destroy the air we breathe. In this time when pigs become lumps of sorrow soaked in preservatives and people register their personal decay in solitary massacres . . . yes I will break the pattern of your summoning. I will sow the seeds of chaos and disorder about your donkey-dung shoes. I have a cake baking in the oven, can you smell the vanilla? Come here. Closer than that. I am going to transform *you*, but not before I have had a bath to give me psychic immunity from all the television screens that go on at night.' Her bones crack against the white porcelain of the bath. 'I am an antibody fighting the diseased putrescent body of this

56

society ... Come closer, Lapinski, with your rotten stumps for teeth and rancid breath, you will be Marie Antoinette.'

I am Marie Antoinette. My bouffant of white cotton-wool hair is tangled with barbed wire and birds; soldiers shoot out of my curls. I am standing outside a blue bank in the high street, a great hooped dress swirling about my Russian hips. My lips red as glacé cherries. Two men who call themselves Aides stand on either side of me. They wear mirrored sunglasses and one of them looks a little like Freddie; a white worm wriggles on his shoulderpad. 'Who's your worm dancing for?' an old woman asks him, sucking a boiled sweet. 'God.' She shakes her fist and calls the worm an antichrist. A huge cake stands on a silver trolley in front of me, iced with a map of the world. I have a metre ruler in my hand and as people go by I ask them if they would like a piece of cake. If they say yes, I ask which part of the world they would like me to slice up. They think and point and nudge small islands, whole continents, dictatorships, democracies, deserts, rain forests, oceans. I put their portion of the world on to a banking slip one of the Aides passes to me, with EAT CAKE in the little boxes where it says ACCOUNT NUMBER. The Anorexic Anarchist plays the trombone behind me, sometimes stopping to wheeze the concertina hung on leather straps around her neck, or to nibble sunflower seeds which are the only thing that keeps her alive.

When the world is eaten, we take the soldiers out of my hair and bury them under a spindly sapling trying to grow in a crack in the pavement. A little boy makes a wreath out of his milk-shake carton. Two lovers kiss on the grave, a small city-dance of leather and suede. I think of my father and mother and how they made love on the marble slab of a war memorial – perhaps it is the shame of the same species murdering each other so often that demands an affirmation of life, murdering each other in the heart, lung, arm, head, thigh, groin; not so different from love play.

We are in a rowing boat. I am rowing. The Anorexic Anarchist rubs Nivea into her sparrow arms. The sun is warm and gentle and I ask her what the difference is between happiness and contentment. She closes her eyes, lids delicate, transparent, slivers of tiny veins. With her eyes shut she looks like a leaf. She trails her fingers in the lake, 'Contentment, Lapinski, is going to meet someone you love on a full stomach. Happiness is going to meet someone you love on an empty stomach.'

She invites me to lunch. On the floor is a clay bowl and inside it two glistening spinach leaves. Her room smells of the wax candles she burns by the dozen while playing the piano. And of bread. It is in her bread that she creates the most beautiful anarchy. She puts everything into it, beer, rice, lentils, cumin, rye, yoghurt, depending on what she wants the bread to do to whoever eats it. It is the coming together, the convergence of everything she yearns for in the world. She makes bread as she wants life to be. Today she wears nothing but a pair of outrageous knickers made from fake fur, lace, silk and wool. She looks like a hermaphrodite as she oils her emaciated legs and arms, and is teaching herself how to walk a tightrope. The rope is just six inches above the floor and her little feet grip it as she shuffles across, arms flapping on either side. On the fifth step she stops, straightens up and points to the two spinach leaves. 'Eat your spinach, Lapinski.' She walks another step, it seems to take a hundred years. 'I have this little thing I do, Lapinski, when I put food on a fork, it can never touch my lips.' She smiles. 'I have walked

58

the tightrope all my life. Now I'm trying to learn how to get to the other side.'

On the meatbelt blood is being spilled. Seashells scatter across the floor. The hands of the clock on the wall have stopped and someone's hands are no longer attached to their wrists. The light is very bright. Women pick up the shells and put them in the pockets of their overalls. They do not know whether they are awake or asleep. Monster burgers slide down the belt, unattended as makeshift bandages are stripped from clothing and women haul themselves back from places of their own making — back to this scene, this room where the very real smell of blood is soaking into the paisley print of someone's headscarf, wrapped around the wrists of a mutilated woman. The meat creates its own dimensions, patterns, becomes itself, a herd of beasts. The smell of blood mingling with perfumes dabbed on the temple and pulse points, and the ghostly fragrance of scents that have been imagined only five minutes before, the skin of a lover, the creases of a child, cardamon in a curry. Two bewildered women hold the shells to their ears — the sea sounds poisoned, slow and heavy as if she pulls towards the moon but cannot get back again. The women feel dizzy with the light, and time stopped, as in the hands of the clock which measures out meatbelt life, and blood, so much blood trickling about their ankles. They wander about like dazed Ophelias. No flowers. No song. Just workers on the meatbelt. Sleep-walkers incapable of their own distress.

What a cunt. When I told that Lapinski I am happy with who I am and what I've got, she told me I have no imagination. Who do they think they are? Why do they think they've got a right to happiness as if it was a debt the world owes them? In fact I've got quite a lot of things to look forward to. When they privatise prisons and water, I'll be there for a slice of the cake. Yesterday I went to a pink and chrome pleasure dome with a colleague. We had steak, as a matter of fact. Then we came back here and got rat-arsed on a bottle of Scotch and watched the video. I didn't feel a hundred per cent this morning. The boss crept up to me in his famous soft soles and said something like 'We don't carry any fat, you know.' Well I suppose fear is an executive tool, but fat? My mother went without so I could sleep at night without eating my fists. I visited her last weekend, she was playing chess with her neighbour and when I walked in (dressed specially in a new shirt) she said, 'Son, you're a prat. Look after your queen, Mrs R.' One day I'll shoot her and it'll break my heart. Dunno how she wanted her son to grow up. Dunno what she wants of me. Tonight I'm going to a charity ball to help raise money for a children's hospital – they're raffling off a helicopter. If I win I might just walk right into the blades of its propeller. If I don't I'll get wrecked on champagne and watch the puffed chiffon of shimmering blondes ooze small clues to men in bow ties, and all for babies with bone disease.

The sun is bloody today; my cufflinks are melting and my head aches. If I was to become strawberry jam under a tube train, the computers would carry on dealing without me; there are plenty more like me to feed the cannon, to stuff full of credit, to fill the bars and toy-town houses, to eat the quiche, to spray tear gas into a million eyes should they be given another sort of uniform. People in my home town still sing the songs my father wrote. He is a well-missed man.

Hopefully the firm will relocate me soon. To the South-East or around. No Lapinski there. No glue sniffers there. No Greek sausages, salt fish or mangos in the shops there. I am not a church-goer myself but it gives me a feeling of security and comfort when I'm near one. There's a sense of order in that part of England, it has the gentle sort of sun I like, the flower beds have no weeds in them and no one stands out in a crowd. The pubs don't let children in, not even in the garden, nor adults with muddy shoes or wearing clothes like John the Baptist.

I feel frightened and I don't know why.

Last night I dreamt I got sucked into the telly.

A whole fresh salmon wrapped in foil with butter and herbs bakes in the oven. The napkins on the table are pale pink French linen, the cutlery silver, the glasses the thinnest, most fragile crystal. Marlene Dietrich croons from the compact disc player.

I, Lapinski, am in front of the mirror again. It seems The Banker and I are destined to meet backwards through the reflective surface of this glass. It was by the mirror my grandmother used to watch herself cry, first as a child and later as an adult. She was too proud to show her tears; instead when she felt the need to weep she would take from the drawer one of her many handkerchiefs, fold it on her lap, take off her eyeglasses and ritually begin. When she married and her husband caught her weeping one day by the glass he shook her by the shoulders so hard her hair, which she always scraped into a bun, fell loose and her combs scattered on the floor. 'Why are you so cross?' she had asked him. He replied tenderly putting the combs back in her hair, 'Never to cry is to be only half a person. I cry often because I always hoped I would marry a beautiful woman – and what did I fall in love with? A woman with a wart under her arm and a mouth like a crack in a pie.'

So they cried together in front of the glass, and when the crying turned to laughter they opened a bottle of vodka kept for special occasions, talking about their sad days and happy days and the future they both looked forward to; it was only when they had finished half the bottle they remembered their daughter (my mother) was skating that afternoon to an audience of hundreds. They arrived drunk, dishevelled and flushed, and embarrassed my mother by singing loudly and badly throughout her dance; afterwards she said their breath melted the ice and made her slip.

Through the looking glass I can see The Banker. She is slipping into a charcoal silk dress, goosepimples on her arms. Eduardo is shaving in the bathroom and shouts at her for leaving water on the floor after her bath. She sprays herself with perfume and says the maid will clean it up in the morning. Eduardo calls her 'catsbreath' and playfully holds the razor up to her throat making slicing gestures. 'This is how you slice Parma ham,' he says, and then cracks open a pistachio nut.

Outside, the Innocents sit by the river drinking a bottle of sweet sherry. The girl has a violin bow in one hand and a cigarette in the other. She bows the boy's ear and he makes the noise of a violin in his throat. Fifty yards away a policeman watches over them, The boy now takes the bow and runs it over the girl's ear. She makes the noise of a violin in her throat. When they have finished the sherry they throw the bottle in the river. A helicopter hovers above them.

Jerry puts the last touches to his dinner table. With his golden ringlets curling under his ear lobes, watery blue eyes and dimples he looks like a baby angel. At twenty-nine he has developed a slight lisp and when he smiles his tongue sticks out between his cupid lips. A pianist/composer, quite famous in particular circles, his forte is to set the songs of Brecht and make a kind of laissez-faire Brecht. He gives concerts for the Conservative club at Cambridge, for small aristocrats in their rural homes, at stately houses rented for the evening and at numerous glitzy dinner parties. His plump hands, giggles, lisp and love of shortbread baked by his adoring grandmother, who he lives with and who is also getting dressed for supper, all make him a delicious slightly wayward little treat. He is much sought after and well-fucked by the sons of lords and dukes.

At this moment Grannie Bird, as she is called, is clipping a pair of ancient jet earrings on to her ears. She powders her soft smooth cheeks and remembers that she left her pot of rouge in the box at the Opera House in Paris.

The boy and girl watch the bottle of sherry bob up and down on the water. After a while the girl takes out a little box and shows it to the boy. Inside the box is a perfect set of long white false fingernails. She begins to put them on and the boy pushes back her cuticles with his own bitten fingernails. The policeman peels a banana.

Eduardo, The Banker, Jerry and Grannie Bird sit at the candle-lit table drinking a light white wine with their fennel and Parmesan salad. Marlene sings 'Fallink in love again' and Eduardo, who has taken off his shoes, searches for his wife's thighs under the table. Jerry is telling everyone about his last concert and how the host has promised to take him skiing in Europe for a weekend. Grannie Bird smiles; her teeth are like porcelain, and her blue eyes small and bright. 'You will look like a little angel flying over the snow. Be sure to keep your fingers warm.' The smell of salmon cooking wafts through the kitchen. Suddenly she says, 'My dear, you smell of roses.' She moves nearer The Banker and breathes deeply. 'Roses and roses and roses.' She gazes up into the chandelier. The Banker tells her there must be rose in her perfume. 'Ah that is what it must be,' sighs Grannie Bird, putting her knife and fork together. Eduardo tells them he has commissioned an artist to make prints of Warhol into tiles for their bathroom. The Banker tells Jerry she lost a hundred thousand pounds in the computer that morning and how it took her an hour to find it again. Eduardo nudges his toe under her knicker elastic. Jerry wraps one of his ringlets round and round his plump finger. Marlene sings 'I can't help it'; Grannie Bird wipes each corner of her lips with a napkin. Suddenly she moves back her chair and begins to tell a story.

'On the tube this morning three Irish children, they must have been five, seven and nine years old, got into my carriage, and in their hands, my dear,' she smiles at The Banker, 'were the most beautiful pink and red roses. Long-stemmed and alert as a rose should be, they smelt like you, Gemma, it is your fragrance that reminds me. And these children started begging from passengers. First the little girl came up to me, held the rose under my nose and said, "Give us some money for food then." I shook my head and she went away. Then the little boy came up to me, his eyes as green as green, his hair shaved off, face heart-shaped and ...' Grannie Bird puts her fingertips together, 'tragic. He also pinned the rose right under my nose and said, "Give us some money for food then." I shook my head. He said, "Please please please please please please please," in a little whine pushing the rose into my face until I found myself blushing and delved into my pocket for some loose change. He said, "Give us a pound, I don't want less than a pound." I gave him substantially less than a pound, just the few coins I had. Perhaps twenty pence. All the time he pressed the rose into my face. "Please please please please please please."'

Grannie Bird makes the sound of a little dog, Jerry giggles and makes a rose from his pink napkin, which he presents to her with a little bow of his golden head.

'Thank you, Sir.'

She smiles at Eduardo.

'That rose smelt like the roses of my childhood. Of the world I grew up in. The woods a haze of bluebells, oh they looked like a Monet, and the light . . . if you appreciate light . . . early-morning mists, cuckoos in spring, the woodpecker, pheasants, wild rabbits. That rose made me think of my mother in her gardening gloves, pruning her rose bushes; she planned her roses every year and people who visited from the city always took one or two back with them. English roses. When they were full-blown, petals would fall on the walnut sideboard, there were vases of them all over the house, and I would gather them in the palm of my hand and save them to press in heavy old books.'

Eduardo shuts his eyes. He is bored. His toe wriggles from side to side, Gemma silently mouthes 'EEEEEEK'; Marlene sings 'Vhat am I to do?' and Jerry fills everyone's glass.

'My world was a peaceful thoughtful world. We talked about literature, great literature, in gardens we ourselves had created. Gentle sunlight, straw hats, white gloves, scones, homemade jams, lazy days picking blackberries in September, fragrant days, happy days. We knew the names of the children of all our servants and never forgot their birthdays. Bees hovered about the lavender bushes, muslin to make sachets of the stuff for our top drawers. My parents honeymooned

66

in Europe for two years in a horse-drawn caravan. The house was always full of artists and actors. I spent my childhood on horses and my adolescence posing under the apple tree for young men in silk scarves. My father was a wonderful host and my mother, although she never made much fuss about it, painted little water-colours with brushes especially imported from China. Dragonflies, my uncle tickling trout, rugs and hampers and lemonade. A hundred strokes to the hair last thing at night. We appreciated life. Lived it to the full, wanted it to last for ever and ever. Do you know, my dears, I have seven generations of earls in my larynx ... '

Jerry nudges her arm. 'Grannie, tell us about the little boy.'

'Oh yes. I gave him the money and he went away. I shouted GIVE ME THE ROSE THEN ... he looked as if he was going to kill me. You see, although other passengers had given money, they had not asked for the rose. They were just glad to be left alone. I am made of sterner stuff, and shouted again, "I gave you the money now you give me the rose." So he gave it to me. And then he started to cry. His sister rummaged in her pockets and found a pencil which she gave to him and he went round with that instead, holding it under people's noses as if it was a rose. And when someone gave him money and demanded the pencil his sister gave him her hair slide ... she just took it out of her hair there and then ... and he went around with that saying, "Give us some money for food then?" And when someone took the hair slide his younger sister turned out her pockets and found a half-eaten sandwich. So he put that under some gent's nose and the man said, "You've got food," pointing to the sandwich. "What do you want money for?"'

The Banker claps her hands. 'Play for us, Jerry.' Eduardo joins in, 'Play play play play.' Grannie Bird leaves the table, her long black velvet dress whispering along the carpet as she walks to the kitchen and opens the oven. The candles flicker as Jerry sings

'Oh Susannah won't you answer
with her hand her face she's hiding
some adventure, some adventure I shall see'

Eduardo is telling his wife about his meeting with a Japanese financier at an oyster and champagne bar in Soho. How they both agreed when the deal had been made that business was not too difficult and totally immoral which is why they both liked it. Jerry tosses his ringlets:

'With her hand her face is hiding.'

Grannie Bird carries in the salmon. It is so big it flops over the sides of the baking tray. She puts it down on the table. It is steaming. She unwraps the foil and is just about to poke a long thin knife into its belly, when the salmon seems to take its last breath. It rises from the dish and gasps. Melted butter runs over its eyes. The Banker, who has been embarrassed by fish before, looks at it with interest. She bites her lip. Grannie Bird says to Jerry, 'Cut the fish will you darling.' Jerry takes the knife from her, his little plump hands shaking slightly. Eduardo moves his toe inside his wife's knickers. The Banker says, 'Eeeeeeek.' Grannie Bird fiddles with the cutlery. Jerry cuts into the fish and Eduardo's plate is held out for the first sliver of pale orange pink flesh.

The terrible strange sight of ten minutes ago is uncommented on, as if saying something will confirm it actually happened. No one touches their salmon. They eat the petit pois, potatoes, broccoli, break bread rolls and dip them into the mayonnaise and parsley sauce, pushing the fish to the side of their plates, talking of summer holidays, the exchange rate, property, obituary columns, and magazines they subscribe to.

68

Grannie Bird puts a bottle of port, five jade glasses and a whole Stilton on the table. She tells them the way to eat it is to scoop out the middle with a little silver spoon. Jerry hands round a bowl of walnuts, singing.

This is shameless
what presumption!
I forbid you to come near.

Grannie Bird pops chocolates on her grandson's tongue and peals with laughter as he pretends to pant for more. Eduardo puts his shoes back on and sits on the cream leather settee with a glass of port. A block of passion-fruit sorbet melts unnoticed on the trolley. The Banker looks at the salmon. She is curious and takes a flat silver knife to cut a tiny piece of flesh off its belly, puts it on her tongue and chews it very slowly as if assessing its flavour. I catch her eye as she spits it out into her napkin and re-glosses her lips. She gargles with rosé and spits that out into the napkin too. As she breaks a match in half and picks her teeth with it, she turns to me, cheeks flushed.

'I think, Lapinski, this is the terrible trick of one of your friends. This fish has the possessed eye of a poet and tastes just as useless. In fact it tastes like a melancholy misfit. I have always hated poetry, I prefer hard mathematics or even hard drugs. Do you really think that in consuming this pescado I would consume its ideas? I have spat them out again and again. Wept them away on a king-sized bed in New York and timed my silly little pain.

'And what is The Idea? That there are thirteen ways of looking at a blackbird? Give it to me, I'll take it to the market and show you sixty ways of looking at it. Poets are fuckwits. They try and legislate with language but

69

they don't have the roubles to bribe. On my aunt's salmon farm they stroke the belly of hen salmon to squeeze out their eggs for breeding. Well, I have squeezed you out too.'

This is shameless
what presumption
I forbid you to come near

Jerry sticks his tongue into the middle of the Stilton, eases it in a little further and looks at Eduardo.

'Do you think I am a cannibal, Lapinski? That I eat consciousness? You fucking piss-artist. That you should try and infiltrate me so deviously. You have delusions of grandeur.'

so coy then
just to tease me . . . la la la
I know why you're waitin' here

Jerry's tongue is covered in Stilton. Eduardo has fallen asleep.

'You fucking village idiot. You've spent too long in steamy kitchens crying useless tears into Ukrainian pork stews, making dumplings and *kasha* for broken people in broken shoes.'

She looks for her car keys.

I do like to be beside the seaside
I do like to be beside the sea

Grannie Bird sings in a quivering high voice, swaying her velvet hips in time with the piano.

The Banker slams her foot down on the accelerator of her Mercedes; smoke streams out of the exhaust and her hands, on the wheel, are white with fury. It is as if years

70

of anger and fatigue are burning through her charcoal silk body. This time when she looks into the mirror she does not cut me out. Her eye is blue as petrol.

'You, Lapinski, are the dinosaur trapped in ice from the age of slow-moving beings. I sit on trains rolling through the remains of the industrial revolution in a first class carriage reserved for me, briefcase by my side, computer on my lap, telephone under my chin, all the while eating warm baked cheese cake. These are the crumbs offered to me, along with tickets for musicals, dinners at Maxims, trips in hot-air balloons, cruises on the Thames, for the stress, for the erosion of my heart, for the thumping of my blood-pressure, for my loss . . . of life. I understand myself perfectly. I do not have to search for reason or meaning or seek the services of a problem prostitute on couches in clinics. I know who I am and what I do.

'I own a prestige apartment facing the sparkle of the river, with south-facing views, a private car park, porter, video security, entry phone, swimming pool and a sauna to nurture my health, which is after all my wealth. I am given all this for good reason. I am valued; I am an irresistible proposition to men in parliaments, writers of pornography, film directors, record producers, tycoons of all kinds; my condom case bulges with the promise of liaison and adventure. I am the new pioneer; the great adventure of my generation is to shake up the world, men, women, to destabilise everything and everyone.

'In my prestige apartment I am Madam de Sade. My phone never stops ringing; it is my Beethoven, speaking into it is oral sex, my shining black cock, I press buttons, phone up New York every evening, find out how the markets close, and sometimes, when Eduardo goes down on me, I wrap the cord around his neck until he begs me for mercy. If he survives, we go out to eat, or see

71

another musical, or go to the first night of a movie, or the opening of an exhibition. I have a very special kind of love play, my instruments are straps and straddles, and bulls and bears, and strangles and strategies, and bells and bonds and whistles. I play my own and other people's destruction silkily and easily. I calculate crashes; I am a whore in the market place, I do a lotta rough trade.

'I don't dream. I fuck and hit the pillow and sleep as if I've died. Under my bathrobe I am covered in bruises. My lovers and I trace each other's scars with lustful fingers, we like to abuse and use each other, it keeps us on our toes. I hate them and they hate me, this is our liberation. Yesterday I dug my nails into the flesh of a young dealer from Berlin, he bled for hours, came for hours, in the back seat of his Golf GTI, blood and sperm staining his seat covers, testimony to our wild afternoon in the maze of an underground car park, impaled on each other in fumes and ecstasy. Last week it was a computer millionaire, a high-flying technical whizzo; he programmed me and I flew until we both crashed into the leather of his swivel chair, screaming. We are exhausted and wide awake, berserk, full of radio-activity, the first generation of beautiful mutants. And we, Lapinski, have won the moral freedom to wound. We dabble our bodies and minds and energy and money in the soils and lakes and seas and mountains of the world. We own the world.'

The bottle of sweet sherry bobs up and down on the water near where The Innocents are sitting. She spreads her long white fingernails, fingers taut so they look like claws. They watch a Mercedes speed past them, and at that moment the girl thinks she can see twenty red parrots, wings on fire, fly into the sun, and the boy thinks he can see a rhino poke its horn through the moon. They share a packet of crisps.

The Banker pulls into a petrol station. She is electric, possessed. The taste of the salmon is still in her mouth; she spits, opens a Diet Pepsi, eats chocolate, smokes a cigarette, gargles with the Pepsi. She says, 'Fuckwit fuckwit fuckwit ... ' Her dress sticks to her body; she seems to be sweating and shivering at the same time. The garage attendant rubs his eyes. With her American Express card she buys a hundred gallons of petrol, which she demands be loaded into her car, the boot, the back and front seat, and on the roof. He does this for her in a daze. She crashes the car into a wall, buckling the front of the Mercedes, starts it again, her hands covered in blood and glass from the shattered windscreen. This time she crashes past the barrier in the zoo car park.

When my hands got mashed in the meat machine, all I remember is the women's eyes as they bent over me; it was as if they had woken from a deep sleep in a strange room and could not place themselves. And then the Alsatians began to bark. Dizzy and dripping I thought perhaps I am a late-twentieth-century martyr, I who lost limbs for production statistics. In the end we are all just meat.

What is described as an Industrial Accident is my left and right hands guillotined somewhere below the wrist and minced with multi-national beef. This means a whole batch of hamburgers will consist of me. Tourists will buy my flesh in a sesame bun with pickle. They will sit in buses and not even know they have eaten me. I am not in pain. My arms are in plaster. My mother has to feed me. Today she cooked me leek soup; every time my father sees me his eyes fill and he has to leave the room. My nights are full of bird song and I don't know where it comes from. No tears. The seashells I once plaited through my hair are long-gone. I am stripped. Even the jagged lifeline I stared at so often in the palm of my hand has gone. No fucking tears.

Once, in a rock pool, I saw baby crabs floating on their backs in the salt water. Further down the beach, dead birds spread on the shore. The sand rippled, marked by the tides. Someone had carved a year of their life into a rock; recorded election results, pop songs of the moment, the birth of a child, the number of winkles found dead every day, recipes, names of people. Who was that stone-carver, he or she who came down to the beach every day for a year with a chisel? I used to paint my fingernails orange – they looked like a shoal of tropical fish. Is there anything still alive on that beach? There is not much left of me. I mean I am losing parts of my self. Literally. We say we have lost our heart to someone; we lose our minds, our hope, our health, our faith, our pride, our dignity. We walk around with bits of our selves missing and do not even know it. No tears. Just bombs. Prisons. Electrodes on genitals. I mean, if you have hands you might as well do something intelligent or erotic or witty with them. As a child I watched sweet peas grow in between stones.

A rope is being strung from two telegraph poles above the zoo. First it is slack and then it gets tighter. Two ladders sway against the hour before dawn. The Anorexic Anarchist looks down. She is starving and her lips are parched. Wearing nothing but her finest bloomers, made from silk and rose petals, she tests the rope with her toe. The Banker shouts, 'I am bored and burning,' as she opens the boot of her car. She carries two of the petrol cans into the zoo, runs back to the car, takes out another two, does this again and again until they are spread out like metal corpses on the turf; the spikes of her heels sink into the mud but she does not take them off, she just keeps running to the car and back again, the beating of her heart a small earthquake that shakes early-morning London. The llama and Freddie sleep on. When Freddie wakes up he sees The Banker in her charcoal silk and stilettos carrying petrol cans and piercing them with a car aeriel. Her hands are bleeding. He rubs his eyes.

The monkeys begin to shriek, gathering their children, calling out to other animals, burying their heads under their arms, nuzzling and nudging against each other; the gibbons make loud whooping calls that echo through the city, into nightclubs and cinemas and traffic jams; the call is sixty-five million years old, it slithers under the foundations of buildings and rests there, it is answered in the dense forests of the gibbons' origin, it breaks the windows of the local police station.

Twenty men put on their boots, jump into a van, and head for a well-known pub where they think 'the trouble' comes from; they want to smash the sound with truncheons, it upsets them. The van smells of frightened animals, fists, rubber, uniforms and peppermints, The Banker disappears into the aquarium trailing blood from her cut hands, into the aviary and reptile house. Freddie discovers he has an erection as he watches her pour petrol through the bars of cages, splash it through every gap she can find, he watches her run for what seems like miles, in circles and zigzags, a silver streak of fury and sweat and ... roses ... and a will whose pulse beats harder than the elephants' stamping feet as they lift up their trunks (at the same time the policemen lift up their truncheons) and bellow (just as three young boys hit in the stomach bellow), ears spread out to the sky. The panda who has fathered twins in Madrid and Washington spits out bamboo, hits his own belly and tries to die. He watches the giraffe become a tower of flames and collapse into itself, ankles broken, tongue hanging out, the seven bones of its neck bowing down, one by one, curving into the earth. The folds of the elephants' skin crumple as the rings of time within it burn; some roll on their backs in the mud to put out the flames, one sits in a pool of water. The lion sees the strange sight of fire over water and roars into the dream he once had, under the acacia tree. As the flames grow and animals butt their heads against walls and bars and each other, the zoo becomes a museum of murmuring lit up by a thousand eyes, and in them Freddie can see himself; he is so aroused he can hardly stand up. Birds spread their wings of fire and try to fly but there is nowhere to fly to; they die in a ball of flames in mid-air, colliding into each other, scattering feathers and seeds. The rhinoceros from Java also attempts to fly; he digs his horn into the earth so that his body is in the air for one miraculous second until the horn breaks and he becomes a putrid hulk, a smouldering monster pointing its broken ivory stub at an invisible moon. The Banker's fingers are hot and articulate, her eyes water but she does not fumble or flinch or lose her balance; she sets fire to the litter bins as if she has been rehearsing for this all her life. She looks around her. There is nothing left of the chief gorilla except his liver which lies burning on the floor of the cage like some joke sacrifice to a wayward god. The one kangaroo that manages to jump out of her allotment runs straight into the litter bin where she falls, whimpering amongst soft drink cans and chocolate wrappers. Many of the animals are unconscious from the smell of petrol and burning flesh alone. In the aquarium the tanks shatter and fish who took so many years to fly (unlike the heavy ostrich who tried to take off in one moment of panic and broke its wings) by developing the habit of jumping to enlarge their fins, now jump straight into the flames. The eels, which when old and sexually mature grow darker, the small fish hibernating at the bottom of the tanks, all fall into the fire, a cluster of tiny scaly stars; the sting-rays spew out poison and writhe in flames that burn purple and black, the silvery-brown spotted piranha sizzles in its own oil, the fish with eggs in their mouths drop them into the flames. Outside, the last of the elephants rolls on his back, legs in the air. There is so much of him to burn in the unquenchable flames of a raging woman.

The llama desperately tries to turn herself into water. She becomes earth, sawdust, stones, but this is not enough to put out the fire inside The Banker; her desire is to destroy and it is hard to break desire. No matter how hard she tries, the llama cannot do it.

She becomes The Poet. Her black boots are covered in ash, her hair singed; perhaps it is the memory of nurses trying to soak her strength with buckets of icy water that prevents her; that time in a Northern European city where she lost all reason and the nurse told her to moderate her passions. She watches the leopards standing on their hind legs clawing at the sky, absorbs the image and tries to reshape it. She changes herself into remorse, hate, bitterness, love and finally salt.

Freddie stares at The Banker. She is vomiting over her stilettos. He stands up and walks through the flames towards her. As the smell of burning flesh fills his lungs and makes him retch, he spits on his little finger, moistens the blisters on The Banker's lips, and presses his tongue into the burning furnace of her mouth.

I can smell burning. I'm glad my flat is insured. The sky is on fire. Reminds me of the time a computer blew up in the office. The night afterwards I dreamt I was on fire and fell from the sky into the sea. As the water filled my ears, a voice said, 'You are the Dirty Young Man Of Europe,' and then I realised I was shitting in the sea, it was pouring out of me, gallons of it, and I was screaming 'SAVE ME', the sea turning brown and I drowning in my own shit. And then a blue marbled whale swam towards me, came to save me, butterflies playing around its head, singing, but as it came closer it began to flounder in the stuff coming out of me. I prefer swimming pools. At least you know what's on the bottom.

Duke is cringing under the chair, whimpering. He did this once before under the bed of a lady I was having my way with and it turned out he could smell a dead budgie − I saw it tucked into a shoe when I dragged him out. Perhaps she's a mad cunt. I like it better in the car − we've fucked through three massacres together, the city pulsing outside, rain, the wipers going backwards and forwards like myself and the guns setting up a nice rhythm, her face squashed into the seat, knickers on my briefcase, doner kebab and a thousand cigarettes afterwards to set me up for the day to come and the days after that. The sky is thick with smoke. Hitler didn't get us out − we're staying put.

I'm saving up to buy something. Tomorrow is always another day because you can always buy something. To date I own a car phone, microwave, video, calculator that is also a diary/radio, tea maker that is also a radio, bicycle machine, vacuum to get rid of the hairs in my car, shower radio, cassette player that is also a clock/television/radio, compact disc player and recently I bought myself an Ansaphone. When I made the message to leave to people I got Duke to bark three times by standing on his tail. Peter rang, said something clever like 'My wife never sounds like that when I do it to her.' He's hoping to become a Conservative MP next year.

Days, weeks go by and there are often no messages on the machine – I thought it would change my life, that it would be full of people trying to contact me. Needing things is like being tortured. You're open to suggestion and your resistance is low. So the torturer beats you senseless and says, 'You need gold taps on your bath don't you?' and you say *yes*. And then he says, 'What you really need is a Cornish pasty up your arse, isn't that right?' and you say *yes yes I need a Cornish pasty up my arse*. I am more needy than I've ever been. Am I the torturer or the tortured?

In sleep I find myself in the belly of that blue marbled whale, dancing across the sea ... and then the whale heaves, begins to vomit me up ... thrashes about until I am thrown out of the centre of its belly. Forever.

The Anorexic Anarchist walks above the flames of The Banker's boredom on her tightrope. A black cat with a pearl collar sits on her shoulder staring at her sister lioness burn below. She takes three steps, her bare feet as slow and as sure as a tortoise; she pauses and breathes deeply; the heat is almost unbearable. Thick coils of smoke circle her head like a halo. On the seventh step she balances herself with her arms, fingers outstretched, dripping with sweat, and says

derangement is the subversion of order
i am deranged
i am starving
i have taken the pain of the world into my self
i have not walked on water but i have walked above fire
this action is my substitute for freedom

She loses her balance, stumbles, adjusts herself with flailing smoke-blackened arms. Her palms are full of blisters.

i am one of history's little jokes ... albeit a starved sickly one
i am doing this for the sins of the pimps in parliament, in the press, in the army, in multi-national torturocracies
i am as old as the eye and the hand and the heart
i do not carry a cross i carry a cat. it found me.

i will use humour to rise above the pathological
politics that shaped me
i ride above this miserabilism
i sabotage the official culture of manufactured sorrow

   She takes another three steps, her green hair blowing
in the putrid wind.

   The Poet stands in her black boots on a mound of salt.
Her belly heaves. 'I grew up on salt soil, pricked myself
on the spikes of plants growing on the dunes, salt was
used to purge, to heal, to preserve meat, I am surrounded by burning meat, there is nothing left to preserve.' She staggers out on to the city streets, blinking
away the fur in her eyes, spitting balls of ash over
discarded machines and broken chairs in the gutter,
walks for hours in zigzags through the middle of roads
and down alleys, singing over the rattle of trains speed-
ing to secret destinations, carrying secret substances
and people with secrets of their own locked deep inside
them; she walks and walks, comes to what looks like a
bridge of black bone, trips over the sprawled legs of a
boy and a girl, The Innocents, sleeping under a blanket
that has absorbed the smell of dying animals, their
heads resting on a white DIAL A PIZZA box. The girl, sores
on her lips, clutches a smaller white box to her breast
and in it, neatly arranged, are the ten white fake
fingernails, the boy nuzzling into her neck, spiked hair
sticky with tea leaves: he is dreaming of Jerusalem,
which he pronounces Jar-oos'a-lam, where he finds
wild sage growing in the cracks of the wailing wall; he
wants to find water to boil and brew the sage to give to
the girl who is murmuring softly, sometimes drowned
by the trains, 'No babies ... I don't want babies ... no
babies.'

Freddie withdraws his tongue from The Banker's mouth. He says, 'I find your fire sexy, Miss.' Their shoes are sticky with vomit. 'Why do you find me sexy, son of a bitch?' She slaps his face and neck and ears. 'Why Why Why?' Freddie catches her hands – which are tearing the skin on his face – with his own hands, and squeezes them until the knuckles go white.

'Because I too want to act on my worst desires, to love my wickedness. I have fought this tendency in myself but now I want to give up the good fight. I want to glory in the truth of my worst nightmares. I want to live on adrenalin and deceit, to pluck the feathers off niceness, to drip scalding wax on my old utopian visions, to stick my fingers up the bums of newly weds ... of rosy optimism ... I want to fuck you in the flames. If the world is your playground I want to play with you; teach me to play. I will be your disciple. I want you to be my teacher, to scold and whip and kiss and suckle me. I want you to offer me a dangerous future. You are the woman I have yearned for all my life. You smell familiar to me. I have found you and do not fear our difference. I have found the hidden jagged edges of myself in you, found forbidden desire in you, found my meanest self in you, in your womanly form ... and I want you.'

The Banker screws up her eyes, watches the flames throw shadows over the golden contours of his body. 'Come here then. Fuck this top Goddess in the flames and I will be your chairwoman.' She lifts up her torn silk dress and tells him how she wants him to move.

'I am the first transsexual who's performed her own operation. I am a man-woman, and you, Freddie . . . I see you have been feminised . . . learnt the language of women I despise. I killed that woman in myself long ago. Drowned it in my husband's semen, drowned my disgusting neediness in the silicone heart of a machine better than my body. I pay no attention to the moon of blood and back ache. I stopped all that long ago. I am totally in control. I have no appetite for love. None at all. I am love's arsonist, burnt it out of myself, where it was is now a smouldering field full of stubble. I am beautiful and brutal, soft and hard; a myth in a techno-logical age. I have mistressed that age and become its master with my womanly contours, hairless skin, perfect breasts and tears. I woo seduce confuse and legislate . . . SUSTAIN IT BADBOY OR I'LL BREAK YOUR LEGS WITH MY WILL . . . HARDER HARDER HARDER . . . Inside my womanly structure I can achieve what no man can even hope for. I am witch, mother, sister, mistress, maiden, whore, nun, princess. I am raping you with archetypes you yourself invented . . . listen to the peacocks howl like hyenas, who would have thought it of such a pretty bird . . . COME COME YOU BASTARD COME!'

She pulls down her dress and asks Freddie to brush her hair. He walks behind her, tenderly untangling knots, smoothing, caressing, stroking. She smiles. He puts on his trousers, limp and breathless and happy. Her breath, which smells of petroleum, is his wind of liberation. He feels abused, soiled, burnt, ecstatic.

She says, 'Breakfast. Croissants, coffee, orange juice, newspapers. I'll pay.' He takes her arm and they walk through the flames to the car park. She drives him to her favourite café where a waiter guides them to The Banker's private table, under an arch of stone.

At the precise moment they sit down on the wicker

chairs, The Anorexic Anarchist imagines she can see three elephants sprout wings and begin their long journey back to the rivers and red dust of Africa and India. 'Ah,' she thinks. 'They might survive us in body, but we will survive them in soul.' Below her she can hear the noise of fire engines, police sirens, the babble of journalists, the flash-lights of photographers. Petals fall from her bloomers as she takes her next step.

'So you see,' says The Banker, dipping her croissant into her cappuccino, crumbs on her glossed lips, she pauses while nostalgic Muzac from a war-time movie washes gently over the walls and little baskets of warm bread rolls. 'We, the stupid, will inherit the earth.' She watches the waiter slice oranges and put them in the juice extractor. 'How many corpses have you got in your mouth then?' She smiles at Freddie who blinks and bites into his bacon sandwich.

In a traffic jam on the A3, the smell of cigar smoke soaks into the air. A man sits in every car and all of them are smoking cigars. It is 7.15 a.m. The man in the electric Porsche smokes the biggest cigar of all. It sticks straight out of his mouth, erect, smouldering. Suddenly his roof slides ten inches, thrusts up to the sky and rolls back. It could be a travelling circus crawling into the city for another performance.

'Fuck it all, Lapinski,' says The Poet, waving her hand in the direction of the café with arches and domes and a striped canopy, 'they will die stuffed and empty at the same time.' Tonight, the moths that circle the light of my lamp like a wreath have wings that are singed at the tips. My cat Krupskaya seems to be dizzy. The pearls on her collar have melted and every time she tries to walk she falls down. The Poet tickles her under the chin and says something to her that makes her feel better. She begins to wash her ears and prance about like a tsarina with a hangover. The poet holds out her rose-coloured glass for a last cup of tea. 'A friend of mine recently lost her hands on the meatbelt, you know ... better to lose your marbles than your hands, don't you think?' She buries her face in the glass. 'I think in my next metamorphosis I'm gonna be a Professor of Medicine and I'll say to my students, 'If you want to know what health is, first you must know what sickness is.' In my sickness I found images sufficiently challenging to make them offer me a number of forms of crucifixion available to them, like shock boxes and drugs to numb my very useful pain. Most reasonable and healthy of them, don't you think? All praise to reason.' She stands up and smashes the rose-coloured glass. 'And when my students know what sickness is we will have a party in the laboratory, get drunk like so many rats in our own experiment. Give me a puff of your cigar. Aaah ... It's time you left off the vodka, Lapinski, you should see the veins in your cheeks, they look like a map to guide people to a spa on the Black Sea to heal their livers; and, Lapinski, why did you go for that job interview in what were so obviously your pyjamas despite the yellow frou-frou you slung on top, tobacco tucked behind your earring, reeking of that sweet chypre oil you rub into your hair? They'll never have you in the civil service if you go on like that.' She kisses me goodbye and makes her way to the coach which is waiting to take her and other workers to the factory.

In another part of London, Jerry sings

for-give ... me
for-give ... me
for-give ... me

And Eduardo joins in

per-do-no
per-do-no
per-do-no

At night, lit up, the factory is the building that marks
place and distance for weary drivers on the motorway.

In the little restaurant which pays my rent, with a bit left over for lipstick and cigars, and where people eat stews watered by my secret and shameful tears, the woman with the broken Chinese umbrella sits opposite me and says, 'Lapinski, my friend is dying.' I pour salt on to the aubergines I have just sliced and she watches it turn the flesh of the vegetable brown. 'At the hospital, by his bed, we no longer talk about what is right or wrong. We talk about small incidents.' Her eyelashes, mascaraed blue, shimmer against the bravado of her cheekbones. 'He said he always wanted a Guardian Angel that smelt of gin, so I am glad to have been useful to someone.' She smiles and the sun shines on her. 'I am clearing out his room for him. It is not his personal correspondence that makes me feel strange – it is his objects. They seem suspended in time, like a miracle.' In her eyes I can see a great plumed fan that opens and closes, but I do not tell her. She takes my hand and leans forward. 'You know what the story of our time is? The fight, the struggle,' she thumps her chest, 'between the state of the heart, and the heart of the state.' I say, 'That is an old story,' and she says, 'I am an old woman.' She takes the aubergines and squeezes them hard in her hands until their water trickles into a saucer. 'I don't know why people don't cry all the time, Lapinski. If I had a kitchen I would cook for you and then you would taste my discontent. Someone charitable asked me how I was feeling. I said, smashed up ... here and here.' Her